THE CHILD'S CONCEPTION OF TIME

The Child's Conception of Time

JEAN PIAGET

Translated by
A. J. POMERANS

LONDON
ROUTLEDGE & KEGAN PAUL

Translated from the French
Le Developpement de la Notion de Temps chez l'Enfant
Presses Universitaires de France 1927
First published in Great Britain in 1969
by Routledge and Kegan Paul Ltd
Broadway House, 68–74 Carter Lane,
London, E.C.4
Printed in Great Britain
by Western Printing Services Ltd, Bristol
English Translation

SBN 7100 6358 x

Contents

Collaborators in this work

Mlle Esther Bussmann, Senior Assistant at the Institute of J. J. Rousseau, Geneva; Assistant at the Psychotechnical Institute, Berne (Chapters Three, Four and Five).

Mlle Edith Meyer, Senior Assistant at the Institute of J. J. Rousseau; Assistant Professor at the Children's Hospital, Boston (Chapter Eight).

Mlle Vroni Richli, Teacher in Zürich (Chapter Six).

Mlle Myriam van Remoortel, Senior Assistant at the Institute of J. J. Rousseau, Geneva (Chapter Nine).

Foreword

This work was prompted by a number of questions kindly suggested by Albert Einstein more than fifteen years ago[1] when he presided over the first international course of lectures on philosophy and psychology at Davos. Is our intuitive grasp of time primitive or derived? Is it identical with our intuitive grasp of velocity? What if any bearing do these questions have on the genesis and development of the child's conception of time? Every year since then we have made a point of looking into these questions, at first with little hope of success because, as we quickly discovered, the time relationships constructed by young children are so largely based on what they hear from adults and not on their own experiences. But when, after trying to apply the idea of 'groupings' to the development of the child's conception of number and quantity,[2] we went on to apply it to the concepts of motion, velocity and time, we discovered that the problems of duration and temporal succession had become greatly simplified. The results are presented in this volume; those bearing on the child's conception of motion and speed are reserved for a later work.[3]

Now, the study of the child's conception of time is not simply the psychological analysis of the development of scientific concepts. Bergson's entire philosophy, as well as the large number of purely psychological works influenced by it, have stressed the great importance of the concepts of inner duration and of

---

[1] The French original was published in 1946. Translator.
[2] Piaget and Szeminska, *La Genèse du Nombre chez l'Enfant*; Piaget and Inhelder, *La Développement des Quantités chez l'Enfant*, Delachaux & Niestlé (Neuchâtel and Paris), 1940 and 1941; Piaget, *The Child's Conception of Number*, Routledge & Kegan Paul, London, 1941 (Third Impression, 1965).
[3] *Les Notions de mouvement et de vitesse chez l'Enfant*, Presses Universitaires de France.

psychological time. Yet far from seizing on the possible convergence of Einsteinian time and 'lived duration', Bergson himself tried to contrast them in a little work that caused quite a stir at the time.[1] In the third part of our study we shall see what genetic research has to say on the subject of this apparent dichotomy.

Moreover, psychopathologists, too, often come face to face with the problem of time. Now, it is fairly well known to what extent the interpretation of pathological concepts is conditioned by the genetic study of corresponding concepts in child psychology. As far as time itself is concerned, J. de la Harpe has endorsed the claim of a well-known psychiatrist that the analysis of duration must be based exclusively on Bergsonian ideas and on phenomenology, and that the problem of the development of the conception of time in children must be ignored on principle.[2] We nevertheless hope that the results we are about to present will prove of use to all those psychopathologists who wish to base their work on the laws of real development rather than on *a priori* dialectics.

Finally, teachers and educational psychologists constantly come up against problems raised by the failure of schoolchildren to grasp the idea of time. A clearer understanding of the constructive processes that go into the development of the fundamental concepts of temporal order, simultaneity, and the equality and colligation of durations, at a stage when the child does not yet suspect that time is common to all phenomena, will no doubt prove helpful to them in their work. It is partly because of the possible educational applications that we shall be quoting so many concrete examples.

The first part of this book (Chapters One and Two) is entirely devoted to a discussion of a laboratory experiment (flow of liquid from one flask into another and reconstruction of successive levels of the liquid by means of diagrams) and to the methods young children use in ordering successive events and in estimating durations. The second part (Chapters Three to Eight) deals with various operations in physical time (order, simultaneity, synchronization, colligation and addition of durations,

---

[1] *Durée et simultaneité*, Alcan, Paris.
[2] J. de la Harpe, *Genèse et Mesure du temps*, Neuchâtel, Trav. Fac. Lettres, 1941, pp. 10ff.

and measurement). The third part (Chapters Nine and Ten), finally, analyses 'lived time' (the notion of age and psychological duration) in the light of the first two sections, i.e. in the light of the analysis of the time schemata constructed by the subjects in the course of their adaptation to the outside world. Some readers might prefer to start with Section 3, go on to 2 and finish with 1 and the Conclusion: in either case, it is important to understand the close connection between Parts II and III.

J.P.

PART 1

Elementary Operations: Time and Motion

The aim of this section is to set the development of the concept of time in the kinetic context outside which it can have no meaning. We are far too readily tempted to speak of intuitive ideas of time, as if time, or for that matter space, could be perceived and conceived apart from the entities or the events that fill it. Much as space is often conceived as an empty box into which bodies are fitted, so time is conceived as a moving film consisting of stills that follow one another in quick succession.

But space is not just a simple 'container'. It is the totality of the relationships between the bodies we perceive or imagine, or rather, the totality of the relationships we use to endow these bodies with a structure. Space is, in fact, the logic of the apparent world or at least one of the two essential aspects (the other being time) of the logic of things: the process of fitting its parts into a meaningful whole (colligation) is analogous to the colligations and series that classes and relations introduce among concepts, and its metric system is that of numbers and numerical operations. Because it is a form of logic, space is above all a system of concrete operations, inseparable from the experiences to which they give rise and which they transform. But as the mind gradually learns to perform these operations outside their factual context, the operations may become 'formal' and it is at this level, at which geometry becomes pure logic, that space appears as a container or a 'form' independent of its content.

Now, exactly the same thing happens with time, the more so as time and space form an inseparable whole. As we shall see again and again throughout this book: no matter whether we are dealing with physical displacements or motions in space,

1

or with those inner motions that memory recalls or anticipates, we shall find that time plays the same part in regard to them, as space does in respect of stationary objects. More precisely, space suffices for the co-ordination of simultaneous positions, but as soon as displacements are introduced, they bring in their train distinct, and therefore successive, spatial states whose co-ordination is nothing other than time itself. Space is a still of time, while time is space in motion—the two taken together constitute the totality of the ordered relationships characterizing objects and their displacements.

But though, in the case of space, we can ignore time to construct geometrical relationships (to do so we need merely postulate a fictitious simultaneity and describe motions as pure displacements at infinite velocity or as displacements independent of their velocity), when it comes to time, we cannot abstract the spatial and kinetic relationships, i.e. we cannot ignore velocity. It is only once it has already been constructed, that time can be conceived as an independent system, and even then, only when small velocities are involved. In the course of its construction, time remains a simple dimension inseparable from space and part and parcel of that total co-ordination which enables us to correlate the kinetic transformations of the universe.

If this is the case, the study of the genesis of the concept of time must prove highly instructive. If time is really the co-ordination of motions in the sense that space is the logic of objects, we must expect to discover the existence of *operational time*, involving relations of succession and duration based on analogous operations in logic. Operational time will be distinct from *intuitive time*, which is limited to successions and durations given by direct perception. Operational time itself may be *qualitative* or *quantitative*, depending on whether the operations involved are analogous to those involved in classes and logical relations, or whether a numerical unit comes into play.

Which then are the elementary operations that lead us to simultaneity and succession as well as to durations of different order? The answer will be attempted in the first section of this book, where we shall analyse the reaction of children at various stages of mental development to a simple experimental situation: the flow of liquid by successive stages from one container to another. Two simple motions are involved: a drop of level and a rise of level. The time operations involved are: (1) fitting the various levels into the series $A + B + C$, etc. by means of 'before' and 'after' relationships (seriation is impossible if the relations are 'simultaneous'); and (2) fitting together the respective intervals (terms) AB, AC, etc. (AB is of shorter duration than AC, etc. and A_1 and B_1 or A_2 and B_2 are synchronous).

If temporal relations resulted from direct intuitions or from intellectual abstractions independent of their content, it is clear that these problems would not face the child with any fresh difficulties—after all, the events take place before its very eyes. But if time, as we suggest, is the operational co-ordination of the motions themselves, then the relations between simultaneity, succession and duration must first be constructed, one by one. It is the general nature of this construction that we shall examine in the first two chapters.

CHAPTER ONE

The Sequence of Events

In our attempt to determine the rôle of time in human experience generally, and that of children in particular, we invariably discover that temporal ideas are linked to memories, to complex causal processes, or to clearly defined motions. One might suppose that memory involves the direct intuition of time; that Bergson's pure memory and intuitive ideas of duration constitute an absolute reference system on which every psychological analysis of the concept of time must be based. But memory is a reconstruction of the past, a 'narrative' as P. Janet has put it, and this applies at the higher and verbal planes no less than at the sensory-motor level. As such it necessarily involves causality. Thus when one memory seems earlier than another, the former is deemed to be causally anterior to the event recalled by the latter. If, for example, I recall that, ten days ago, I put on my tie before giving my morning lectures, this is not because these two memories are indelibly engraved on my mind in a precise order of succession; it is because I am certain that the first of the two acts is a necessary preparation for the second. The order of succession of two independent events is purely fortuitous, in the sense that Cournot defines chance as the mutual interference of two distinct causal series. It is not, therefore, because it eludes causality but simply because it is involved in chance, i.e. in a tangle of causal series, that a given sequence of events is so difficult to remember; we can only recall it by reference to inner causes or to indirect connections, i.e. to other causal series. Even in our memory, time is therefore involved with causality: it is the structure of our own history but only to the extent that we construct or reconstruct it.

To determine time, we must therefore appeal to causal operations, i.e. establish a chain between causes and effects by

5

explaining the latter in terms of the former. Time is inherent in causality. It is to explicative operations what logical order is to implicative operations.

That is why we decided to begin our analysis of the child's conception of time with an examination of the way in which children link two events into a simple causal chain, for instance the motion of falling objects:[1] the child is presented with photographs of the falling body at various phases of its descent chosen at random and asked to put these into the right order. Now this technique, which we shall be discussing in some detail in the next chapter, has enabled us to demonstrate an apparently paradoxical fact, namely the operational, non-intuitive way in which children grasp time sequences—in effect, the reconstruction of an irreversible succession of events presuppose a reversibility of thought, i.e. the performance of operations that make it possible to run through each sequence in both directions. In particular, we observe that up to the age of seven or eight, the child, having adopted any sort of sequence (which in general is the one first presented to him) has great difficulties in changing his mind when presented with a better one (84 per cent of our six-year-old subjects but only 15 per cent of the eight-year-olds). Clearly, therefore, before the age of seven or eight, children are not yet capable of reasoning about several possibilities at the same time. In other words, they lack the power of operational reversibility needed for the selection of various possible orders, whereas eight-year-olds can make use of that power and thus reconstruct the true and irreversible order of events.[2]

If time is linked to causality and to the irreversible course of events, it follows that the temporal operations needed for the construction of a particular order of succession must be akin to explicative operations in general, i.e. precisely to those operations that enable one to reconstruct the displacement of objects in space. What, in effect, is causality if not the co-ordination in time-space of motions of which time is one dimension?

However, instead of studying time in complex causal series of the kind we have mentioned, we can confine our analysis to a more restricted motion in space, such that the successive posi-

[1] Krafft and Piaget, 'La notion de l'ordre des événements et le test des images en désordre', *Arch. de Psychol.*, 1925, XIX, pp. 306–49.
[2] Cf. *ibid.*, pp. 346–9.

tions of the moving object are, *ipso facto*, the reference points of the time sequence. The disadvantage of complex series is that, though they help us to determine the order of succession, they do not necessarily enable us to co-ordinate durations, whereas the study of isolated motions helps us to do just that.

§1. *Technique*

1. We present the child with two flasks or jars, one on top of the other. The upper flask (I) is in the shape of an inverted pear. It is filled through a hole at the top, and emptied by means of a glass tap communicating with the lower flask (II). The latter is perfectly cylindrical, fairly slender, and of the same capacity as (I). (I) is filled with water coloured with fluorescein. At regular intervals, fixed quantities of liquid from (I) are allowed to run into (II) until (II) is full and (I) is empty. The quantities run out from (I) correspond to graduated increases in the level of (II).

2. The subject is supplied with a series of cyclostyled drawings, showing the two empty flasks with a space between them. From the beginning of the experiment, when (I) is full and (II) empty, and thereafter at each change of level, including the last, the child is asked to indicate the respective levels in the two flasks by drawing a horizontal line on the paper in green pencil. For each new level, a new sheet is handed out and the experimenter must make sure that the levels of both (I) and (II) are drawn in clearly enough for the child to distinguish them afterwards. When all the liquid has been transferred, the sheets (6–8) are shuffled and the child is asked to put them in order:

3. 'Put the first drawing you made here (on the left). Next (to the right of the first) put down the drawing which you made when the level of the water first began to drop. Then the one you made immediately afterwards . . . (and so on).' The child's arrangement is noted. If it is incorrect, questions are asked about the mistakes and the child is prompted until it has achieved complete success.

4. Every sheet is now cut in two with a pair of scissors so as to separate the drawings of (I) from those of (II). If the child has produced the correct order (3) without assistance we pass

7

directly to (5). If not, i.e. if it needed prompting, a further question is asked. All the drawings of (I) and (II) are shuffled together and the subject is again asked to put them in order. Naturally, this task is more difficult than (3) because (I) has to be arranged in descending order and (II) in ascending order of levels, and the two have to be put into one-one correspondence.[1] The subject is again prompted to correct any possible errors.

5. After the drawings have again been shuffled, the subject is asked a number of questions of the following two types: (1) 'Was the water here (e.g. in I_2)—(if I_1 I_2 I_3, etc. = levels of I; then II_1 II_2 II_3 = the corresponding levels of II)—before or after it was here (e.g. in II_3)? (2) When the water was there (e.g. in I_5), where was the water in the other flask (II)? Find the drawing you made at the same time as this one (I_5), etc.' To answer these two types of question the child must, of course, re-arrange the drawings. However, he is not asked explicitly to do so; he is simply asked to find a successive or simultaneous relationship and it is up to the child himself to understand that this relationship cannot be established without partial or complete seriation.

Once the questions in Sections 3 and 5 have been analysed, the experimenter can go to the determination of intervals or the evaluation of durations:

6. Experience has shown that it is useful to begin by asking a question about the equality of two synchronous intervals, even when the child assumes the simultaneity of the two corresponding levels in (I) and (II)[2]: e.g. 'Does the water take the same time to drop from here to there (from I_1 to I_2) as it takes to rise from here to there (II_1 to II_2)?'

7. Next, the experimenter can ask a question to discover whether the subject realizes that the whole is larger than its parts. 'Which takes longer: for the water to drop from I_1 to I_3 or from I_1 to I_2? For it to drop from I_1 to I_3 or for it to rise from II_1 to II_2?'

8. Next comes a quantitative problem concerning the equality

---

[1] Here we have a multiplicative 'grouping' of the relations whereas in (3) an additive 'grouping' suffices. See below Chapter Two, §5.
[2] The fact that the two levels are only approximately simultaneous does not affect the experiment in any way.

or inequality of two successive durations: 'Does the water take the same time to rise from II_1 to II_2 as it takes to rise from II_2 to II_3, to drop from I_1 to I_2 as it takes to drop from I_2 to I_3, to drop from I_1 to I_3 as it takes to drop from I_3 to I_5?' etc. etc.

9. Finally, the experimenter can investigate whether or not the child sees a connection between equal time intervals and the flow of equal amounts of liquid. To that purpose, he can use two distinct methods. In the first, he asks questions (8) and (9), and after the child has admitted or denied the equal duration of the change from II_1 to II_2 and II_3, it is asked whether there is an equal increase in water level from II_1 to II_2 and II_3, etc. In the second method, the experimenter starts at once with question (9) or, if need be, even states that the quantities of liquid that have been transferred from I into II are equal and then puts questions (6) to (8).[1]

Let us note that, if need be, questions (6) to (9) can easily be simplified. Thus if the child should find the drawings too abstract, successive water levels can be marked on the wall of flask I by means of dark lines and on the wall of II by means of elastic bands. The child is now asked: 'Does it take more, less or the same time for the water to change from here to there?' It goes without saying that the experimenter can then ask the subject to correlate his drawings with the marks and this is, in fact, essential if he wishes to analyse the relationship between ordination and measurement.

We see then that, taken as a whole, this experiment is a simple generalization of the picture-arranging experiment, but with this useful addition: seriation is complemented by the co-ordination of intervals and, finally, by measuring operations. In this way, the arrangement of the drawings is related to the overall time relations.

Having said this, we shall postpone the discussion of questions (6) to (9) (estimation and measurement of duration) to the next chapter, and merely show that three stages of mental development can be distinguished in the answers to questions (3) to (5) (order of events). During the first stage, children are unable to

---

[1] Strictly speaking, the flow of equal amounts of water is not, of course, synchronous—due to a gradual change in pressure. But this does not affect the experiments.

9

arrange the shuffled, uncut drawings in correct order, at least not immediately, thus showing that they fail to grasp the order of succession of the various water levels. During the second stage, children are able to arrange the unseparated drawings correctly and at once, but as soon as figures (I) and (II) are cut, they again find themselves at a loss. At this stage, therefore, they have a coherent intuition of the physical process of flow and of the corresponding time factor, but fail to transform this intuitive order into an operational system of relations of simultaneity and succession. In the third stage, finally, they are able to establish the correct serial correspondence.

§2. *The first stage: Difficulties in reconstructing the complete series*

Though the least advanced children are at first incapable of putting even the uncut drawings (sub-stage I A) into order, they succeed in doing so at the end of the stage by trial and error (sub-stage I B).

Let us take a few examples from sub-stage I A:

AUD (5; 11) draws the successive levels with keen interest and even interrupts the work to ask *Would you like to lend me your machine? I'd find it useful. I'll bring it back tonight.* Nevertheless he is quite incapable of arranging his (uncut) drawings in chronological order. In fact, he constructs the series $D_1 D_5 D_2 D_3 D_6 D_4$.[1] We now remove D_1 and D_6. Which of them was first? (D_1) Why? *Because at the start of the test this one* (I) *was full.* Right. And which of these two (D_2 and D_5) came first? *This one* (D_5). Why? . . . And which of these (D_2 and D_5) is fuller? *Oh, that one* (D_2). All right then, arrange the drawings so that the first one you made is put here and the next one there, and so on. . . . He produces the series: $D_1 D_2 D_5 D_3 D_6 D_4$, thus repeating the previous series with only one change.

RIC (6½) makes the following arrangement: $D_6 D_3 D_4 D_2 D_5 D_1$. Which was drawn first, this one (D_6) or that one (D_1)? *This one* (D_1) *because it's full.* All right then, arrange them in the right order, etc. . . . (He starts again and produces $D_1 D_3 D_2 D_5 D_4 D_6$.) Which of these (D_5 and D_4), came first? *This one* (D_5). *Why?* (He looks at the two flasks I and II attentively but does not answer.)

What is the meaning of these failures? Clearly, while the water was actually flowing, the child must have had a rough idea of the

---

[1] By $D_1, D_2, \ldots$, we refer to the uncut drawings.

actual succession of levels because he drew them correctly and appreciated the fact that while the water level in I fell that in II rose. Why then, having watched and correctly reproduced this process in his drawings, does the child fail to arrange the drawings in the right order?

Now it seems likely that the difficulty is simply bound up with the convention inherent in the arrangement of the drawings, for this convention is, in fact, more complex than it looks. On the one hand, the transformation of a time sequence into a (one-dimensional) linear series is not at all self-evident, but implies the uniquity of time, i.e. that all relations involving 'earlier' and 'later' can be fitted into a unique time series. Moreover, as Luquet has shown, a child of that age (7–8) does not customarily represent a story by successive drawings corresponding to successive periods of time, but rather combines anachronic features into one and the same drawing. Now, in our previous study of children's reconstruction of a story from a series of drawings, we, too, found[1] that it is precisely because they are unable to elaborate a story that children fail to understand the method of successive pictures. We may therefore put it that the two problems of thinking of time in the shape of a linear series and of representing events by a succession of distinct pictures in space are in fact identical.

This suggests that once the observed events have taken place, the child fails to reconstruct their order of succession because it cannot fit them to unique points in directed time. In other words, faced with two drawings representing two distinct pairs of levels (I, II), the child cannot clearly decide which of the two is prior to the other, and this because he can no longer perceive the displacement of liquid from the top to the bottom (I) or from the bottom to the top (II), but is left with a series of static spatial relationships (constant levels), which he is then asked to reconstruct after the event in the form of a time sequence. It may be said that, in that case, the problem becomes one of reasoning and ceases to be one of time. But what is the concept of time if it is not this very reconstruction? And are not the relationships involved in this reconstruction precisely those that

[1] See Margairaz and Piaget, 'La structure des recits et l'interpretation des images de Dawid chez l'enfant', *Arch. Psychol.*, XIX, pp. 211–39; and Krafft and Piaget, *op. cit.*

are also involved in perceptive judgements? We shall see that this is so in Chapters Three and Four—that establishing time sequences or simultaneity presupposes a capacity for operational co-ordination.

An analysis of reactions at sub-stage I B fully corroborates this assumption, for at that stage the child, though originally unable to arrange the drawings in order, ends up by improving his original reconstruction after a series of trials and errors. But—and this is interesting—though children at sub-stage I B can correct a number of mistakes—and it is in this respect that they are superior to children at sub-stage I A—they cannot yet grasp the overall order of events—precisely because they lack a systematic method of reconstruction:

BER ($5\frac{1}{2}$) has just finished his last drawing: Tell me what you've drawn. *The water ran from there to here* (he points to two levels in flask I) *and then right to the bottom, and it rose to just there* (pointing to flask II). Good. Now you can arrange your drawings in the same way. Put the first drawing you made, when the water was right at the top, here, then the next one here, etc. (He produces the series $D_2 D_3 D_1 D_5 D_6 D_4$). Is this right? *Yes.* Where was the water right at the start? *It was at the top in the first drawing.* And in the bottom flask? *There was no water.* Well then, is this right (with D_2 at the top)? *Oh, no.* (He changes D_1 and D_2 to produce $D_1 D_3 D_2 D_5$ etc.). And at the end? *The top flask was empty.* Well, then? (He changes D_6 and D_4). Are all the drawings correct now? *Yes.* Have a good look. *Yes.* What about these two (D_3 and D_2)? Which came first? (He looks at II_2 and II_3). *This one* (D_3). Look at the top flask. *Oh, no.* (He changes D_3 and D_2). Is everything right now? *Yes.* Have a good look. (He traces the levels on I with his finger and changes D_4 and D_5.)

The drawings are now cut, shuffled and the child asked to arrange them anew. 'Put them back together exactly as before.' He puts II_1 (the empty, lower flask) at the top, and looks for I_1. Then he puts II_4 next to II_1 and looks for the corresponding I: he looks at the apparatus and puts his finger on flask I at the level he thinks will correspond to II_4; then he finds I_3 and puts it on top of II_4. He continues using the same method and ends up with $I_1 I_3 I_2 I_5 I_4 I_6$ on top of $II_1 II_4 II_5 II_2 II_6$. 'Is that right?' *No.* (He takes I_4 and I_3, examines them and replaces them as before.) 'And now?' (He puts I_6 between I_1 and I_3 and then shifts it to the tail end.) 'What's the water doing in the top flask?' *It drops down all the time.* 'So?' (He arranges some of the I's at random and seems satisfied.)

LIN (6; 4) produces the series of (uncut drawings) D_1 D_3 D_2 D_6 D_4 D_5. Why did you put this one (D_3) after that one (D_1)? *Because the jar was full here* (D_1). And here (D_6)? *It was empty. Oh, of course.* (He puts it at the end). Are the rest correct? *Yes.* Just look at them. ... What's the water doing in the top flask? *It runs out.* Well, then? (We point to D_2 and D_3.) *Ah, yes.* (He corrects the mistake.)

The drawings are now cut and shuffled and the subject is asked to 'arrange them as they were before'. Lin looks for II_1 and puts it down. On top of it he places I_2; next he forms a second pair of I_4 and II_3 judging them by eye without making further comparisons. In the same way he combines I_5 with II_6; I_3 with II_5; I_6 with II_4 and I_5 with II_2, continuing to disregard all other pairs and acting as if the levels in both jars kept dropping. When the arrangement is completed, Lin realizes that it must be wrong and tries to correct his mistakes. But instead of changing the drawings round individually, he changes them by pairs, as if once I_2 has been placed on top of II_1 the two can no longer be separated. The result is a fairly correct arrangement of I's but an utterly confused arrangement of II's, on which he is unable to improve.

At sub-stage I B, therefore, children show an initial failure to arrange the uncut drawings but gradually correct their errors under questioning or by spontaneous trial and error. Once the drawings are cut, however, they are quite unable to construct the correct series.

The water ran from here to there (I) *right to the bottom, and rose up to here* (II), Ber said without hesitation in answer to our very first question. Why then do some of these children fail to put even the uncut drawings (D) into order?

Let us note at once that since, by and large, the subjects grasp the order of succession while the water is actually flowing, their understanding must be more than a merely passive form of registration—it clearly involves a complex structuring of time. Leaving aside the correlation of corresponding levels in flasks I and II respectively, to which we shall return when we discuss stage II, we merely note here that even the sequence of levels in either of the two flasks (e.g. in I) poses a perceptive problem. As has often been shown, a sequence of perceptions does not in itself constitute a perception of a sequence nor (let us add, *a fortiori*) a comprehension of this process. Let us assume, for argument's sake, that a baby, which knows nothing about the flow of water, notices the decrease in level every time the tap of the flask is opened. But as there is a pause in the flow at every level (the time it takes to make a drawing) the reconstruction of the total flow requires a coherent recall of all the preceding stages, and the baby lacks the power to do this. The fact that our subjects have this power (as shown by the experiment with Ber) is due not simply to the registration of a series of successive perceptions but to a kinetic interpretation of the flow process as a whole.

Now, during the actual experiment, this interpretation and the associated reconstruction are facilitated by direct and continuous contact with the actual flow. Every new drawing of a given level thus becomes part and parcel of a general process, i.e. takes its correct place between the preceding drawing and the following one, and this practical arrangement is imposed by the facts themselves. On the other hand, once the drawings have been made and shuffled, they are no longer parallel to perceptions or actions; the general motion must now be imprinted upon them, as it were from the outside, and to do that is something quite other than to observe the actual process or to record it as it happens. Practical seriation must give way to mental seriation and it is here that the nub of the difficulty resides.

Whereas the subjects at sub-stage I A fail completely in this task, those at sub-stage I B accomplish it more or less successfully, and we shall now examine why this should be so. What precisely enables these subjects to correct their own mistakes? The simple answer is that they are able to associate the spatial order (the height) of the various levels with their memory of the actual flow process. Before making this co-ordination, they are already capable, as Ber has shown quite clearly, of describing the flow, but this verbal ability does not yet help them to put the various levels into the correct series. They would, however, have succeeded in this task, had we given our questions a purely spatial rather than a temporal form. 'Put the drawing with the greatest amount of water in I on top, next the one with slightly less water, and so on until flask I is empty.' What they cannot do, however, is to express the water levels in terms of motion, or motion in terms of a series of states. Now, it is precisely this

14

co-ordination that constitutes the comprehension of time sequences.

Ber, for example, having first explained the overall flow in the two flasks, went on to construct series consisting of three un-co-ordinated segments. He placed D_3 correctly after D_2 but then constructed the series D_1 D_5 D_6, later adding D_4. In other words, he had to recall the beginning and the end (D_1 and D_6) of the general process before he could begin to arrange the complete sequence. All this suggests that, faced with individual drawings, the child loses sight of the total process, and needs a considerable effort of recall and reconstruction to place them in their total context. Lin, in the same way, began by joining the three pairs D_1 D_3; D_2 D_6; and D_4 D_5 and failed to correct his mistakes until he had clearly exclaimed that the water 'falls', as if this came to him as a sudden revelation.

In short, much as the perception of a sequence is quite different from a sequence of perceptions because it combines states that, taken in isolation, do not involve the time factor, so the intellectual grasp of a time sequence presupposes a seriation that is quite distinct from the spatial order (of levels): to transform spatial into temporal successions we must first be able to correlate the several states in terms of an overall motion. Now, though children at stage I are capable of recalling the overall motion (flow) intuitively and of arranging successive levels by their purely spatial characteristics, they are unable to treat these levels as so many successive positions of a moving body, i.e. as a function of the flow. Subjects at sub-stage I B have this ability in part, but thanks only to intuitive and mnemonic recall, so that they, too, fail to produce a general co-ordination. As for the seriation of the separated drawings, it goes without saying that it is quite beyond them, but this raises a more general problem, and one we shall meet again at stage II.

§3. *The second stage: The correct arrangement of unseparated drawings (D) but failure to seriate the separated drawings (I and II). The first sub-stage (II A): Inability to produce a complete series.*

At sub-stage II A, as at sub-stage I A, children are quite in-capable of seriating the separated drawings but remarkably quick in seriating the unseparated drawings (D). Let us look at a few actual cases:

BAUD (6; 8) rapidly arranges the six drawings D. When they are shuffled and when any two are offered for comparison, he immediately chooses the one 'drawn before the other': *It's because the water is higher* (in I). On the other hand, when the drawings are cut and I is separated from II, and he is presented with I_5 and asked to find the corresponding II, he chooses II_2 simply because it has the same level as I_5. Which of these two (I_2 and I_5) was drawn first? *This one* (I_2). That's right. And of these (II_2 and II_5)? *This one* (II_2). Good. And which of these (the II's) did you make at the same time as this one (I_4)? (He chooses II_3 at random.) Try and put everything back as it was at the start. (He arranges I_3 I_1 I_2 I_5 I_6 above II_1 II_5 II_6 II_3 II_2 II_4.) Is that right? *Yes.* What was it like at the top when we started? *Oh, I see.* (He swaps I_1 and I_2.) And what about these (I_3 and I_2)? *Yes, they're also wrong.* (He swaps I_3 and I_2 as well as II_5 and II_6 as if II_5 were inseparably tied to I_3 and II_6 to I_2.) What happens here (II)? *The water rises.* Well, what about these two, then (II_6 and II_5)? *Oh, yes.* (He swaps them again but at the same time swaps I_2 and I_3.) A few more corrections are made, but he continues to swap drawings in pairs. He then gives up and explains his jumble of levels by saying: *The water rises, and then it goes down again.*

POR (7; 1) makes seven drawings D and, after shuffling, re-arranges them without difficulty. They are shuffled again and two drawn out at random. Asked which one was made first, he gives the correct answer. Later the sheets are cut and he is asked to find the level of II corresponding to I_3. He points to II_4: Why? *Because up here* (I_3) *it's the same thing as down there* (pointing to the empty space in II_4). But how do you know it's the same thing? (He based his decisions entirely on the heights without bothering about differences in width and volume.) *I was wrong.* And which corresponds to this one (I_2)? *That one* (II_5). Why? (He points to the levels in I_2 and II_5 as if they were directly and not inversely proportional.)

Would you now like to arrange all the drawings as before? He correctly joins I_1 to II_1, and II_7 to I_7, then forms the series I_1, I_2, I_3 and joins I_2 to II_6 and I_3 to II_5, again as if the levels were directly proportional. Finally, he establishes the inverse relationship of several pairs and ends up with general confusion. Look at these (II_5 and I_3). *Yes, I have put them the wrong way round.* (He corrects his error by removing the pair I_3 and II_5 but without separating them.) He then makes some further corrections by moving a number of 'inseparable' pairs and finally gives up.

16

MAY (8 years) correctly arranges the D series and easily determines which of any two is antecedent. On the other hand, after the drawings have been cut, he thinks that II_4 corresponds to I_2 (direct ratio) and II_3 to I_2 (inverse but arbitrary ratio). When asked to arrange the I's or II's separately, he reconstructs the two series correctly, but when presented with the I's and II's together, it does not occur to him to reconstruct a general series. Asked to do so, he starts with $I_1, I_2, \ldots$ I_6 (correctly), then puts II_1, II_6, II_5 underneath them, and declares that II_4 has no corresponding elements. Are these right (I_2 with II_6)? *Yes, because there is the same amount of water in both.*

HAB ($9\frac{1}{2}$) is at the most advanced level of sub-stage II B. He arranges the D's at once. When the I's are separated from the II's he starts by correctly explaining that I_1 precedes II_4 *because here* (I_1) *the flask was full and here* (II_1) *it was empty when we started.* On the other hand, he thinks that II_4 corresponds to I_3: *They were made at the same time because the water in the two is in the middle.* How can we make sure? He arranges them arbitrarily in pairs. Can't you do better than that? . . . And if you arranged them as before? (He constructs the series $II_1\ II_6\ II_5\ II_3\ II_4\ II_2$.) Is that right? *Oh, no.* (He changes it to $II_1\ II_6\ II_5\ II_4\ II_3\ II_2$ placed above $I_6\ I_2\ I_3\ I_4\ I_5$.) By questioning every mistake in turn, we eventually get him to arrange the I's and the II's in two correct but separate sequences, which he seems unable to co-ordinate. Getting more and more bogged down, he concludes: *I must look at these* (the levels marked on the flasks) and arrives at the correct answer by tracing the marked levels on the flask with his finger.

These subjects were all in the age group 6 to 9 years (mean age 7–8 years). All of them could (1) arrange the D's and I's and, generally, the II's in correct order, but failed to correlate the I's and II's. Moreover, if they tried to arrange the I's and II's simultaneously, they failed to arrange one or the other. (2) All of them failed to grasp spontaneously that the correspondence (simultaneity) of levels I and II is determined by their double seriation. (3) While recognizing in principle that the levels in II rise as they drop in I, none of them was able to remember this relationship throughout the construction of his series. (4) All of them considered as more or less inseparable two levels they had linked together however arbitrarily, and however glaring the resulting errors.

Perhaps it will be said that these reactions at sub-stage II A (and no doubt at sub-stages I A and I B as well) fall more into the province of the psychology of seriation, and hence of reasoning, than into that of time. At first sight it seems, in effect, that children have a correct grasp of the succession of the various levels in I and even in II, as well as of their general correspondence, and that it is only the reconstruction of the details that eludes them: this would suggest that their reasoning alone is at fault and not their grasp of time. But here we are precisely concerned to discover whether or not the failure to grasp the ordered relationship constituting a series of events, is not in fact a failure to grasp time sequences. It is for this very reason that we must dwell at some greater length on the four difficulties we have listed.

1. To begin with, we find that even those children who have no difficulty in arranging the D's will fail to arrange the I's when thinking of the II's and *vice versa*. It was for this reason that Baud, having correctly arranged the D's, in 'putting everything back as it was at the start' produced the series $I_3 I_1 I_2 I_5 I_4 I_6$, as if he were no longer capable of grasping the regular drop in the level of I, and the series $II_1 II_5 II_6 II_3 II_2 II_4$ as if he had forgotten that the water rose regularly in II. We may therefore suppose that, losing sight of the overall process, he was unable to construct two corresponding series and contented himself with combining a series of pairs made up of elements I and II chosen by sheer guesswork. In the same way, Por managed to put the D's into order but, as far as the separated drawings were concerned, could only put the extreme elements in their correct position. The case of May was even more curious, because he was able to arrange the D's and the I's and II's separately, but failed to associate the I's with the II's. Hub did no better until he checked his drawings against the levels marked on the flasks.

Why is there such a wide discrepancy between the ability to arrange the D's correctly and the failure to correlate the separated drawings? The answer is quite simple. It is not only that a double series, or correspondence, is inherently more complex than a simple one, with a smaller number of elements,[1] but also that, in this particular case, the time relations involved in the

---

[1] Cf. Piaget and Szerminska, *La Genèse du Nombre chez l'Enfant*, chaps. V, VI and IX.

double series are much more complex than those involved in the simple arrangement of either I or II. In the case of a single flask, in effect (and hence in the case of the D's which can be arranged by paying attention to only the I's or the II's), our subjects are not called upon to co-ordinate two motions operationally; all that is required is a simple reconstruction of a single motion (the drop of the liquid in I or its rise in II), in which the problem of 'before' and 'after' completely coincides with that of the successive levels in the flasks. That even this reconstruction goes beyond perceptive intuition has been mentioned in §2.

However, perceptive or direct intuition and operational reasoning are separated by more than one step. Thus we refer by 'articulated intuition' to that phase in the development of temporal concepts in which the child can reconstruct the phases of a single motion, but is not yet able to relate them to phases in the motion of other bodies. A case in point is the separate seriation of the D's, I's and II's. The correlation of the I's and II's, on the other hand, calls for something quite different: the co-ordination of two motions at different velocities (gradual fall in level I and rapid rise in level II) and it is precisely this type of co-ordination that constitutes an operation as distinct from an intuitive conception of time. In effect, to establish the correspondence of levels in I and II, the child must (1) consider the order of succession in I and in II separately; (2) appreciate the fact that the water level drops from I_1 to I_2, etc. while it rises from II_1 to II_2, etc., the drop in I being much slower than the corresponding rise in II; (3) grasp the approximate simultaneity of I_1 and II_1; I_2 and II_2, etc.

The correlation of the various levels in I and II respectively, therefore, depends not only on the fact that the two sets can be put into series separately but also on the operation of a correspondence principle, to wit simultaneity. Now to establish or reconstruct that principle, the subject must either grasp the equality of the synchronous durations $I_1 I_2$ and $II_1 II_2$ or else he must bear in mind that the water stops flowing in II whenever it stops flowing in I, and *vice versa* (zero succession). In either case, the differential rate of the flow presents the subject with the same problem: the operational co-ordination of two distinct motions.

2. How, in fact, do children at this stage reconstruct the simultaneity of corresponding levels? Simply by guesswork and by relying either on the equality of the levels in I and II (e.g. for May, I_2 corresponded to II_6 'because there is the same amount in both', and for Hub, I_3 corresponded to II_4 'because the water in both is in the middle') or else on the equality of the unfilled space in II and the remaining liquid in I (Por: 'Because up here it's the same thing as down there'). Now, in either case, the child establishes the correspondence without taking into account the differences in shape and volume of the flasks I and II, i.e. without bearing in mind the essential fact that the level of II rises much faster than it drops in I (in the wider part of the pear). In short, the child establishes simultaneity by the absolute value of the levels and not by their corresponding order of succession. Particularly when presented with the separated and shuffled drawings I and II and asked to reconstruct the actual rather than the apparent simultaneities, the child proves incapable of grasping that the correct answer calls for a process of double seriation. Conversely, when he tackles the double seriation, the child ends up with elements lacking partners, thus ignoring the fact that every level of I must be simultaneous to a level of II and *vice versa* (see the cases of May and of Hub).

If these various facts occurred in isolation, one would hesitate to give them such an interpretation. But as we shall see in the course of this book, children invariably hesitate to describe as simultaneous either points at a distance or motions at different velocities, and it is precisely this hesitation which explains why children at sub-stage II A should find it so difficult to establish simultaneities by means of double seriations or even to grasp the underlying idea.

(1) and (2) can therefore be summed up by saying that if the child can arrange the uncut drawings D and the separated I's and II's, but cannot cope with the double seriation of the I's and the II's nor grasp the idea of simultaneity based on this double seriation, then it is because whereas (a) arranging the drawings D, I and II separately calls simply for the intuitive reconstruction of a single motion (articulated intuition), (b) pairing I and II calls for the co-ordination of the respective phases of two motions differing in velocity, i.e. for operational co-ordination.

3. We can therefore understand the more or less systematic difficulties that our subjects experience in trying to correlate the inverse flow in I and II, even though they have only just been watching the actual process and had themselves sketched the successive levels. Baud paired II_2 and I_5 because both were low levels, and this despite the fact that he realized II_2 came before II_5. He thus vacillated between the direct and the inverse relation and arrived at this absurd conclusion: 'The water rises and then it goes down again'. The same was true of Por. May was quick to grasp the order of the II's while arranging them separately but, when tackling the double seriation, he, too, began by pairing the two extremes correctly and then went on to pair the rest as if the changes in level were in direct ratio.

Instead of thinking of a double motion in two opposite directions, all these subjects were bogged down by the details, evidently because, once again, they failed to master the operational mechanism governing simultaneity.

4. Now, this failure goes hand in hand with a fourth peculiarity which holds the psychological key to the first three, although, at first sight, it seems to contradict them. This is the rigid way in which our subjects try to correct their mistakes. For example, Baud, in changing round I_3 and I_2 which he had paired with II_5 and II_6, also moved the last two as if they were inseparable from the first. Only some of the older subjects at this sub-stage who have sufficient mental mobility to eschew this rigid type of correction.

Now, this rigidity in performing detailed operations is not only part and parcel of our subjects' general failure, but may well be its explanation. For what, in effect, enables them to put the two series I and II into correspondence, and hence to demonstrate that they have grasped the double direction of the motions involved? Despite the irreversibility of the actual flow of the water, they must, in fact, be able to perform a reversible operation, to wit an operational 'grouping'.[1] As we have shown in the article quoted at the beginning of this chapter, reconstructing events in their correct sequence presupposes an ability to go up and down the time scale, i.e. to construct a series

---

[1] See Chapter Two, §5.

A → B → C ... such that the arrows can stand for 'precedes' as well as for 'follows'. Now, in establishing this logically reversible series based on an irreversible course of events, our subjects must have sufficient mental mobility to choose from all the possible sequences only those in which the arrows can be given a consistent interpretation. Much as the children discussed in our earlier book (1925) lacked the mental reversibility needed to organize a series of pictures into a story, so the subjects now under review lack the mental reversibility demanded by the reconstruction of the flow of a liquid.

It is worth while pursuing this initial difficulty even further, because it is essential to our entire interpretation of the child's construction of time. Let us recall that the children tested in 1925 could at best change a few pictures about; they simply accepted the story as it was presented to them in a random arrangement of the pictures. They invented complicated stories to explain the quite arbitrary series; later, in spite of a few corrections and even when shown the correct sequence, they produced new stories that partly or wholly repeated the old ones. (This applied to 84 per cent of the new stories told by 6-year-olds but only to 15 per cent of the new stories told by 7-year-old subjects.) Now, the fact that by the age of 8, children have acquired the ability to correct their initial errors suggests that, whereas younger children suffer from a viscosity of thought that prevents them from accepting fresh hypotheses, older children no longer suffer from this handicap and are therefore able to give their narratives a consistent direction.

Now, it is precisely this combination of irreversible mental rigidity with the absence of an overall direction that we also find in the present experiment. Does this mean that it is because of difficulties in reconstructing the general motion of the flow that our subjects have so much trouble in forming the correct combinations of drawings, in splitting pairs once formed, or is it rather that they fail to construct the correct series because they lack the necessary mental reversibility? Needless to say, these two phenomena are complementary: any series of successive relations constitutes an 'operational grouping', i.e. a reversible construction. To say that, at sub-stage II A, children fail to give their constructions an overall direction or lack reversibility of thought, is to proclaim the same truth, namely that they cannot yet handle time by operational 'groupings', but do so by rigid and unco-ordinated intuitive methods.

All children at this sub-stage may therefore be said to have common difficulties in constructing overall series, in appreciating the fact that simultaneity is determined by double seriation, and in handling the inverse relation of the drop of liquid in I and the rise of liquid in II. Moreover, they all lack enough mental mobility to correct their errors. All these difficulties are but complementary aspects of their tendency to think of time in terms of simple intuitive relationships rather than of reversible operations.

§4. *The second stage: Sub-stage II B: initial failure followed by empirical success*

Nothing provides a better verification of the preceding remarks than an examination of subjects who arrive at the correct solution by trial and error, rather than by operational techniques. If conceptions of time arose independently of the operational grouping of successions, we might expect them to exert an 'external control' on the child's ability to form double series from the outset. On the other hand, if the grasp of temporal succession develops with the ability to construct series, we should find that the trials and errors leading up to this construction go hand in hand with the gradual development of the concept of simultaneity, considered as a link between two series.

Here are some examples:

EPA (7; 10) correctly points out which of several pairs of drawings chosen at random was made first, e.g. D_4 was drawn before D_5 *because* (I) *is higher and* (II) *is lower*. Whereupon he arranges the six drawings without hesitation.

We then cut the drawings in two. *Aha*, Epa exclaims, *you're going to ask me to put them together again.* That's right, but first of all tell me which of these drawings (I_3 and II_4) was made first? *I don't know. Perhaps they were done at the same time.* What must you do to make sure? *I don't know.* If I give you all the drawings, would you be able to tell? *No.* (He forgets that he is expected to re-arrange them.) You can look at the other drawings, too. (Confusion. He compares I_3 with II_2, II_5, etc. at random; later he compares the empty space in I_3 with the full space in II_4 but does not try to arrange them in series. Then he combines $I_1 II_1$; $I_6 II_6$; $I_5 II_5$; $I_2 II_3$; $I_3 II_4$, and $I_4 II_2$.) Is that right? *No.* (He swaps I_2 and I_3 as well as II_4 and II_3 and makes some further corrections, always by pairs, which has no effect on the final result.) Which came first (I_3 or I_4)? *This one.* (correct.) And if they were arranged as before? (He constructs the correct series $I_1 I_2 \ldots I_6$ but without separating the I's from the II's with which he had previously combined them.) What about these (II_3 and II_5)? *Ah yes.* (He corrects the mistake.) Was this one (I_3) drawn before, after or at the same time as that one (II_3)? *Oh, at the same time.* Why? *Because, because* (he shows that a slight tear in each of the two halves of the sheet fits together precisely!)

MAT (8 years) makes seven drawings of D. Which of these two (D_3 and D_5) was made first? *This one* (D_3). Why? *It's higher here and lower there.* And which of these (D_4 and D_5)? (same reasoning). Would you like to sort them? He constructs the correct series without hesitation.

The sheets are cut. Was this one (I_5) made before or after this one (II_4)? *Before.* Can you be sure? *Not really.* How could you make sure? *By looking at all the drawings.* Very well. (We mark II_4 and I_5 with a cross to remind him of the problem.) (Mat spreads out all the drawings in front of him and looks at them.) What are you looking for? *For the place where it all fits together. That one* (I_5) *ought to be lower* (to fit II_4) *and that one* (II_4) *ought to be higher* (to fit I_5). Well then? (He combines I_3 with II_4, then I_7 with II_1 and exclaims:) *Oh no.* (He puts I_1 with II_1, I_7 with II_7, I_2 with II_2 and I_6 with II_5.) And now which of these (I_5 and I_4) was drawn first? *This one* (I_4) *because it's lower* (I_5). *But I can't be sure.* Can't you find something to make sure? Have you any idea? *No, not yet.* I'll help you. (We put down $I_1 I_2 I_3$.) Would it help you if I arranged the lot? *Yes, it would help but we still couldn't be sure.* All the same, we'd be a little bit surer? *Only a little bit.* Let's try. (Mat correctly arranges the I's, then, after some groping and re-arrangement, the II's as well.) Are we sure now that this one (I_4) was made at the same time as that one (II_4)? *I'm not very sure.*

GEN ($9\frac{1}{2}$) at once puts the 7 D's into order. They are cut and he is shown II_1 (empty) and I_4 (half-full). Which was made first? *This one* (I_4). Why? *This one* (II_1) *came last because it is quite empty.* Which one was empty at the end of the test? (We show him the apparatus.) *This one* (flask I). Well then, which of these two (I_4 and II_1) came first? *This one* (II_1). Good. And which of these (I_4 and II_2, i.e. I half full and II a third full)? *It's difficult to tell.* Why? *Because this one* (I) *is getting empty so we can't tell any more.*

You are right, it's difficult to remember. Now I shall give you all the drawings. (He looks at them and picks up II_3 and I_2). *This one* (II_3) *came first because it is not yet full.* And this one? *Came later because it is getting empty.* How can we be sure? *We could try them all. I'll look for the first* (He takes I_6). *No.* (He takes I_1 I_2 I_3 etc. and arranges them I_1 I_3 I_4 I_5 I_6 I_7, leaving I_2 on one side, then II_3 II_4 II_5 II_6 II_7.) Well, then, which of these (I_2 and II_3) was drawn first? (He looks at the series but in putting the I's on top of the II's he shifts the entire lower series so that the extremes II_1 and I_7 are left without corresponding items.) *These* (I_2 and II_3) *were made at the same time.* (For a time he continues to base all his answers on his mistaken arrangement and not on the correct order.) Are the drawings placed correctly? *Yes.* This one (I_1) was made at the same time as which? *As this one* (II_1). Good. And do these two (I_7 and II_7) go together? *No, because this one* (II_7) *is full so this one* (I_7) *comes after.* (We tell him the story of the gentleman who buttoned his waistcoat up the wrong way and thought he had one button too many at the top and one buttonhole too few at the bottom. He laughs but fails to see the connection.) These two (I_1 and II_1) are right then, are they? He puts them on top of one another. And these two (I_2 and II_2)? *They are right as well.* (He corrects the series up to I_4 and II_4 and then stops.) And these (I_7 and II_7)? *Ah yes.* (He corrects them.) *They were made at the same time.*

We could hardly expect to find clearer answers to the question we asked at the end of the last paragraph, namely what is the precise relationship between the development of time concepts and the mental reversibility and mobility needed to construct operational series? Does the failure to handle reversible seriations spring from a failure to operate with time or is it rather of a purely logical nature? Does the grasp of time result from 'groupings', or does it precede them? Now, at the point in sub-stage II B when the child produces his first double series by trial and error, he is only just beginning, and with great difficulty at that, to grasp the connection between simultaneity and the order of events in time.

We saw that these subjects (like those at sub-stage II A)—and this cannot be stressed enough—are capable of forming series of the uncut drawings D or of the cut drawings I or II separately. Moreover, they are capable of saying without hesitation which of two drawings I_x or I_y (or II_x or II_y) 'came first'. One might therefore suppose that they would be able to put a series of events into order and understand the serial character of time, and that only the co-ordination of two series in opposite directions and relating to motions with different velocities faced them with any difficulties. This is true, but we must stress again and with some insistence, that it is only by the co-ordination of at least two motions with different velocities that purely temporal relationships can be distinguished from spatial relationships or from intuitive ideas about motion. When he is merely asked to reconstruct the successive positions of a single moving body (the levels in I independently of II, and *vice versa*), the child need master only two techniques: (1) he must be able to arrange heights as such, i.e. to construct a spatial series; (2) he must, moreover, understand that these heights are relative to a motion, and must therefore be able to recall the motion as a whole (cf. §2). It is the combination of these two abilities which we call the 'articulated intuition' of temporal successions. Now, when only a single movement is involved, the time sequence ('before and after') coincides with the space sequence (in our particular case, 'above' and 'below'): in other words, the order of events coincides with the order of positions. The intuitive recall of an isolated movement therefore does not call for a special, differentiated time framework. On the other hand, when two motions with different velocities have to be co-ordinated, articulated intuition, which is the product of motor or kinetic intuition and of operations with space, no longer suffices; what is called for now is the determination, by specific temporal operations, of the order governing the succession and the simultaneities. True, each of the moving bodies in turn passes through positions whose temporal succession coincide with a spatial succession, but the correlation of the order of succession (or simultaneity) of the positions of two moving bodies calls for the co-ordination of their velocities. In other words, whereas space is a system of positions or 'placements' and of changes of positions or 'displacements', the latter being considered as 'stills', time emerges with the appearance of 'co-placements' and 'co-displacements', i.e. with the co-ordination of the respective positions of two or more moving bodies. Each 'co-placement' would then define a simultaneity, each correlation of distinct 'co-placements' a time sequence, and each 'co-displacement' would engender duration and velocity. It follows that the operations of seriation and co-seriation (serial correspondence) are prerequisites of the construction of time (order of co-placements) and not its consequence.

Now, in respect of co-seriation as such, we find that children at sub-stage II B start off by making the same mistakes as those of sub-stage II A. Thus Epa quickly combined a number of associated pairs but did not think of arranging them in a series; next he seriated the I's without separating them from the II's to which he had originally joined them (rigid pairs). Mat proceeded in the same way, but produced some changes in the course of his attempts. Gen, who found it easier to arrange the I's and II's separately (he was $9\frac{1}{2}$!), combined the two but shifted the entire lower series one space to the right. The only difference between these subjects and those at sub-stage II A is, therefore, that after making the same initial errors, the more advanced group arrives at the correct answer by trial and error. This raises the question of what precise conception of time corresponds to their final results.

Now, on this essential point, their answers are quite clear. As Mat put it in the most explicit fashion, the double seriation of the I's and II's 'would help us' to determine the simultaneities, 'but we still wouldn't be sure . . . only a little bit'. In other words, the child, who had himself drawn the levels I_1 to I_7 and II_1 to II_7 on uncut sheets of D, was no longer absolutely certain that the separated I's must correspond item by item to the separated II's. Thus when he fitted II_4 to I_4 he was not entirely convinced that the two were simultaneous: 'I am not quite sure.' Now Mat realized that to establish these simultaneities he would have to look at all the drawings. Furthermore, he grasped the causal principle underlying the sequence: D_3 comes before D_5 'because it is higher here (I) and lower here (II)'. Why then did he not realize that simultaneity is determined by serial correspondence, and anteriority by inequality of level? Is it evidently because, to him, serial correspondence still lacked any deductive or 'operational' significance, and hence did not yet constitute a reversible 'grouping'. As a result, he was forced to supplement his understanding of temporal operations with an intuitive appreciation of isolated states: 'I look for the place where it all fitted together'. In the same way Epa, who had even greater difficulty in constructing his series, trusted them so little in his search for correspondence that he had to look for irregularities in the scissor marks to guide him! Gen was even more explicit when he stated bluntly that 'one can't be sure because this one (flask I) is getting empty so we can't tell'. This highly instructive formulation simply means that, since time is part of the irreversible flow of things, it is impossible to reconstruct the sequence of past events! And this is quite true so long as one relies on intuition, or even on articulated intuition—it is only by means of the reversible operations of seriation and co-seriation, whose mechanism or 'grouping' eluded Gen, that the irreversible course of events can be reconstructed. In Chapter Two we shall see that Mog, also at stage II, had this to say on the subject of duration: 'When we've emptied these three space (I_{1-4}) only this one (I_{4-5}) is left, so we can't empty these three spaces (I_{2-5}) all over again'. In other words, past duration cannot be determined simply because it is past! Or to put it differently again, the irreversible intuition of time prevents its reconstruction by reversible operations! And Gen was, in fact, so sceptical about the feasibility of his task that he was quite unperturbed by the disconformity of his two series, maintaining that I_7 (empty) could have been drawn before II_7 (full)!

It is clear therefore that children do not invest serial correspondence with a precise time significance (simultaneity) before they reach the operational stage; while still proceeding by trial and error they simply construct intuitive models. Now their resistance to operational methods is all the more striking because at their age (8–9) they have no difficulty in arranging two series by size alone (e.g. matching 10 dolls in increasing order of height with 10 sticks in descending order of length). Why then are they incapable of co-ordinating our two series of levels by other than purely empirical means? It is because arranging two series by height alone is something quite different from arranging them by height as well as by the co-ordination of the two motions of which there are so many stages. In the first case, the process is purely spatial: there is only a single overall 'co-placement'; in the second case, we have a correlated series of distinct 'co-placements', based on the inherent order of succession of two motions: now this series is nothing other than time itself.

This explains why operational co-seriation is an essential preliminary to the construction of operational time. However, it should be stressed that while co-seriation necessarily leads us to time (once achieved it is the very 'scheme' of time), it is based on purely spatial relations (co-placement) and kinetic relations (co-displacement), though involving at least two motions. The problem, in effect, reduces to this: given that two motions ('co-displacements') of different velocities (the emptying of I and the filling of II) proceed by stages, which positions mark identical spatial states ('co-placements')? Now, since the succession of stages can be determined by articulated intuition of only one of these motions, the new problem is simply the determination of the co-placements. Our subjects fail in this task quite simply because they lack the mental agility to co-ordinate two motions with distinct velocities—as soon as they succeed, they have grasped the idea of time itself. Indeed, how does a subject determine whether two positions are simultaneous or successive, and therefore form part of the same total spatial state (co-placement)? The simplest method is direct perception: those positions that can be seen to occur together are said to be simultaneous. However, as we shall see in Chapter Four, children often deny that two runners stop 'at the same time' if they move at different speeds and do not stop in the same spot. Now, if direct perception is not enough to establish the simultaneity of two events at a distance, intuition must fail *a fortiori*. The child must therefore rely on operations based on his understanding of the motions themselves: if two motions are dependent on each other as in our experiment, they can be correlated in terms of this dependence, and thus transformed into a system of co-placements or simultaneities.[1]

We may therefore take it that it is because of their inability to effect an operational and causal co-ordination between the motions in the two flasks that our subjects fail to grasp the fact that the simultaneities are determined by the double seriation. As a result, they content themselves with an overall, intuitive picture of the double motion, instead of producing a co-seriation based on the exact reconstruction of the co-displacements, and hence fail to endow the co-placements with a precise temporal significance. This will be borne out in Chapter Two, when we shall see that subjects at the same stage do not realize that the

[1] Modern physics has shown clearly that the idea of simultaneity has no meaning outside a material context.

time it takes the liquid to flow out of I is necessarily equal to the time it takes to fill II to the top level.

§5. The third stage: Operational co-seriation of the separated drawings and the grasp of succession and simultaneity

We may call operational all attempts to produce double series, no longer by trial and error, but in accordance with a correspondence principle. Now, experiments show that, as soon as children master the requisite technique of operational grouping, their conceptions of time automatically assume an orderly and no longer purely intuitive significance:

MEIS ($8\frac{1}{2}$): When the water in the top flask was here (I_3), where was it in the bottom flask? (He looks first at II_5, then at II_2, II_3 and II_4.) What are you doing? *I'm looking for where there is as much water down there* (in II) *as there is up here* (empty space in I). *I think it's here* (II_4). Are you sure? *No.* What can we do? (He arranges the II's from II_1 to II_6.) And which one does this one (I_3) go with? (He arranges all the I's and then pairs I_1 with II_1, etc.) *This one* (II_3), *because it was made at the same time.*

LUC (8; 10): Which of these two was made first? *This one* (I_4) *because it has less water* (the empty part of I_4) *than that one* (the water poured into II_5). And what about these (I_5 and II_5)? (He picks up a few I's and II's and matches them against I_5 and II_5.) *I must look.* (He constructs three rows: I_1 I_2 I_3 I_4; I_5 II_1 II_3; and II_4 II_5 II_6 I_6.) What about these two (I_5 and II_5)? (He inspects the three rows without touching them.) *They were together.* And these (I_4 and II_6)? *This one came first* (I_4). And these (I_5 and II_4)? *This one was first* (II_4). Luc thus applies the correct method of mental co-seriation when working with his three rather awkward rows. Couldn't you make a better arrangement? (He places the two series I_1–I_6 and II_1–II_6, on top of each other.) Now look what I am going to do. We place I_1 I_2 I_3 I_4 in a row with I_3 and I_4 beneath II_1 and II_2.) Which was drawn first, this one or that one (I_3 II_2)? *This one* (II_2). Why? *Because when this one* (II_2) *was drawn it was like that one* (I_2). How did you find out? (He points at I_1 and II_2; I_2 and II_2; etc.)

LAUR (9 years). The drawings are separated at once: Can you tell me if this one (I_3) comes before or after that one (II_4)? *Before, I think.* (He looks at the II's and some of the I's.) *Yes, that's so.* He then picks up all the drawings and looks for I_1. He goes through the

I's several times to make quite sure, and then puts down I_1. He finds II_1 without hesitation, puts it down and says: *That's right, it's quite empty.* He looks for I_2 by comparing all the remaining I's, puts it down and puts II_2 beside it: *Would it be this one? I'll put it down meanwhile.* He continues to look through the II's and says: *Yes, that's it* (He puts it underneath I_2.) *Now for the next one.* (He looks for and finds I_3.) *Yes, that's it.* (Having looked at all the rest.) *What goes with it?* (He puts down II_4 tentatively and looks through the rest) *No, it's this one* (II_3). He follows the same method up to the end, always looking for the highest level of the remaining I's and the lowest level of the remaining II's. He thus constructs his entire double series correctly.

Clearly these children have made progress in two directions. In the first place, they have learned to handle double series and correspondences without mental or practical hesitation or errors. Laur, for example, arranged his drawings by relying on the fact that any one of them must show a higher level (I) or lower level (II) than all those following, and that the two series must correspond with each other. Moreover, in applying these two principles, he displayed a consistent mobility of thought, putting down, for example II_1 and II_2 tentatively and then testing his hypothesis, then following with II_4, only to reject it again, and so on. Luc was content with constructing three incomplete rows, and though his particular arrangement did not seem to show an appreciation of the importance of co-seriation, it nevertheless enabled him to establish the correct correspondence: what he did, in effect, was reconstruct the two corresponding series by means of purely mental operations. This is borne out by the fact that he made no mistakes and was able to produce the double series as soon as he was asked to improve his arrangement. Meis, for his part, arranged the I's and II's separately but established their correspondence by pointing to the correct pairs. In short, every one of these subjects had the ability to apply operational techniques systematically, together with a high degree of mental mobility in the handling of hypotheses: from the start, they all treated the relations involved as a 'grouping' or reversible operation, i.e. they thought in terms of corresponding series straightaway and no longer had to establish them by trial and error.

In the second place, and this is essential, the subjects knew from the outset, that every I must have a corresponding II, and it is precisely this prior knowledge that introduces the time factor into co-seriation. Thus Meis, while trying to pair I_3 with a II, asserted that the corresponding element would 'be the one drawn at the same time'. In general, each of the subjects realized that correspondence is equivalent to simultaneity and non-correspondence to succession.

May we then take it that it is only because these children, unlike those in the preceding stages, have precise ideas about time relationships that they are able to produce corresponding series, knowing *a priori* that these will lead them to the correct correspondences? But then, how precisely do they get their precise ideas about time, seeing that such ideas are absent during the second stage and cannot, therefore, be innate or intuitive? In fact, we believe that it is their ability to produce corresponding series operationally, and hence their ability to anticipate the existence of a clear-cut correspondence between individual items in the two sets of drawings, that lead them to the construction of time concepts and not *vice versa*. Both co-seriation and the anticipated correlations it implies, can be very simply explained by the fact that these subjects, in contrast to those at stages I and II, no longer merely arrange heights or levels as such (an arrangement that does not involve any *a priori* assumptions about correspondences) but that they think straightaway in terms of the co-ordination of motions, i.e. of 'co-displacements'. In short, the outflow of liquid from I and the rise of the same amount of liquid in II are treated as correlated motions with corresponding stages, and it is precisely because of the resulting 'co-displacement' that spatial correspondence comes to introduce the time factor. With subjects at stage II, on the other hand, the motion proves an obstacle to co-seriation ('It's getting empty so we can't tell any more').

Viewed in the light of these facts, the general development from stage I A to stage III appears to be quite straightforward. At stage I the child is unable to arrange either the uncut drawings D or the cut drawings I or II separately—it lacks the capacity to place successive heights in spatial sequence, and later, when it acquires that capacity, it is unable to treat heights as functions of a single motion (the lowering or raising of the water level). At stage II, the subjects, using articulated intuition

32

based on their recall of the single motion together with their ability to arrange heights, are able to form series of the D's and of I's and II's separately. However, while they have no difficulty in forming double series with purely spatial magnitudes (e.g. dolls and sticks), they are quite incapable of arranging the levels in I and II: they cannot yet think in terms of combined motions, i.e. of 'co-displacements'. At the third stage, finally, their grasp of co-displacements enables them to handle the technique of co-seriation and hence leads them to the construction of the correct successions and simultaneities.

It may be asked, finally, how this grasp of co-displacements arises in the first place—whether it precedes the understanding of time or whether it results from it. The answer is quite simple: it arises from causality. Subjects at stages I and II are incapable of forming corresponding series because they forget that the levels in flask II result from the flow of water in flask I, while subjects at stage II bear this causal link constantly in mind. In general, co-displacements are based either on direct causal relations (e.g. astronomical time) or else on the mutual interference of several causal series, but such that the motions and velocities to be compared obey common laws constituting a general system. And what else is causality than a system of operations in space-time?[1]

What must be stressed, however, is that the operations involved in co-seriation which lead the child to the construction of transintuitive time concepts are not logical-cum-arithmetical, but infralogical or physical operations, as we have called them in an earlier book,[2] i.e. operations that do not involve classes of objects, relations between invariable objects or numbers, but bear exclusively on positions, states, etc., i.e. on transformations rather than on constant states. As Kant has shown so clearly, time and space are not concepts but unique 'schemes'—there is only one time and one space in the entire universe. However, he was wrong to conclude that time and space were 'forms of sensibility', and hence to deny their operational character. In

---

[1] According to Brunschvicg, the causality principle reduces to the statement: 'There is a universe' (in the precise sense of the term used by relativity theory).
[2] Piaget and Inhelder, *Le Développement des Quantités chez l'Enfant*. See 'Conclusions'.

33

D

fact, space and time result from operations just as do concepts (classes and logical relations) and numbers, but in their case, the operations take place within the object itself, and by the colligations of its parts, play a direct part in the transformation of that unique object which is the universe of time-space.

Hence, to assert that our understanding of the co-displacements constituting time is based on our grasp of causality, is merely to state a tautology: the operational co-ordination of these co-displacements is but a particular case of operations in time-space defining causality. The assertion can, however, become meaningful if we put it as follows: the operations involved in the co-ordination of motions engender the 'scheme' of time, inasmuch as they participate in that logic of objects which we call causality and which 'groups' the totality of infra-logical or 'physical' operations ('placement' or 'displacement' for space; 'co-placement' or 'co-displacement' for time, etc.).

CHAPTER TWO

Duration

Quantitative time is both ordinal and cardinal: the order of events, or the ordinal succession of reference points, corresponds to the cardinal value or duration of the intervals between these points, i.e. the order of events A, B, C, D, etc. corresponds to the inclusion (colligation) of the partial duration a (A–B) in the longer duration b (A–C) and to the inclusion of b in c (A–D), etc. Having said this, we shall now go on to examine the development of the concept of duration in children.

To begin with, we may take it that the child's evaluation of duration must reflect his grasp not only of simultaneity but also of succession. Thus a child cannot be said to have grasped the simultaneity of, say, I_1 and II_1; I_2 and II_2, etc. simply because he explains that they happened 'at the same time' or 'together'— he must also have realized that the duration $I_1 I_2$ is equal to the duration $II_1 II_2$. Similarly, the child cannot be said to have grasped the fact that I_2 precedes I_3 simply because he explains that it 'came first' or even that 'it contained more water', etc.; he must also grasp that the duration $I_1 I_2$ or $I_1 II_2$ is shorter than the duration $I_1 I_3$ or $I_1 II_3$. In brief, we may put it that succession and simultaneity are not grasped operationally unless they lead to the construction of a system of colligated durations, much as durations are not grasped operationally unless they can be placed in one-to-one correspondence with a system of successions and simultaneities.

The child's conception of duration is thus a test of his grasp of the order of events. Moreover, a closer analysis of duration will corroborate our view that time concepts emerge as motions become increasingly co-ordinated. In effect, during stage I, the very concept of duration or of time intervals is so imprecise that if a child is asked to state whether the time it takes the water to run from I_1 to I_2 is longer or shorter than (or the same as) the time it takes from II_1 to II_2, he not only fails to realize that the two are equal because he sees the level in II rising more rapidly than the level drops in I, but also because he fails to grasp that velocity is inversely proportional to time, i.e. that more rapid = less time. During stage II, the child does discover this inverse relationship and begins to appreciate that time intervals may be divorced from speed or distance, but is still unable to co-ordinate these intervals. Thus he continues to hold that the duration $I_1 I_2$ is longer than the duration $II_1 II_2$, simply because the water level drops more slowly in I than it rises in II. Finally, at stage III, the child succeeds in correlating durations with the correct order of events. Here we have direct proof of how closely the concept of duration is linked to the co-ordination of motions and their velocity.

§1. *The first stage: Failure to grasp the idea of duration*

We have distinguished two sub-stages in the child's attempts to arrange the drawings D (or I and II separately), namely complete failure and success by trial and error, and in what follows we shall show that the same sub-stages mark the evaluation of durations. It must be stressed, however, that our questions on duration are no longer based on drawings but on marks on the flasks themselves (ink marks on flask I and elastic bands round flask II):

PEL (6 years): Does the water take as long to rise from here to there (II_1 to II_2) as it does to drop from here to there (I_1 to I_2)? *No.* How long does it take to rise here (II_1 to II_2)? *Two minutes, I think.* And to drop here (I_1 to I_2)? *Five minutes.* Why? *It's bigger and there's more water on top.* (Pel has failed to appreciate that the same amount of water is involved and thinks that the greater displacement must necessarily take longer.) What's the water doing here (I)? *It's dropped from up there to down here* (I_1 to I_2). How much time did that take? *About four minutes* And what happened there (in II)? *It rose to there.* In how much time? *In two minutes.* Didn't it take the same time? *No, first it took four minutes and then it took two minutes.* Why? *Because this one* (flask) *is taller.* And so? *So it takes longer to fill.* Why? *Because the top one is bigger here* (points to the swollen part of the pear shape) *and smaller there* (points to the lower, narrower part) *so it's bound to drop more quickly.*

If we look at this watch[1] how far will it move when the water rises from there to there (II_1 to II_2)? *Up to there* (45 seconds). And while the water drops from here to there (I_1 to I_2)? *Up to here* (55 seconds). Why? *Because it drops down more quickly.* What do you mean? *It'll take up to here* (55 seconds) *to drop and up to here* (45 seconds) *to rise.* Why? *Because it rises more slowly.*

LIN (6; 4) whose errors in arranging the drawings we have already described (Chapter One; §2): How long does it take the water to drop from here to there (I_1 to I_3)? *A short time.* And to go from there to there (II_1 to II_3)? *More time.* Why? *Because it has further to go.* Where was the water in here (II) when it was there on top (I_1)? *Here* (II_1). And when it was there (mark on I_3)? *Here* (elastic at II_3). Did it take the same time here ($I_1\ I_3$) as there ($II_1\ II_3$)? *No.* When the water was here (I_2) where was it in the bottom flask? (He points to II_2.) Does it take the same time to run from here to there ($I_1\ I_2$) as from here to there ($II_1\ II_2$)? *No, it takes more time here* ($II_1\ II_2$).

How long does it take you to go home from school? *Ten minutes.* And if you were to run, would you be getting home more quickly or more slowly? *More quickly.* So would it take you longer or not? *Longer.* How much? *It would take ten minutes.*

CHAP (7; 4). The water is allowed to drop from I_1 to I_2: Did you see that? *Yes, the water dropped here* ($I_1\ I_2$) *and rose there* ($II_1\ II_2$). Did it take the same time here ($I_1\ I_2$) and there ($II_1\ II_2$)? *No, it took longer to rise in here* (II) *than to drop down there* (I). Why should it take longer in here (II)? *Because I could tell.* We're going to let the water run out again (from I_2 to I_3) while you count how much time it takes. (Chap counts up to ten.) So? *This time, it took less time to rise here* (from II_2 to II_3) *than to drop there* (from I_2 to I_3). Why? *Because there was some water in it* (II) *already.* So what does that mean? *Less time.* How much would you have to count from here to there (I_1 to I_3)? *Ten.* And from here to there (II_1 to II_3)? *Eight.* Why? ...

A and B, two of the experimenters, run across the hall, starting simultaneously from the same point and stopping simultaneously, but with A some distance behind B. Did they start at the same time? *Yes.* Did they stop at the same time? *No.* Why? *That one* (A) *stopped first.* Next A and B start simultaneously but A from a point some two metres behind B, and stop simultaneously at the same point: Did they start at the same moment? *Yes.* And stop at the same moment? *Yes.* Did they go at the same speed? *No, that one* (A) *ran more quickly.* Did they run for the same length of time?

[1] The laboratory stop-watch.

No, that one (A) *took longer*. How much did that one take (B)? *Five minutes*. And this one (A)? *Ten minutes*.

How long does it take you to go home? *One hour*. And if you are in a hurry? *I go more quickly*. Does that take more or less time. *More time*. Why? *Because*.

Now watch this. If I let the water run first from here to there (I_1 to I_2) and then from there to there (I_1 to I_3), which will take longer? *That one* (I_1 to I_3). And from here to there (I_1 to I_3) and then from here to there (II_1 to II_2)? *That one* (II_1 to II_2). Why? *It's a longer way*.

In Chapter One, we saw that the idea of time involves the co-ordination of at least two motions—in the case of a single motion, temporal succession coincides with spatial succession (i.e. with geometrical distance in the direction of the motion), so that no specific time problem is posed. On the other hand, once two motions at different velocities have to be co-ordinated, the correlation of their successive positions does pose a specific temporal problem, i.e. one that can no longer be solved in terms of spatial succession—hence our assumption that the schema of time is constructed operationally by means of 'co-placements' and 'co-displacements'.

Now, what we have just learned about the evaluation of durations at stage I agrees with this assumption and, moreover, fully bears out what we have said with respect to the corresponding stage discussed in Chapter One (§§2–3). So long as only a single motion with uniform velocity is involved, e.g. the displacement of the water level in either I or II, the child has no apparent difficulties in estimating durations, simply because the latter do not appear as such but merely as functions of the displacements in space.

It was thus that Chap gave the correct answer, when he said that it takes longer to cover the distance I_1 to I_3 than it takes to cover the partial distance I_1 to I_2. This suggests that, in the case of a body moving with uniform velocity, young children have an intuitive conception of duration based on the appreciation that the whole (B = A + A') is greater than its part (A). But the moment two distinct motions are introduced, this intuitive conception breaks down, as witness Chap's assertion that the total duration $I_1 I_3$ was shorter than the partial duration $II_1 II_2$, simply because the rise in level from II_1 to II_2 looked bigger than the drop in level from I_1 to I_3. In other words, Chap failed to distinguish duration from distance. All in all, therefore, the concept of duration, like that of succession, involves the co-ordination of two motions with distinct velocities.

This helps to explain two essential aspects of all the reactions we have just been analysing: when comparing two simultaneous motions, children at stage I fail to grasp the equality of synchronous durations, and this because they fail to appreciate the inverse relationship between time and velocity. This failure, better than anything else, explains not only the initial difficulties besetting the intuitive evaluation of durations but also the fact that operational time is the co-ordination of co-displacements.

For no matter whether they are dealing with two changes in level or with two people running a race, children at stage I invariably assume that the body moving more rapidly must necessarily take longer. Thus, from the fact that the water level in flask I dropped more quickly than it rose in flask II, Pel deduced that the water took 4 or 5 minutes in the top $(I_1 \, I_2)$ as against only 2 minutes in the bottom flask $(II_1 \, II_2)$. Again, when asked to predict the respective durations on the stopwatch, he said: 'It'll take up to here (55″) to drop, and up to here (45″) to rise—because it rises more slowly'. Clearly Pel felt that the water in II rises more slowly than it drops in I, simply because he was thinking of the greater effort that climbing generally entails. Lin, by contrast, paid no heed to this aspect of the problem but simply argued that the water had a longer way to go from II_1 to II_2 and therefore must take more time. Both these children, as well as Chap, also declared that the quicker of the two simultaneous runs takes longer, i.e. that time is directly proportional to velocity. Chap, finally, argued that the water in II took more time to rise when the flask was empty and less time when 'there was some water in it already', no doubt because he felt that, in the second case, there was less work to be done, i.e. a smaller distance to be covered.

What precise significance attaches to all these stage I responses? The answer is relatively simple. To the adult, who is used to measurements and steeped in the ideas of classical mechanics, distance and time are the primitive concepts from which velocity must be derived: $v = s/t$. But we might equally hold—and observations of children at stage I support this belief which, moreover, agrees with the finding of quantum mechanics—that the primitive concepts are, in fact, distance and velocity and that it is time which is gradually derived from them by the correlation of co-displacements. It follows that, at stage I, time would, of necessity, be confused with velocity or distance (space traversed or change in water level).

Here we should say something about the intuitive nature of such concepts as displacements and velocity, the more so as there are several levels of intuition, each characteristic of a particular stage. As we said earlier (Chapter One, stage II), it is possible to distinguish clearly between 'articulated intuition' which, though bound up with perceptive relationships, involves semi-operational co-ordination, and 'direct' or 'amorphous' intuition, in which perceptive relationships are reproduced directly—some correctly and others incorrectly—but never fitted into a coherent whole (stage I). Thus 'direct' intuition leads to the correct appreciation of *fairly large displacements* involving moving bodies that start from superposed points and travel in the same direction along parallel straight lines, but not of bodies starting from points differently aligned. Similarly with velocity, 'direct' intuition yields the correct answer provided one of two bodies overtakes the other; however, once the two bodies end up in the same point, even if they started from distinct positions, their velocities are judged to be equal. In particular, when the two bodies pass each other out of the observer's view (for instance inside two tunnels, one of which is quite obviously longer than the other) but are seen to start and stop simultaneously, their velocities will generally be judged equal. It follows that, at first, velocity is not grasped as a ratio or relationship.[1]

Needless to say, the development of the time concept is intimately affected by this, so much so that we may well ask whether there might not also be a 'direct' intuition of duration. Now, direct intuition, in the case of two motions, only leads to correct estimates when the two bodies move with the same velocity, and start from the same point at the same moment but do not stop simultaneously: the motion of the one that stops first is then rightly judged to be of shorter duration, but

[1] The details of these experiments will be described in my forthcoming *Le Mouvement et la vitesse chez l'Enfant*.

only because it has covered a shorter distance. In much the same way, 'inner' duration leads to the correct intuition when one of two tasks performed with equal speed is discontinued first (for example, writing out the numbers 1–50). But in the second case, as in that of motion, the shorter duration is simply conceived as being directly proportional to the decrease in the work done. Now, it goes without saying that this type of 'direct' intuition only applies to equal velocities—the moment the velocities differ, direct intuition must make way for articulated intuition or for operation. This is because duration has become divorced from the space traversed or the work done and must now be constructed by the co-ordination of the motions themselves: physical time consequently assumes the form $t = s/v$, and psychological time that of the ratio of the work done to the rate of activity. We shall see that it is precisely because of their inability to co-ordinate co-displacements by means of 'direct' intuition that, during stage I, our subjects confuse duration with velocity and displacement.

We might note here that direct intuition does not even suffice to determine simultaneity (as we saw with Chap) unless the moving bodies come to rest in the same point in space (or in two distinct points after travelling with equal velocity). Thus Chap believed that one of two runners finished 'before' the other in time, simply because he finished before the other in space. It follows that the only correct 'direct' intuition of temporal succession is limited to the case of two bodies moving with equal velocity, or to the successive positions of a single body (and hence to the actions of a single subject). Now, it may well be that the obstacles in the path of the intuitive grasp of order, which we encountered in Chapter One, also impede the intuitive grasp of the relationship between time and velocity: unable to dissociate temporal from spatial succession (see Chapter Three) the child may fail to appreciate that the more quickly moving body must needs reach a given point in space 'before' the other one does; in other words, the child has not yet equated 'more rapid' with 'less time'. Moreover, since during stage I there is no clear co-ordination between succession and duration, the intuitive grasp of order does not entail a correct appreciation of the relationship between duration and speed.

Here it becomes clear why the direct intuition of duration,

based as it is on length of activity, can entail the relationship 'quicker = more time' as well as its converse. In fact, once we are not simply considering the motion of a single body or of two bodies moving with equal velocity, we can determine durations in two ways: we must either dissociate them from velocity and distance (which is precisely what children at stage I cannot do) or else we must somehow apply the intuitive idea that 'duration = increase of activity' to the co-displacements (which our subject cannot yet co-ordinate for lack of a differentiated concept of duration). In the second case, do we argue that the slower body has need of greater activity, and hence will take more time to complete a given course or task, or do we rather extend the meaning of activity and say that the more rapid body is, in fact, also the more active, i.e. that time varies as the velocity? Now, the association of the slower body with greater activity presupposes a high degree of abstraction and an inversion of apparent relationships, which, in the absence of operational techniques, can only be effected by 'articulated intuition': this is precisely what happens at stage II. While the child relies on direct intuition alone (stage I), it cannot but attribute the greatest activity to the quickest body. This would explain the strange idea that 'more rapidly = more time': its customary evaluation of time by the work done or the distance traversed, enables the child to make correct assessments of durations involving equal velocities, but once the velocities differ, it will attribute a longer duration to the quicker motion simply because it covers a larger distance. Thus Chap, while appreciating that the two runners started and stopped simultaneously, nevertheless contended that the one starting some distance behind the other took 'more time' because he was running faster (10 minutes as against 5 minutes). In other words, for Chap, duration depends neither on succession nor on simultaneity, but simply on activity. One could simplify things by saying that for these subjects 'more rapidly' = 'further' (overtaking) and 'further' = 'more time', irrespective of all other factors involved.[1] This explains why Pel thought that the same amount of water takes 'two minutes' to rise from II_1 to II_2 and 'one min ute' to drop

[1] See Chapter Eight for the reaction of children who, after having counted up to 15 while the hands of a watch advanced to 15″, predict that if they count more quickly the hands will go further.

from I_1 to I_2—in his view water 'naturally' takes longer (more activity) to rise than it takes to drop. Lin apparently used the opposite argument to arrive at the same result: ignoring the fact that $I_1 II_1$, $I_2 II_2$, . . . etc. are simultaneous, he failed to appreciate that the durations $I_1 I_2$, $II_1 II_2$, etc. are equal and argued that, since one of the two synchronous displacements of level 'had further to go' (the rise from II_1 to II_2), it also took 'more time'. For Pel, therefore, length of duration is a function of activity; for Lin it is a function of distance (change in level). As for Chap, he explained that the water took 'more time' to rise from II_1 to II_2 than it took to drop from I_1 to I_2 but that it took 'less time' to rise from II_2 to II_3 than to drop from I_2 to I_3 'because there was some water in it (II) already'. In other words, he felt that it takes longer to fill an empty flask than to empty a full one, but less time to continue filling the first than it does to continue emptying the second. There is no better way of illustrating the purely intuitive and 'active' character of primitive evaluations of duration: what Chap undoubtedly wished to convey was the idea that by continuing to fill the narrow flask II one is nearer the end of the action than by continuing to empty the wide flask I. In other words, he was evaluating the velocity by the final result and the time by the velocity, i.e. once again by activity.[1]

All in all, therefore, children at stage I have as little true understanding of duration as they have of the order of events— in both cases because they rely purely on 'direct intuition' and have not yet reached the stage of 'articulated intuition' let alone of operational 'grouping'. Now, though this failure is obvious within each of these two spheres (duration and order of events) taken separately, it must also be stressed that, before the emergence of operational techniques, the two spheres themselves remain unco-ordinated: the longer duration of a motion is not identified by the fact that it ends 'later' than another, and two simultaneous motions are not necessarily deemed to be of

---

[1] It might be objected that the relation 'more rapid = more time' is a purely linguistic one, based on the fact that both involve the term 'more'. However, it is simple to show that children produce the same evaluation of time even when they are not asked about velocities, i.e. when the word 'more' is not introduced. The linguistic similarity may increase the confusion, but does not create it.

equal duration. It is not until we reach stage III that we find a consistent correlation between order and duration.

§2. *The second stage: Articulated intuition of duration but lack of co-ordination: I. The equalization of synchronous durations*

The reader will recall from Chapter One that children at stage I were able to seriate the uncut drawings D but that they failed in the co-seriation of the drawings I and II. In other words, they had an intuitive grasp of the overall order of events but were unable to correlate them two at a time—they used 'articulated intuition' but had not yet reached the operational stage. Now the same thing is true of their grasp of duration. Children at this stage have begun to appreciate that time and velocity are inversely proportional but here, too, they rely on articulated intuition because they still lack the operational co-ordination needed to deduce the equality of the synchronous durations $I_1 I_2 = II_1 II_2$, to correlate durations with the order of events, and, finally, to fit different moments of time into a unified system.

When it comes to the equality of synchronous durations, we can say at once that the reason why children at stage II so often fail to establish the identity of the intervals $I_x I_y$, $II_x II_y$, is simply that, because the water level changes more quickly in I than it does in II, they think it must do so in a shorter time. Here are some examples, beginning with a subject half-way between stages I and II and ending with one half-way between stages II and III:

WAR ($6\frac{1}{2}$): Did the water take the same time to go from here to there ($I_1 I_2$) as it took from here to there ($II_1 II_2$)? *No, it took longer in the bottom* ($II_1 II_2$). Why? *Because the water dropped more quickly but rose more slowly.* Does running home from school take you the same time as walking? *No, when I run I get home more quickly, it takes less time.* Look at this (two figures on the table which are kept in motion for the same time but with A moving more quickly than B.) How long did this one (B) take? *Five minutes. They were running the same* (simultaneity of start and finish) *but this one was quicker and so he went further.* And how long did that one (A) take? *Less time.* Look at the flasks again (the level is allowed to drop from I_2 to I_3). Did that take the same time as this ($II_2 II_3$)?

44

It took less time on top and a little longer at the bottom. Try to count. (War counts to 8 while the level drops from I_3 to I_4.) Well, how much time did it take? *It took 8 on top and 8 at the bottom.* So is it the same time? *No, it takes longer to rise; the one on top dropped more quickly.*

DUC (6; 5): When the top flask was full, what was happening at the bottom? *This bottle (II) was empty.* And now (I_6)? *The one on top is empty and the bottom one is full. All the water has run down.* Did it take the same time to empty that one as it took to fill this one? *No, the water took longer to rise because it went higher* (in II); *it drops down much more quickly.* But you were looking at the watch; how long did it take to drop? *That much* (30 seconds) And to rise? *That much also.* So it took the same time? *No, it dropped more quickly and took longer to rise.*

LIL (6; 10), same answers. But how long did it take from here to there ($I_1 I_2$)? *Two minutes to drop down.* And to rise? *Two as well, oh no, that's wrong, four minutes.* How could we make certain? *We would have had to use another glass exactly like this one* (II), *and fill it right up to here* (II_6). In other words, for Lil, durations can only be compared in the case of identical vessels!

FLEI (7 years). ($I_1 I_4$ and $II_1 II_4$): *It takes more time here* ($II_1 II_4$) *because it goes on longer.* Why? *It takes more time in the bottom* (II) *because it's bigger and taller; it takes less time to drop down than to rise.* Look carefully ($I_4 I_5$ and $II_4 II_5$). How long on top? *That much* (30″). And below? *That much* (90″). Why? *Because it's rising at the bottom.* But look carefully. (The experiment is performed and instead of paying heed to the simultaneities he notices that the change in level is greater in II.) *Oh, no, it's the other way round, it takes this much* (30″) *in the bottom and that much* (90″) *on top.* Look at these two pencils. (They are moved along the table, starting from the same point and stopping simultaneously, but one in front of the other.) Did they start together? *Yes.* And stop together? *Yes.* So did they move for the same length of time? *Yes.* (hesitation) So what about the water here and there ($I_5 I_6$ and $II_5 II_6$)? *It took more time on top.*

NIC (8½). ($I_1 I_2$ and $II_1 II_2$): *It took more time to drop down because the water ran less fast.* And here ($I_2 I_3$ and $II_2 II_3$)? *It took more time to drop because the water was running more slowly.* How could you tell? *It changed more here* (the levels in II; a correct observation), *because the water rose more quickly.* How much time did it take to run down? *Five minutes.* And to rise? *One minute.* Why? *Because the water rose more slowly.*

We run a race with him through the hall, starting and stopping at the same time: *You went more quickly, so you took more time.* But didn't we start together? *Yes.* And stop together? *Yes.* Then didn't we take the same time? *No, it wasn't the same time because we didn't go at the same speed.*

HEN (9 years): Does it take the same time from here to there $(I_1 I_3)$ as from here to there $(II_1 II_3)$? *Yes, its the same, it's the same number* (= amount of water). Why? *Because it gets less here* (I) *and rises there* (II). And that takes the same time? *No.* Why? *It takes more time here* $(II_1 II_3)$. Why? *Because it's higher, no, it takes less time because it's quicker.* Show me on the watch how long it takes here $(I_1 I_3)$. *That much* (15″) . . . *Oh, it's the same thing. It's the same thing because it's the same number* (amount of water).

What is so interesting about these reactions is that they are similar in all respects to those we met at stage I, except for the fact that duration has become inversely proportional to velocity. It should be stressed that this development represents a regular chronological succession. Thus amongst the hundreds of subjects we have examined, some (stage I) held that velocity was directly proportional to time but failed to identify equal durations $(I_x I_y = II_x II_y)$, others (stage II) believed that time was inversely proportional to velocity and also failed to equalize synchronous durations, but there were none who were able to equalize synchronous durations while yet believing that t varies directly with v (except for momentary lapses).

Now, the fact that the comprehension of duration involves two stages—one in which duration is considered as being inversely related to velocity and in which two synchronous motions at different velocities are not thought to be of equal duration, and the other in which synchronous durations are equalized—is clear proof that the idea of time results from the gradual co-ordination of motions or co-displacements. But how can we explain the gap between these two stages? The only reasonable answer would be that the relationship children discover first (i.e. that time is inversely proportional to velocity) is the more intuitive of the two, while the relationship they establish next (i.e. the equality of synchronous duration) must involve a more highly operational approach. Now, an analysis of our subjects' answers shows, in effect, that to grasp the inverse relation between time and velocity the child need merely distinguish

46

between two intuitively apprehended aspects of activity, while the equalization of two durations, synchronous or otherwise, calls for operational grouping and hence for decentration with respect to activity.

The belief that time is *directly* proportional to velocity is rooted in the mistaken idea that *activity* and the *work done* can be combined into a single concept. Now, when two tasks are performed at a uniform rate, time can, in fact, be measured by the work done: it takes longer to draw 30 strokes than it takes to draw 20 at the same rate. However, when one of two people draws 30 strokes *while* the other draws 20, the first is obviously working harder, whence the illusion that it takes him longer. In other words, when work is done at unequal rates, the result is no longer a reliable measure of duration, unless it is coupled to an introspective assessment of the activity, and quite particularly of the various factors governing the speed of the action (P. Janet).

In brief, the essential difference between subjects at the first and second stages is that the former judge duration purely by the results (work done or distance covered), while the latter dissociate the work done from the activity itself and judge duration by the introspective characteristics of the latter. Now, depending on the factors governing the speed of an action (acceleration, effort, enthusiasm, etc., or boredom, fatigue, etc.), durations may 'feel' longer or shorter after an action than they do while the action is being performed: work done with great absorption seems to be finished very quickly. In other words, the child has to use introspection before it can conclude that velocity and duration are inversely proportional. We see, therefore, how the idea that time and velocity are in inverse proportion results from the simple articulation of intuition, based on the analysis of the action itself, while belief in the direct ratio is due to a direct or amorphous intuition based on the results of the action alone. A detailed confirmation of this hypothesis will be found in Chapter Ten, where we shall deal with time and action.

On the other hand, when it comes to the identification of the two durations $I_x\,I_y$ and $II_x\,II_y$ by reference to the simultaneity of the levels I_x and II_x and I_y and II_y (or to the identity of the mass of water leaving I and entering II), the child must be able to make a correlation surpassing both direct and articulated

47

intuition. Thus while subjective time is plastic—expanding during the performance of slow tasks and contracting during faster action—objective time is homogeneous and uniform, and can only be grasped by the decentration of thought away from subjective ideas of duration. Hence, in our experiment, the child cannot simply project his own time into each of the motions in turn—a characteristic of egocentric intuition during the first two stages—but must conceive of a homogeneous time common to two motions, i.e. independent of the velocities of either. In brief, what is called for is the co-ordination of co-displacements and not the separate assessment of two distinct displacements in the light of the activity involved. Now this type of co-ordination is a characteristic of operational decentration (grouping) and as such the very opposite of intuitive centration (egocentrism), so that it is only natural that it should not occur until stage III.

During stage II, in effect, the child, even while recognizing that two tasks may be begun and finished at the same time, does not conclude as to the equality of their duration. For example, War, regarding the two figures on the table, claimed that they 'were running the same' but that one of them took 'less time' because it finished up behind the other. Next he counted while the water level dropped from I_3 to I_4, and found that 'it took 8 on top and 8 at the bottom' but nevertheless concluded that it 'takes longer to rise [because] the one on top dropped more quickly'. Similarly, Duc explained that the changes of level in both flasks took 30″ but nevertheless contended that the level in II 'took longer to rise' because it rose more slowly. Lil, again, stated quite categorically that it is impossible to compare durations with flasks of different shape and hence with unequal changes of level. Flei managed to identify the synchronous durations of the two motions on the table, but did not see any similarity between them and the flow of the water. Nic asserted that 'it wasn't the same time because we didn't go at the same speed'. Finally Hen, who began like the others, ended up (thus reaching the boundaries of stage III) by assuming the equal duration of $I_x I_y$ and $II_x II_y$ for this very interesting reason: 'It's the same thing because it's the same number (amount of water)'.

Thus we find that in all these cases (except for the last) the child behaves as if it were incapable of conceiving that two motions with different velocities could possibly have the same duration or a common time: there is one time for the water flowing out of flask I and another for the water pouring into flask II. As far as these subjects are concerned, length of time is simply a matter of displacement.

In brief, though they have come to appreciate that time is inversely proportional to velocity, they argue that since the velocity of the flow is greater in I or in II, one of the synchronous durations must be longer than the other. As for the velocities themselves, it should be noted that precisely because they fail to treat time relationships by operational grouping, these children continue to evaluate them in a purely intuitive fashion. In general, they feel that a rise in level takes more time because a drop (over an equal distance) is more rapid. This, for example, was Flei's view; however, when he looked more closely at the actual displacements and observed that the change was greater in the bottom flask, he changed his mind: 'Oh, no, it's the other way round,' he said, and Nic and Hen were of much the same opinion.

Now all these reactions raise the question of why there is this initial failure to grasp the unicity of time, at least as far as duration in the external world is concerned. Let us note first of all that this failure demonstrates clearly that intuition, and even articulated intuition, is incapable of engendering physical time, even in its purely qualitative (intensive) form. All instants and all durations are part of one and the same time, said Kant, to stress its intuitive rather than conceptual nature: a unique reality, however complex, is bound to be an object of intuition, by contrast to the sensuous ingredients of experience whose correlation calls for a synthetic act of judgement. And, to the average adult, time is, in fact, an 'a priori form of sensibility'. However, we know that, at very great velocities, durations vary from observer to observer. Moreover, we know that when it is first constructed, time is not conceived as something unique (when Aristotle postulated a 'subjective time' he was thinking of the time of children and not of that of the relativists). All in all, it is of considerable psychological interest to discover the precise nature of a conception (the unicity of time) that is lacking at first, appears quite naturally at a certain level of intellectual development, and is then surpassed, much as the space of common sense was surpassed and reduced to a particular case by the emergence of non-Euclidean geometry.

49

Now, the Kantian contrast between the unity of complex objects, based on intuition, and that of manifolds based on concepts, does not exhaust all the synthetic possibilities for, as Kant himself realized, the set of integers constitutes a unity that falls neither into the first nor into the second category: it is a 'schema', i.e. a procedure of the imagination by which the categories of the understanding are applied to sensuous intuitions. Now, the set of integers constitutes a group, and in modern mathematical language, we may say that this particular 'group', or every type of logical 'grouping', is an example of a system that is operational rather than intuitive, and not necessarily conceptual.[1] True, in the case of the 'grouping' of classes and logical relations we are entitled to claim that the system is of a conceptual kind, but only if we remember that the whole system, i.e. the 'grouping' itself, is not a simply-ordered set but a well-ordered set and thus contains its unity as such. But side by side with logical 'groupings' and with arithmetical and discontinuous groups, we can also construct 'groupings' of infra-logical or space-time operations (partition and placement or displacement) on the logical model, and continuous 'groups' on the mathematical model. Now, these systems correspond to the type of unity that Kant was wrong to describe as intuitive. Poincaré has proved this for space, when he emphasized the genetic rôle of the 'displacement group', and it is worth pointing out that this group may correspond to qualitative 'groupings' based on the simplest of all operations.

To apply a similar solution to the problem of time strikes us as having two advantages. In the first place, just as the Euclidean sub-group can be associated with non-Euclidean sub-groups in which the unicity of space governing relatively slow motion on our macroscopic scale no longer holds sway, so the Galilean group, which expresses time on our slow scale, may be considered a first approximation of the Lorentz group.[2] In the second place, if the unicity of time does, in fact, depend on the continuous nature of the group characterizing it and on the 'infra-logical' nature of the corresponding 'groupings', it be-

[1] For 'group' and 'grouping' see §5 of this chapter.

[2] In which time is expressed by $dt' = dt \sqrt{1 - \dfrac{v^2}{c^2}}$, where c is the velocity of light.

comes clear why the postulate of a unique time should emerge as soon as the child begins to 'group' perceptual and conceptual relations, and why it should elude children at stages I and II, whose thought is completely perceptual or intuitive. For while intuition enables the child to predict that by slowing down a motion we increase its duration, it does not help him to compare the respective durations of two motions; to do so the child must needs pass beyond intuition towards the construction of an operational system based on succession and serial correspondence.

Now, psychological experiments do, in fact, bear out the above interpretation: before the unicity of time is grasped, elementary grouping operations continue to elude our subjects; both are constructed simultaneously at a later stage. What precisely are these elementary operations?

As far as the order of events is concerned, the reader will recall that they consist of a double seriation (I_1 I_2 I_3 . . . etc., II_1 II_2 II_3 . . . etc.) and of a correlation or co-seriation based on the recognition of simultaneities (I_1 II_1; I_2 II_2; I_3 II_3; . . . etc.). Now, these infra-logical operations of 'co-placement' (and 'co-displacement') correspond to 'partitions' in the qualitative evaluation of durations. Between any two successive points of the co-series, we can, in effect, cut off an interval having these two points as its limits, and this interval is a duration by definition (if the two points are not successive, the duration is zero (simultaneity)). It follows (1) that two intervals I_x I_y and II_x II_y lying between the corresponding points I_x II_x and I_y II_y must be of equal or synchronous duration; and (2) that when three points I_x I_y I_z (and the corresponding points II_x II_y II_z) are successive, the duration I_x I_y ($= II_x$ II_y) must needs be shorter than the duration I_x I_z ($= II_x$ II_z) of which it forms a part. The reader will notice that nothing at all need be known about the absolute value of these durations nor about the precise relation between I_x I_y ($= II_x$ II_y) and I_y I_z ($= II_y$ II_z). In other words, the two operations are infra-logical and qualitative (intensive) and not quantitative or extensive. It follows that it must be possible to construct a 'grouping' of durations by fitting them as so many parts into an ever-increasing whole, and also that such a 'grouping' will correspond to that of the order of events.

Now we have seen that children at stage II are unable to

perform operation (1), i.e. to equalize synchronous durations. We shall now attempt to show that this failure, and also that of performing operation (2), i.e. the colligation of partial durations, is due to a failure of 'grouping'. Before we do so, it might be as well to mention that there is yet a third operation (3) by which this qualitative grouping is transformed into a quantitative group, and which is, psychologically, no more complex than the other two.

3. The moment our subjects, either by reference to the amount of water run out from flask I, or to the height of the levels in the cylindrical flask II, introduce the equality of two successive durations (for example $I_x I_y$ and $I_y I_z$ or of $II_x II_y$ and $II_y II_z$), the colligation of durations (2) assumes a numerical character: $I_x I_y (= II_x II_y) = 1$; and $I_x I_z (= II_x II_z) = 2$ units of time, no matter whether the time is measured by a watch, a sand glass or any other means. Let us merely note that, in all these measurements, the equalization of two successive (and no longer synchronous) durations involves the implicit or explicit reliance on the principle of the conservation of velocity: the water, the hand of the watch, or the sand, must be thought of as moving at a constant velocity, i.e. as covering the same distance in the same amount of time.

§3. The second stage: II. The qualitative colligation of durations and their measurement

Now, as we shall see below, neither the qualitative operation (2) nor the quantative operation (3) is grasped by children at stage II. Our analysis has been based on the use of the uncut drawings I and II, level markers, a cardboard clock whose single hand is moved forward 5 minutes with every change of level, and a stop-watch (tap shut every 10 seconds). Here are some of the reactions we obtained:

TAR (6; 8) is shown the drawings $I_1 I_2 I_3 I_4$ and $II_1 II_2 II_3 II_4$ in exact superposition and in correct serial correspondence: What do you know about the time it took the water here (I_1 to I_3) and there (II_2 to II_4)? *It took more time here* (II_2 to II_4). Why? *There was more of it.* Didn't we move the hands forward twice between here and there ($I_1 I_3$)? *Yes.* And here ($II_1 II_3$)? *Also.* So did it take longer or not? ... If you let the water run in from here to there (II_1

to II_3) while your friend lets it drop from here to there (I_2 to I_4) would it take the same time or not? *It would take longer here* (II_2 to II_4). And what about these two ($I_2 I_4$ and $II_1 II_4$)? *It would take longer here* ($I_2 I_4$).

CLAN (6; 10): How long does it take the water from here to there (II_1 to II_2, marked with elastic)? *That much* (15″). And from here to there (II_2 to II_3)? *That much* (15″). So does this one ($II_1 II_2$) take the same time as that one ($II_2 II_3$)? *Oh no, that one always takes longer, there is more water in it.*

MAGA ($7\frac{1}{2}$): Did it take more, less, or the same time here (II_1 to II_2) and there (II_2 to II_3)? *Less time for this one* ($II_1 II_2$). Why? *Because this one* (II_2) *was already a bit full.* (Maga, therefore, thinks like Clan that it takes longer to add water than to pour it into an empty jar.) Did you look at the watch while the water was running from here to there ($II_1 II_2$)? *Yes.* And from here to there (II_2 to II_3)? *Oh yes, it's the same thing.* So would you say it took as long from here to there ($II_1 II_2$) as from here to there ($II_5 II_6$)? *It takes longer here* ($II_1 II_2$) *because there was nothing there before.* How much water was put in here ($II_1 II_2$) and there ($II_5 II_6$)? *The same. The same amount of water was put in both times.* And in the same amount of time? *No.* Which took longer? *This one* ($II_5 II_6$). Why? *If it hadn't taken longer it wouldn't have risen to the top.* Did it take the same time from here to there ($I_1 I_3$) as it took from here to there ($II_1 II_2$)? *No.* Why? *It took longer here* ($II_1 II_2$) *because there was nothing there before.*

MAT (8 years): Which took longer, for the water to go from here to there ($I_1 I_3$) or from here to there ($II_1 II_2$)? *This one took longer* ($II_1 II_2$). Why? ... And from here to there ($I_2 I_4$) or from here to there ($I_6 I_7$)? *That one* ($I_6 I_7$). Why? ...

HEN (9 years): Did it take the water the same time to drop here (I_1 to I_3) as it took to rise in there (II_1 to II_4)? *There was more water here* (II_4) *than there* (empty space in I_3, which he indicates on the drawings). And what about these (I_3 to I_4 and II_3 to II_5)? *It took the same time.* What about these two ($I_1 I_3$ and $I_5 I_7$)? *It ran out three times in both cases.* The same time? ... And what about ($I_1 I_5$) and ($II_1 II_4$)? *More water ran out here* (II). What about the time? *The same.* And what about ($II_1 II_4$) and ($II_1 II_5$)? *It took longer here* (correct).

Now for some children questioned by means of the second of the techniques described in Chapter One (§1): instead of using watches, we simply tell the child in advance (or remind him at the appropriate moment) that the same amount of water is being run out every time:

DEL (7; 7), working without drawings or a watch: ($I_1 I_2$ and $II_1 II_2$) *It takes longer to drop down.* Why? *Because each time the water runs out the bottom one gets higher.* So? *It takes more time* (= more work). And here ($I_2 I_3$ and $II_2 II_3$)? *More time at the bottom.* Why? *Because it's got further to go.* What about the water? *It's the same.* So? ... And what about ($II_2 II_3$) and ($II_3 II_4$)? *It takes the same time because it's the same lot.* And this ($I_1 I_2$ and $I_4 I_5$)? *It takes less time here* ($I_1 I_2$) *because that one* ($I_4 I_5$) *is bigger.* Is it the same amount of water? *No, more here* ($I_4 I_5$). And what about the bottom? (We point to $II_1 II_2$ and $II_4 II_5$.) *The same.* And on top? *Oh, yes, because it's running out the same way.* The same time? *Yes, because it's the same amount.* And what about ($I_5 I_6$) and ($II_5 II_6$)? *It takes the same time because it's the same amount of water*. . . . *No, it drops down more quickly, so it takes less time to run out.* And what about ($I_1 I_3$) and ($II_2 II_4$)? *Less time here* (I) *because it's a longer bit.* Same amount? *Yes, it's higher at the bottom but the same amount.* And what about the time? *It takes longer at the bottom because it's rising. It goes more quickly on top, so it takes less time.* Del thinks that it would take the same time to fill two flasks, one wide, the other slim, to the same level *because it's the same height*: And what about these ($I_1 I_3$ and $II_1 II_2$)? *More time here* (II).

MOG (8 years): What about these ($I_1 I_2$ and $II_1 II_2$)? *It takes more time here* (II) *because the bottom one fills up less quickly than the top one empties out.* And ($II_1 II_2$) and ($II_4 II_5$)? *It takes the same time because it's the same thing: there's the same space between these two lines* (elastics) *as there is here* ($II_1 II_2$). And what about these ($II_1 II_3$ and $II_2 II_4$)? *It's the same, because there are two* (spaces) *in both.* And ($I_1 I_4$) and ($II_1 II_4$)? *The same time because the water fills this one* (II) *and empties that one* (I) *in the same time.* Is there the same space here ($I_1 I_4$) and there ($II_1 II_4$)? *No.* Does it take the same time? *No. It takes longer here* (II). And what about ($I_1 I_4$) and ($I_2 I_5$)? *More time here* ($I_1 I_4$) *because when we've emptied these three spaces* ($I_1 I_4$) *only this one* ($I_4 I_5$) *is left, so we can't empty these three spaces* ($I_2 I_5$) *all over again.*

And what about ($I_2 I_5$) and ($II_3 II_5$)? *It takes longer at the bottom* ($II_3 II_5$) *because there's more water in it.* How many spaces? *Two in the bottom, three on top.* So? *But it's only three small spaces.* What about the amount of water? *More in the bottom.* (incorrect) And if we poured this one ($II_3 II_5$) into the top, how many spaces would that make? *Two spaces.* (correct) So which takes more time ($I_2 I_5$ or $II_3 II_5$)? *More time for the two spaces in the bottom because there's more water in them.*

On watching two men run, Mog admits that they started and stopped at the same time, but nevertheless contends that 'the quicker of the two spent less time because he was running faster'.

BOIR (8; 11) similarly vacillates between estimates based on the quantity of water and those based on the displacement or the rate of displacement of the levels: Do these ($I_1 I_2$ and $II_1 II_2$) start and finish at the same time? *Yes, they are the same.* So do they take the same time? *No, this one ($II_1 II_2$) takes longer.* And what about these ($II_3 II_4$ and $II_4 II_5$)? *Same thing, because the elastics are the same.* And ($I_3 I_4$ and $II_4 II_5$)? *No.* And these ($I_3 I_4$ and $II_4 II_5$)? *They took the same time because you let out the same amount of water.* So what about these ($I_3 I_4$ and $II_4 II_5$)? *It wasn't the same time. This one (II) took longer because it's higher.* But was it the same amount of water? *Ah, yes, it took the same time.* One moment you say it wasn't the same and the next moment you say it was. *No, it's not the same because it's higher there ($II_4 II_5$) so it fills up more slowly and takes more time. The top empties more quickly so it takes less time.* But when the water was down here (I_4) hadn't it come up to there (II_5)? *No.* And did the water come up to here (I_6) and there (II_6) at the same time or not? *Yes, at the same time.* So which of these ($I_4 I_6$ and $II_5 II_6$) took longer? *This one ($II_5 II_6$).* Why? *It just took longer.*

MIR (7; 10) finally, reached the boundary of stage III: ($I_1 I_2$ and $I_2 I_3$) *It takes the same time, because it's the same distance.* And ($I_1 I_2$ and $II_2 II_3$)? *More time below because it's longer.* And what of these ($I_5 I_6$ and $II_5 II_6$)? *More time on top.* How much water? *Ah, it's the same amount and it takes the same time.* And what of the distance? *It's longer on top but it takes the same time.*

Every one of these replies is highly instructive in itself, and if we compare them generally with those described in §2, we begin to understand why children, even at this stage, are unable to grasp the idea of unique and homogeneous time: they cannot as yet produce a coherent 'grouping' of the relations involved. Let us now see what precisely are the operations involved in such a grouping.

If we ignore quantitative time, i.e. all units of time, the 'grouping' of durations is simply a colligation by operational partition: the interval $D_1 D_2$ of duration *a* is part of the interval

$D_1 D_3$ of duration b (whence the interval $D_2 D_3$ is of duration $b - a = a'$); b in turn is part of $D_1 D_4$; whence $D_3 D_4 = c - b = b'$; etc.). Is this type of colligation, which is simply based on the fact that the part is smaller than the whole, understood by our subjects (Operation 2)? The facts show that it is not.

No doubt, if they were merely asked to compare a partial duration measured by the flow of liquid in a single vessel, to a total duration measured in the same vessel, they would encounter no difficulties. Thus when Hen was asked to compare the durations $II_1 II_4$ and $II_1 II_5$, he replied at once that the second was longer. But this is simply because he confused time with the duration of a single motion and because he could ignore the behaviour of all other moving bodies. In that case, and in that case only, a partial duration is readily seen to be shorter than a total duration. Now this recognition is based on a primary intuition (much as the intuitive grasp of simultaneity is based on spatial coincidence, and that of the order of succession on the motion of a single body), and cannot yet be called a proper colligation of durations, since the whole is still, so to speak, in the same plane as its parts and hence the simple, intuitive, extension of these parts in space.

By contrast, when it comes to the comparison of the partial duration of one process (for instance the flow $II_1 II_4$) to the total duration of a different process (e.g. the flow $I_1 I_5$), it is no longer possible to fit the part into the whole by spatial perception alone. Simultaneities and successions have also to be taken into account: I_1 and II_1 are simultaneous, but II_4 precedes I_5, therefore $I_1 I_5$ is of longer duration than $II_1 II_4$. Now this kind of colligation, which is based on co-displacements and is therefore specific to time, is quite beyond children at stage II. Thus Hen, though quite capable of coping with durations in II, nevertheless contended that $I_1 I_5 = II_1 II_4$, because he ignored the simultaneities and successions and merely paid heed to the height of the levels. Does that mean that the child simply forgets the order of events? No doubt it does, but precisely because, at this stage, durations, though constructed from 'intervals' between seriable events, are still evaluated quite independently of one another. If we remind our subjects of the successions, as we generally do, they make no deductions as to the durations: thus Boir agreed that I_6 and II_6 were simultaneous and that I_4 preceded

II_5, but nevertheless thought that the duration $II_5 II_6$ was greater than $I_3 I_6$, simply because he thought that the level in II changed more slowly. Conversely, Tar thought that $I_2 I_4$ was of greater duration than $II_1 II_4$ because it changed more slowly, etc., etc. Mog went so far as to recognize that $II_3 II_5$ represents 'two spaces' and $I_2 I_5$ 'three spaces', but since the latter were 'small', he thought it would take 'more time for the two spaces in the bottom because there's more water in them'.

In brief, subjects at this stage are quite incapable of colligating durations, simply because they are unable to relate duration to the order of succession. Now before we can establish that $I_x I_z > II_x II_y$ or $II_x II_z > I_x I_y$, we must be able to understand that $I_x I_y = II_x II_y$, i.e. we must be able to equalize synchronous durations. The operations (1) and (2) are therefore closely related and it is natural that if there is a failure to perform the operation (1) or the equalization of durations, it will be the same with operation (2) or the colligation of durations.

Now if that is what happens with simple qualitative colligations (i.e. with logical or rather with infra-logical colligations) it goes without saying that children at this stage will be unable to perform operation (3), i.e. the equalization of successive durations or the measurement of time.

In effect, the construction of a time unit m, calls for the correlation of at least two equalizations. Thus, in the case of two successive durations a ($=$ e.g. $II_1 II_2$) and a' ($=$ e.g. $II_2 II_3$) such that $a + a' = b$ (where $b = II_1 II_3$), our subjects have to grasp that the synchronous durations a and m are equal and that the synchronous durations a' and m are equal as well, and must then deduce that $a = a'$ and $b = 2a$. This type of co-ordination clearly calls for both the equalization of synchronous durations and also for the colligation of durations (operations (1) and (2)), so that, quite obviously, operation (3) cannot precede the other two. In addition, the common measure m must remain unchanged even while it is being displaced, and this presupposes a grasp of the principle of the conservation of velocity: once velocity is conserved, a duration m can be identified as a given distance covered at a constant velocity. In our particular case, in order to construct m, the child can either consult a watch ($=$ distance covered by a hand moving at constant velocity), or it can refer to the flow of water: equal changes in level, $II_1 II_2$ or $II_2 II_3$, etc. correspond to equal amounts of water flowing at a constant velocity (changes in pressure and other factors affecting the regularity of this particular clock are too small to affect the general results).

Now, the simple qualitative colligation of durations based on the order of events, is already a form of operational grouping (but of an infra-logical rather than quantitative type): as such it implies the reversibility of thought. To grasp that the duration $a \, (= II_1 II_2)$ is shorter than the duration $b \, (I_1 I_3 = II_1 II_3)$ once the water has reached $II_3 \, (= I_3)$, the child must, in effect, go back in thought to $II_1 \, (= I_1)$, and hence be able to traverse the intervals $II_1 II_2$ and $II_1 II_3$ in either direction. But in that case, it is thought alone which becomes displaced: the child moves a mental clock in such a way that an hour in the past is always equal to an hour in the present or an hour in the future. In other words, before it can equalize $a \, (= II_1 II_2)$ and $a' \, (= II_2 II_3)$ and pose that $b \, (II_1 II_3) = 2a$, the child must first be able to 'mobilize' the time m of the watch ($=$ the flow of the water at a certain velocity over a given distance $II_1 II_2 = II_2 II_3 = II_2 II_3 = $ etc.) so as to apply it equally well to liquid that has flowed in the past, to liquid that is still flowing, and to liquid that will flow in the future.

Now, this precondition of reversibility either of thought itself (qualitative operational time) or else of the 'mental clock' (quantitative operational time) is absent in subjects at stage II. It is thus that Mog volunteered the following remark (in response to our request that he compare $I_1 I_3$ with $I_2 I_5$): 'When we've emptied these three spaces ($I_1 I_3$) only this one ($I_1 I_5$) is left, so we can't empty these three spaces ($I_1 I_5$) all over again'. From which he concluded that $I_1 I_3$ is of longer duration—the only space he was prepared to compare it with was $I_3 I_5$! To the adult, this behaviour seems utterly astonishing, but, in fact, it is easily explained and, moreover, holds the key to the construction of operational mechanisms or groupings.

In an earlier experiment, children were shown a box containing some twenty wooden beads, two of which were white while the rest were brown. The children were then asked which would make a longer necklace: all the wooden ones or the brown ones. Now all of them replied that the brown necklace would be the longer of the two because only two white beads would be left. In other words, thinking by irreversible images and not by reversible operations, or more specifically by concentrating on one of the parts (the brown beads) only, the children lost sight of the whole. Now precisely the same mechanism operates in the comparison of a partial duration (e.g. II_2 II_3) with a total duration (e.g. I_1 I_3): because of irreversibility, the child limits its comparisons to the distances, with the result that the part is considered larger than the whole. One of our subjects, Laur,[1] threw a great deal of light on the secret processes of infra-logical thought when he explained that once we had made a necklace of brown beads, the latter, though admittedly made of wood as well, had been used up so that we were only left with white beads for the wooden necklace. Such interpretations, though far from being stupid, nevertheless stress the natural contrast between intuitive thought 'centred' on activity alone (irreversible centrism) and logical thought which 'decentres' action by rendering it reversible. Now for reversible thought, the brown necklace is simply a hypothesis, and there is no reason why, once it has been made, it cannot be destroyed again to be incorporated into, and compared with, another hypothetical necklace containing *all* the wooden beads. In a 'mental experiment' repeating an irreversible action, on the other hand, a string once constructed in theory is a string constructed in practice, and so prevents the construction of other strings with the same beads.

Mog argued in a similar way when he contended that, once the water has run out from I_1 to I_3 it is impossible to compare I_1 I_4 to I_2 I_5. More precisely, imagining the water back at I_2 is incompatible with the existence of a duration I_1 I_4, since the latter depends on the fact that the water is in I_4 and not in I_2! It is therefore their lack of reversible mobility that prevents subjects at this stage from estimating durations or from reconstructing the overall order of events. Paradoxically enough, time can only be understood as duration (by contrast to present, 'lived' time) once thought has become reversible. We might even say that the schema of time is characteristically reversible and that only its contents are irreversible. What we call 'the course of time' is, in fact, nothing other than the sequence of events, but if 'time' represents all the relations of co-placement

[1] See Piaget and Szeminska, *Le Genèse du Nombre chez l'Enfant*, p. 203.

and co-displacement relating to these events, then it must needs be reversible because succession involves two directions and only the contents follow a straight path. It is thus that, though a past event cannot be resurrected, we can nevertheless reconstruct the past in thought: while the content ceases to be 'present', the framework persists and can incorporate the memory or mental reconstruction of a past event in the form of a new content. Now, this framework is neither empty nor static; it is the mobile system of successions and intervals engendered by the co-ordination of positions and changes of positions, and hence by placements and displacements—a system that consists neither of events nor of motions but of all their interrelations and that is therefore bound to be reversible.

The failure to distinguish between irreversible events and the reversible mechanisms of operational time is expressed in yet another form: children at stage II are unable to differentiate the duration of two displacements from (a) the order of succession of their end points, and (b) the order of succession of their starting points. It was thus that (case a) Tar and Clan judged the duration of the flow by the end point alone: 'There was more of it,' said Tar when comparing $II_2\,II_4$ to $I_1\,I_3$, and 'that one always takes longer; there is more water,' said Clan when asked to compare $II_2\,II_3$ with $I_1\,I_2$. This was no misunderstanding of the question itself, as we were able to verify, but a simple lack of mental mobility and hence a failure to retrace the course of events from start to finish. In other words, these subjects replace the idea of a reversible relationship between start and finish with that of an irreversible flow towards an end point—they substitute the content of time for its form by 'centring' attention on the flow. This is easily understood if we remember that to primitive intuition, time is simply the 'prolongation of activity'. Thus Maga attributed a greater duration to $II_2\,II_3$ than to $II_1\,II_2$ 'because here (II_2) it was already a bit full', but having had his attention drawn to the stop-watch, he changed his mind and adopted approach (b), i.e. he judged the duration purely by the end point of the action, declaring that $II_1\,II_2$ 'takes longer because there was nothing there before'. Chap (whose answer we now understand) reacted similarly at stage I when, thinking of the action still to be accomplished, he attributed the greater duration to the first change of level, but forgot to compare the end points! After which he returned to criterion (a): $II_5 II_6$ takes longer than $II_1 II_2$ because 'if it hadn't taken longer it wouldn't have risen to the top'.

In brief, children at stage II, as at stage I, fail to dissociate time as a structure from its content, i.e. from events or motions, and hence judge duration by either the starting or else by the end points of an action, but never by the two together. This explains why operation (3), i.e. the comparison of successive durations by the free displacements of a time unit into the past or the future (and hence in two directions), cannot be effected at this stage. To measure duration, i.e. to determine the length of an interval, means thinking in terms of starting points *as well as* of end points. Now, our subjects either base their arguments on one of these points only, or else they are not concerned about the order of succession (as we have already stressed) and hence assess duration either by the (absolute) length of the path traversed or else by intuitive ideas about the velocities.

It is clear, therefore, that, in their attempts to solve problem (3), i.e. the comparison of successive durations, children use precisely the same criteria they employ for solving problems (1) and (2), i.e. the equalization of synchronous durations and the colligation of unequal durations—no matter whether they are being examined by the second method (in which they are told in advance that the same amounts of water are being poured out at every step) or by the first. Now it would seem that once they are told that equal amounts of liquid are being transferred at every step (which, moreover, they can see for themselves by the equal heights $II_1 II_2 = II_2 II_3 = II_3 II_4 \ldots$ etc.) and since, moreover, the water is being run out from I at a constant rate, our subjects should find it easy to grasp that the successive levels are isochronous and that each interval $II_n II_{n+1}$ can be treated as a unit of time. Similarly, in the case of subjects examined by means of the first technique, the use of the watch ought to have obviated the need for all further reflection on the subject of duration. Nevertheless, in both cases, our subjects failed to solve or even grasp the problem of comparing successive durations, and this precisely because they lacked the necessary reversibility of thought.

Now it is quite true that (second method) some of our subjects did, in fact, appear to make use of the information that equal amounts of water were being run out at every step; thus Boir thought that $I_3 I_4$ and $II_4 II_5$ took 'the same time because you let out the same amount of water'. But, in fact, he was looking at two identical shapes (two segments $II_x II_z$ or even $I_x I_y$ and $I_y I_z$ of the same height), and we must therefore ask ourselves if, though speaking of equal amounts of liquid, he was not simply thinking in terms of equal columns. And, in fact, when the shapes of the flasks differ, height (or rate of change) becomes the sole criterion of duration; thus Del, asked to compare $II_2 II_4$ to $I_1 I_3$ said 'it's higher at the bottom but the same amount' and nevertheless judged the time by height and speed alone ('it takes longer at the bottom because it's rising'). In other words, it is not that these children ignore the conservation of quantities when changes of shape are involved, it is simply that they fail to make the complex correlation needed to judge duration by the flow of the liquid: they fail to grasp that, at a constant rate of flow, a given quantity of water is associated with a given amount of time. Now, if the constant rate of flow is not borne in mind, the amount of water tells us nothing about the time, and that is precisely why our subjects, even when told in advance that the same amount of water is being run out with every step, still evaluate time by the length or speed of the displacements.

As for the use of the clock or watch, we noticed how Tar, Clan and Maga remained quite indifferent to this measurement of time: 'Oh, yes, it's the same thing,' said Maga, comparing the durations $II_1 II_2$ and $II_2 II_3$, but 'here ($II_2 II_3$), it took longer ...', etc. In brief, the clock shows its own time and not that of the motions to be timed. Now, this lack of co-ordination is obvious if we understand its basis. To compare t_1 (for example $II_1 II_2$) and t_3 (for example $II_2 II_3$) by means of the time t_2 read on the clock, the child has to argue that, since $t_1 = t_2$ and $t_2 = t_3$ hence $t_1 = t_3$. But since $t_1 = t_2$ and $t_2 = t_3$ are equalizations of synchronous durations and since such equalizations are not yet understood at this stage (see §2), it goes without saying that the general argument has no meaning for the child.

To sum up, when asked to correlate or measure durations, children at stage II try either to correlate durations with the sequence of events, but fail to take into account anything except the starting or end points of the motion, or else they judge durations apart from the order of events and simply evaluate it in terms of distance or (before the emergence of articulated intuition) in inverse ratio to the velocity. In each of these cases, estimates of durations are hampered by a lack of operational reversibility. As a result, time as such is not dissociated from its contents: durations are conceived as being heterogeneous, and each motion is thought to have a characteristic time of its own. As we shall see during our study of stage III, time does not become unique and homogeneous until it is constructed by the reversible 'grouping' of successions and colligations: in the absence of this grouping, synchronous durations cannot be equalized, partial durations are not necessarily thought to be smaller than total durations, and no unit of duration is capable of being displaced in two directions to ensure that an hour measured in the past equals the present hour or one that is yet to come. In brief, the conception of time at stage II is still intuitive, and since intuition, by its very essence, can never embrace more than a single event or a single moment at once, it cannot solve the crucial problem of time: the problem of co-placements and co-displacements, or the co-ordination of positions and motions.

§4. *The third stage: The operational construction of qualitative durations and the measurement of time*

At stage III, all the problems we have been discussing become capable of systematic and simultaneous solution. In general, children at this stage are able to construct a unique time scale embracing all moments and all events. This they can do thanks to an overall 'grouping' culminating in the equalization of synchronous durations and the colligation of unequal durations; moreover, they can 'group' the limiting events of these durations by the co-seriation of successions (including simultaneities). As a result, they are capable of constructing and iterating a unit of time and hence of measuring colligated durations. Let us begin with a few cases tested by means of the first method (use of clock but no assertion that equal amounts of water are released at every step):

CHOL (8; 7): Did it take the same time from here to there ($I_1 I_3$) as it did from here to there ($II_1 II_2$)? *More time here ($I_1 I_3$) because it kept pouring longer.* And between ($I_1 I_2$) and ($I_2 I_3$)? *They're the* *same time.* $(I_1 I_3)$ and $(II_1 II_3)$? *Also.* Why? *It's the same amount of water.* And $(I_1 I_4)$ and $(II_3 II_5)$? *More time here $(I_1 I_4)$ because the water was turned on twice here $(II_3 II_5)$ and three times there $(I_1 I_4)$.*

CIE (9 years): $(I_1 I_3)$ and $(II_2 II_3)$? *More time here $(I_1 I_3)$ because this one (I_1) came before that one (II_2).* And $(I_1 I_4)$ and $(I_3 I_5)$? *More time here $(I_1 I_4)$.* Why? *Because here $(I_3 I_5)$ there were two lots and there $(I_1 I_4)$ there were three.* And from $(I_1 I_3)$ and $(II_2 II_4)$? *They're the same, each is two lots.* And $(I_2 I_3)$ and $(II_3 II_4)$? *The same time.* And $(I_1 I_3)$ and $(II_1 II_3)$? *The same time because it's twice this much $(10'')$ on the clock.*

LAUR (9 years) looking at the drawings arranged in series: Did the water take same time to run from here to there $(I_1 I_2)$? *Yes.* And from here to there $(II_1 II_2)$? *Yes. And I think it took the same time because they were both running at the same time* (spontaneous reply). And what about here $(I_1 I_3)$ and there $(II_3 II_6)$? *Yes, also the same time, because both are three lots.* And here $(II_1 II_2$ and $II_2 II_3)$? *Oh yes, both took the same time.* And now look at these $(II_3 II_4$ and $I_4 I_5)$. Did the same amount of water rise up in here (II) as dropped down in there (I)? *Not quite, because a little more water ran out before (I_4) than did before (II_3). Ah, yes, because here $(II_3 II_4)$ it's not the last lot but it took $10''$ to fill all the same.* (Laur has thus discovered that it is possible to equalize two non-synchronous durations as well as the corresponding amounts of water.) And did the level change as quickly from here to there $(I_1 I_2)$ as it did from here to there $(II_1 II_2)$? *Yes, because they stopped at the same time.* But was it the same speed? *No, it was quicker in the bottom because it's completely different; at the bottom it's like a tube, and on top it's like a pear.* But it's the same time? *Yes, it is.* And did these $(I_1 I_3$ and $II_2 II_5)$ take the same time? *No, it took longer in the bottom because it was being filled more times: 3 times at the bottom and 2 times on top.*

Here, now, two cases examined by means of the second method (in which the subjects are told beforehand that equal amounts of water are run out at every step):

LAD (8; 7): Did these two take the same time $(I_1 I_2$ and $II_1 II_2)$? *Yes, they did, because they're divided the same way.* Are they the same height? *No, this one $(I_1 I_2)$ is smaller but that's because it's bigger* (wider). And what about these $(I_1 I_3$ and $II_3 II_5)$? *Oh yes, they took the same time because two equal amounts were poured out; it's the same parts of water.* And these $(I_2 I_3$ and $I_6 I_7)$? *Oh yes, they took the same time as well.* Why? *Because it's the same* *amount of water* (points to II_2 II_3 and II_6 II_7). And if we poured this lot (II_6 II_7) into here (I)? *It would make a layer like that one* (I_6 I_7).

ANT (8; 10) has no difficulty in co-seriating the cut drawings: (I_1 I_2) and (II_1 II_2)? *It's the same time.* Why? *Because there's the same amount of water in both.* Does the water fall and rise at the same rate? *No, this one* (II) *goes more quickly than that one* (I). So is it the same time or not? *Yes, it's the same time.* Why? *Because the water drops and rises at the same time.* But didn't you say that it rises more quickly? *It's the same time, because the two of them drop at the same time: while this one empties, the other one gets filled.* And what about (II_2 II_3) and (II_3 II_4)? *It keeps taking longer because the water is rising higher and higher. . . . Oh, no! From here to there* (II_2 II_3) *takes the same time as from here to there* (II_3 II_4) *because it's always the same height.* And what about (I_1 I_2) and (II_5 II_6)? *It's the same time because it's always the same amount.*

We can see that these answers differ markedly from those obtained at the preceding stage. To begin with, subjects at stage III have no hesitation in affirming or even in demonstrating the equality of synchronous durations. Some, like Laur and Ant, deduce this equality from the simultaneity of the starting and finishing points: 'It took the same time,' said Laur of I_1 I_2 and II_1 II_2, 'because they were both running at the same time' and 'because they stopped at the same time'. And Ant explained that 'the water drops and rises at the same time . . . while this one empties, the other one gets filled'. Chol, Cie and Lad (and also Ant at the beginning), on the other hand, deduced the equality of synchronous durations (directly) from the identity of the quantities of water run out or from the clock. Thus, for Chol, I_1 I_3 = II_1 II_3 'because it's the same amount of water'. Lad argued that the durations I_1 I_2 and II_1 II_2 were equal 'because they're divided the same way . . .', i.e. since the layer of water is 'smaller but wider' in I_1 I_2 the same quantity of water must be involved. Cie, finally, equalized I_1 I_2 and II_1 II_2: 'it's the same time because it's twice this much (10″) on the clock'; i.e. t_1 (= I_1 I_2) = t_2 (= II_1 II_2) because t_1 = t_2 (= 10″) and t_2 = t_3 (double equalization).

Now this (single or double) equalization of synchronous durations shows clearly that for subjects at stage III time is no longer simply the 'intuitive' duration of a particular action or motion, but a unique structure common to various motions or, in brief, a system of co-displacements. This is why Laur was able to explain that the motions of $I_1 I_2$ and $II_1 II_2$ took place at distinct speeds: 'It was quicker at the bottom because it's completely different . . .'; nevertheless it's 'the same time' because time is common to both motions and enables one to compare their respective velocities.

Children at stage III experience no greater difficulty in colligating unequal durations; this problem, too, is solved by reference to the order of succession of the starting and finishing points of the motion or to the identity of the amounts of water run out. Thus Cie asserted that $I_1 I_2$ took longer than $II_2 II_3$ 'because this one (I_1) came before that one (II_2)'. Now, simple though we ourselves find it to establish this kind of link between duration and the order of succession, we must agree that it is a great advance on reactions at the preceding stages. Chol, on the other hand, based his solution on the quantity of water run out: $I_1 I_3$ takes longer than $II_1 II_2$ 'because there was more water'. In both cases, we therefore have the correct colligation and the co-ordination of colligated durations with the order of succession.

Now, we find that as soon as the child has mastered these operational groupings of a qualitative kind, he becomes able to construct a time scale and to correlate successive moments, and no longer simply moments that are wholly or partly synchronous. As we saw, the qualitative grouping of colligated durations (of which the equalization of synchronous time is only a particular operation) presupposes mental reversibility, since before he can colligate durations, the child must be able to retrace the course of time as well as to project it forward: in that case thought itself plays the part of the moving body. When it comes to quantitative time, on the other hand, thought displaces the clock and its unit of time, and this, by synthesis, no longer of duration and 'placement', but of duration and temporal 'displacement'. How is this new synthesis arrived at? It has often been remarked that the measurement of time raises problems that do not arise in the measurement of space. When measuring two straight lines $a < b$, we need merely apply a to b and split b into two parts, one equal to a and the other equal to a' ($b = a + a'$) and then apply a to a' by a displacement of a. If $a = a'$ we have $b = 2a$, and if $a \neq a'$, we compare a and a' by the same method as a and b. The measurement of a distance is therefore an operational synthesis involving partition and displacement, and is based on the fact that we can displace a straight line without altering its length. But when it comes to the correlation of two successive time intervals a and a', and hence to the construction of a time scale, we cannot displace one of the two directly: thus if $b = a + a'$, we cannot apply a to a' or *vice versa* since the partial interval a' begins when the other partial interval a has come to an end. To equalize a and a' we must therefore 'mobilize' the part-unit a, and the only method of doing this is to reproduce the physical phenomenon whose course (motion) was of duration a and then to synchronize a with a'. This is the principle of all timing devices—clocks, sundials, sand-glasses, watches, etc. —i.e. the synthesis of the partial durations and of the corresponding spaces with displacements in time, or the repetition of the motion engendering unit duration. Time measurement, therefore, introduces a postulate not involved in space measurement, namely the conservation of motion and velocity. This raises the question of what precise 'clock' children at stage III use to equalize successive durations.

Now the examination of our subjects' reactions enables us to give a very simple answer to this question: in the great majority of cases discussed in this book, the clock used by the child is simply the flow of the water. Here we must distinguish two situations, the one in which the water is allowed to run while the stop-watch moves forward 10″ (or the cardboard clock 5′) at a time (first method), and the other in which the subjects are told before every change of level: 'We are running out the same amount of water with every step' (second method). Now it is easy to see that in the first case, in which the clock is imposed from the outside, the uniformity of duration is, in fact, guaranteed by the relationship between the amount of water run out and the lapse of time. Hence there is little difference between the first and second situations: in the first, the equality of the amounts of water has to be constructed and it is this construction which, in fact, ensures the equality of time: in the second, the equality of the amounts of water run out at every step is given, but does not imply the equality of time until the correct relationship between the quantity of water (or the difference in levels), the uniform velocity of the flow and the corresponding duration has first been established.

In effect, how did Chol, Cie and Laur (first method) explain the equalities or inequalities of successive durations? Chol, who established that the duration $II_1\ II_2 < I_1\ I_3$ 'because it was pouring out longer' in $I_1\ I_3$, and that the duration $I_1\ I_3 = II_1\ II_3$ because 'it's the same amount of water', simply transformed his equalization of the amounts of water into a chronometry when he went on to say that $I_1\ I_4$ took longer than $II_3\ II_5$ because 'the water was turned on twice here $(II_3\ II_5)$ and three times there $(I_1\ I_4)$'. Similarly Cie established the inequality of $I_1\ I_4$ and $I_3\ I_5$ on the grounds that 'here there were two lots and there there were three lots' and the equality $I_1\ I_3 = II_3\ II_5$ because 'each is two lots', and it was only for the synchronous case of $I_1\ I_3 = II_1\ II_3$ that he invoked the clock. Laur, for his part, established the equality $I_1\ I_3 = II_3\ II_6$ at once 'because both are three lots', thus again relying on the quantity run out. When asked if the amount of water in $II_3\ II_4$ was equal to that in $I_4\ I_5$ he was first confused by the difference in order, but then corrected himself by saying 'it's not the last lot (II_4) but it took $10''$ to fill all the same'. All in all, therefore, it is the relationship between the time of the flow and the quantity of liquid which represents the true unit of duration. We need only recall how Hen passed from the second to the third stage (§2) when he discovered that 'it's the same time because it's the same amount of water'.

As for the subjects questioned by means of the second method, it is remarkable how Lad, after realizing that the amount of water does not change during the transfer from I into II, went on to affirm that the durations $I_1\ I_3$ and $II_3\ II_5$ were equal: 'Oh yes, they took the same time because two equal amounts were poured out; it's the same parts of water'. He even succeeded in equalizing non-contiguous intervals such as $I_2\ I_3$ and $I_6\ I_7$ by means of quantity: 'Oh yes, they took the same time . . . because it's the same amount of water'. And Lad based this assertion on reversibility: $I_2\ I_3 = II_2\ II_3$; $I_6\ I_7 = II_6\ II_7$ and $II_2\ II_3 = II_6\ II_7$, and if $II_6\ II_7$ were poured back into I 'it would make a layer like that one $(I_6\ I_7)$'. Ant explained that 'it takes the same time because it's always the same height (in II)', thus implicitly acknowledging the conservation of velocity.

In brief, whether the child at this stage discovers the equality of the amounts of water run into the cylindrical flask II by virtue of the equality of the levels ($II_1 II_2 = II_2 II_3 = II_3 II_4 \ldots$), or whether he is told about it in advance, he invariably uses the flow of the water as a clock. Unlike children at the two preceding stages, who measure time by height of column (whence the mistaken view that $II_x II_y$ takes more time than $I_x I_y$) or by the rate of changes in level (whence the inability to equate durations of I and II), children at stage III therefore look upon the changes of level simply as indications of the quantities of water run out and, immediately correlating changes of level in I with those in II, conclude from the equality of the successive levels in II as to the equality of the quantities poured out and, above all, as to the equality of the intervals between each level and the next.

To what factors must this fundamental progress be ascribed? Let us recall that before children can deduce the equivalence of successive durations from the equality of the levels ($II_1 II_2 = II_2 II_3 = II_3 II_4 = \ldots$) they must first grasp the conservation of the velocity of the flow. Now, interestingly enough, when we ask children to mark out the successive daily runs of a miniature car or cyclist which, we explain, travel at constant speed and whose first-day run we ourselves have traced out for them, we find a remarkable parallel with the development of the time concept: it is not until about the age of eight years that children succeed in marking out equal runs.[1] The conservation of velocity is therefore by no means the result of direct intuition, but involves a complex elaboration. Hence it is obvious that quantitative time, which calls for this conservation, cannot be constructed at an earlier stage. But it is also clear that the conservation of velocity demands at least a capacity for qualitative time grouping, so that the grasp of velocity alone cannot help to explain the construction of time.

The essential difference between subjects at stage III and those at stage I and II is therefore bound up with the operational reversibility of thought: while children at stage II clearly appreciate the equality of the quantities of water represented by each level, they do not draw any quantitative conclusions as to the equality of the corresponding durations—for them, the latter

[1] See my forthcoming book on the child's conception of motion and velocity.

remain heterogeneous. We must guard against the belief that time can be discovered from the outside, all ready-made in some physical process or another: physical processes do not have any bearing on the development of the time sense unless they become incorporated into an overall operational structure and it is this structure which we shall now examine more closely.

§5. Elementary operations and their main 'groupings': The order of succession and the colligation of duration conclusion

In our analysis of the three stages in the development of the child's conception of time, we have come up against two series of correlated facts. During stage I, the first stage, the child observes that the liquid flows in a regular way, and gathers that this gives rise to an orderly succession of levels, but as soon as the flow has stopped he fails to arrange even the unseparated drawings D because he is unable to reconstruct the order of events in terms of an overall sequence. When it comes to duration, on the other hand, the child has an intuitive grasp of displacements (space), or relative motion (speed) and of the continuation of activity (beginning of psychological time) but fails to combine or articulate these intuitions even in respect of the inverse ratio of time and speed. In brief, in both cases, children fail to construct a unique time scale, either because such a scale involves moments in the past whose sequence they cannot reconstruct, or else because it involves distinct motions whose co-ordination calls for discrimination between time and distance. During stage II, the child succeeds in arranging the drawings D and the I's or II's separately, but fails to co-seriate the I's with the II's. He appreciates that time is inversely proportional to velocity but cannot equalize synchronous durations or colligate partial durations. In other words, he has begun to correlate the motions themselves but, lacking reversibility, he cannot retrace the course of events and is therefore unable to construct the system of 'co-displacements' which constitutes operational time. During the third stage, finally, co-seriation of successive stages goes hand in hand with the colligation of durations, and leads to the construction of operational time—both qualitative and quantitative.

This development, and quite especially this growing interdependence of succession and duration, underline the operational character of a unique time scheme, embracing all distinct moments as well as all synchronous or successive durations. In effect, while ideas of succession and duration are originally based on heterogeneous and unco-ordinated intuitions, they finish up in a single overall system. In other words, there is a gradual construction of operational 'groupings' of the kind we have met and analysed in our study of the development of logical concepts (seriation of relations and colligation of classes), of numerical concepts and also of general quantitative concepts (mass, weight and volume). There is nothing surprising in all this, since time, like all these quantitative systems, appears first in the form of a rough or intuitive quality or quantity, later to emerge in its double rôle of logical quality and extensive or metric quantity. There is, however, a difference of degree between time and the other systems inasmuch as qualitative time, when it becomes operational, continues to play a much greater practical rôle in the measurement of duration than, say qualitative weight does in the determination of mass. But this difference is explained by the existence of an inner duration, bound up with the memory of our past actions or with the relative difficulties of our present action, while the action of weighing is not affected by such qualitative considerations. For the rest, the construction of time involves a system of operations comparable to that which we have described in our previous studies.

As for these operations, we have described them individually, and can now proceed to the construction of a general scheme in which the gradual operational co-ordination of relationships based on the order of succession and the colligation of durations can be seen in fuller perspective, thus preparing the reader for the more detailed analysis which will be given in the following chapters.

Let us first of all recall what we mean by a logical or infralogical 'grouping' and in what respect it differs from an arithmetical 'group'.

A 'group' is a set of operations subject to the following four rules: (1) The product of any two operations remains in the set [for example the set of integers (positive and negative) constitutes a group under ordinary addition $(+ 1)$, since the product

of any two additions is still an integer (e.g. $+ 1 + 1 = + 2$)].
(2) Reversibility: for every direct operation there is an inverse
operation that annuls the first (e.g. $+ 1 - 1 = 0$). (3) The set
contains one and one only identical operation ($+0$), which is the
product of any operation and its inverse (e.g. $+ 3 - 3 = 0$),
and which can be combined with any operation without affecting
its product (e.g. $+ 3 + 0 = + 3$). (4) The operations are associative, i.e. $(A + B) + C = A + (B + C)$. Thus $(+ 1 + 2)$
$+ 3 = + 1 (+ 2 + 3)$, i.e. $(3) + 3 = 1 + (5)$.

Now we have been able to show[1] that logical operations
constitute 'groupings', i.e. sets more primitive than groups. Let
A, B, C, D, . . . be a set of colligated classes, each part of the
next, so that $A + A' = B$; $B + B' = C$; $C + C' = D$; . . .
etc. In that case we can (1) compose these equalities (principle
of syllogism); (2) associate the operations with their opposites
(exclusion): $B - A' = A$ or $- A - A' = - B$, etc.; and (3)
define an identical 'general' operation: $(A + A' = B) - (A$
$+ A' = B) = (0 + 0 = 0)$. However, over and above the general
identity, every equality is (4) identical to one of its terms (tautology $A + A = A$) or to higher terms of the same sign ($A + B$
$= B$); it follows (5) that associativity is limited to the case in
which operation (4) is applied to both members of the equality at
once, i.e. that the elements of the grouping are not 'classes' as
such, but equalities or statements of the form $A + A' = B$,
etc. In this way, all the possible combinations characteristic
of a system of syllogisms constitute a 'grouping'.

Let us also recall that the same grouping principle can be
applied to a system of asymmetrical relations such that

$$\begin{array}{cccc} & a & a' & b' \\ 0 \to & A \to & A' \to & B' \end{array}$$

('logical or qualitative seriation'). Now it is precisely the combination of this grouping with the preceding one which engenders the additive group of integers (*op. cit.* Chapter Ten): the
fusion of two groupings makes it possible to replace the tautology ($A + A = A$) with the numerical iteration ($A + A = 2A$),
since the terms A, A', B, etc. have become interchangeable and
seriable and hence transformed into 'units'.

[1] J. Piaget, *Classes, relations et nombres. Essai sur les groupements de la
logistique et la réversibilite de la pensée.* Paris, 1942 (Vrin).

Now, the qualitative relations of time can be called 'groupings' once they have ceased to be intuitive and irreversible and are constructed by reversible operations. We shall now examine the various operations and groupings children can perform at the end of their development (stage III).

Once the construction of time has been achieved and operational time goes hand in hand with reversible mobility, it is logically immaterial whether the child starts with the order of succession of events and deduces the system of durations from it, or proceeds *vice versa*. However, psychologically speaking, it is undoubtedly awareness of succession that is the more elementary experience of time and, in fact, as we shall see, it also corresponds to the simplest of the two possible methods of logical construction.

Let the water level in flask I move through the points I_1; I_2; I_3; etc. thus defining the direction (or succession) in space $I_1 \rightarrow I_2 \rightarrow I_3$, etc., where the arrow stands for 'precedes'. We may also express this by:

$$\begin{array}{cc} a & a' \end{array}$$
$$(1) \qquad I_1 \rightarrow I_2 \rightarrow I_3 \ldots \text{etc.}$$

i.e. if I_1 precedes I_2 and I_2 precedes I_3, then I_1 precedes I_3. This series constitutes an 'additive grouping of asymmetrical relations' (qualitative seriation).

It is clear that if the motion in question is real and not fictitious i.e. if it proceeds at a finite velocity, the word 'precedes' must necessarily apply to time as well as to space. Now, in the case of a single motion, these two meanings are inseparable—time is not yet distinguishable from motion.

The moment, however, we introduce a second motion whose trajectory and velocity differ from those of the first, we also have (for the rise of level in the second flask)

$$\begin{array}{cccc} a & a' & b & c \end{array}$$
$$(1a) \quad II_1 \rightarrow II_2, II_2 \rightarrow II_3, \text{etc., and } II_1 \rightarrow II_3, II_1 \rightarrow II_4, \text{etc.}$$

The next step is to relate the successive positions of one of the moving bodies I or II to those of the other. In the case of the experiment we have been analysing, the motion relating successive positions of I to those of II is the transfer of liquid from one flask to the next. We could equally well have used a system of optical signals, or better still the movement of the eye from positions of I to those of II (double displacement $\rightarrow$ and $\leftarrow$). In each case, we introduce a new system of relations between the positions I_1 and II_1; I_2 and II_2; etc. In the case of the flow of water, II_1 will occur slightly later than I_1; II_a than I_a, etc.; in the case of visual observation by one and the same subject, on the other hand, there will be no appreciable interval between I_1 and II_1, etc. In that case, which we have merely quoted to simplify matters, we must, however, introduce a new relation, or rather a limiting form of the relation we have been discussing, namely null succession ($\overset{\circ}{\rightarrow}$) or 'simultaneity':

$$(2) \qquad (I_1 \overset{0}{\rightarrow} II_1) = (I_1 \underset{\leftarrow}{\overset{\overset{a}{\rightarrow}}{a}} II_1) = (I_1 \overset{0}{\leftrightarrow} II_1)$$

Defined in this way, simultaneity corresponds to its apparent psychological structure: it is, in fact, the limiting case of absolute simultaneity, i.e. of simultaneity concurring with spatial coincidence; simultaneity becomes relative the moment the points under observation recede from the observer and as soon as he is forced to have recourse to compensating motions, including movements of the eye. It should, however, be stressed that once quantitative time has been constructed, simultaneity can be calculated and not merely observed, whereupon a precise reference system can take the place of purely qualitative operations. But even in that case, simultaneity remains relative, and loses all meaning in the case of very great distances and very great velocities.

Now, once the simultaneity of the positions $I_1 \leftrightarrow II_1$, $I_2 \leftrightarrow II_2$, etc., has been established, it becomes possible to endow the terms 'before' and 'after' with a temporal as distinct from a purely spatial significance. Every pair or multiple system of simultaneous positions constitutes an overall spatial 'state' or a 'snapshot'. Now these 'states' or 'snapshots' can be arranged in a series and this is precisely the order of succession involved in the complex system of co-displacements constituting the temporal order. To determine this order, we need merely combine relations (1) and (2), and perform what is known as a multiplicative grouping of relations (serial correspondence or co-seriation):

$$
\begin{array}{ccc}
a & a & b' \\
I_1 \to I_2 \to I_3 \to \ldots \\
\downarrow 0 & \downarrow 0 & \downarrow 0 \\
a & a' & b' \\
II_1 \to II_2 \to II_3 \to \ldots
\end{array}
$$

(3)

This 'grouping' of co-displacements has a specific temporal significance, since over and above the order of the spatial positions of I and II, we can deduce from it such relations as 'I$_1$ comes before II$_2$' or 'I$_3$ comes after II$_1$', etc., i.e. relations that are devoid of any spatial meaning.

Since the temporal order represented by a multiplicative grouping of asymmetrical and transitive relations (co-seriation) co-ordinates the various positions of a system of co-displacements, we can show, by following the psychological operations step by step, that this grouping is isomorphous with that involved in the colligation of durations except for one factor: the latter, though based on the order of succession, bears exclusively on the symmetrical relations of the intervals.

If I$_1$ comes before I$_2$ (or II$_2$ and I$_2$ before I$_3$ and II$_3$), it is, in effect, possible, even without knowing anything about the quantitative value of the distances or times involved, to conclude that the interval between I$_1$ and I$_3$ or II$_3$ is greater than the interval between I$_1$ and I$_2$ or II$_2$. Now, the interval between the 'states' I$_1$ II$_1$ and I$_2$ II$_2$ or I$_3$ II$_3$, etc. is nothing other than duration. To express the system of durations by a new operational grouping, we need therefore merely bear in mind that, even if the 'state' I$_2$ II$_2$ invariably comes after the state I$_1$ II$_1$, the interval between them remains the same, no matter whether our thought proceeds from I$_1$ II$_1$ to I$_2$ II$_2$, i.e. follows the course of time, or goes back from I$_2$ II$_2$ to I$_1$ II$_1$. Intervals can therefore be represented by the following symmetrical relations:

$$
\begin{array}{ccc}
a & a' & b'
\end{array}
$$
(4) $\quad$ I$_1$ II$_1$ $\leftrightarrow$ |I$_2$ II$_2$; I$_2$ II$_2$ $\leftrightarrow$ |I$_3$ II$_3$; I$_3$ II$_3$ $\leftrightarrow$ |I$_4$ II$_4$; etc.

Moreover, if we define relations of the $\leftrightarrow$ type as the set of all the relations defined by inclusion in one and the same interval between all possible levels from I_1 and I_2, etc., we are entitled to add them as follows (first type of addition of durations):

(4a)
$$a \qquad\qquad a' \qquad\qquad b$$
$$(I_1 \, II_1 \leftrightarrow | I_2 \, II_2) + (I_2 \, II_2 \leftrightarrow | I_3 \, II_3) = (I_1 \, II_2 \leftrightarrow | I_3 \, II_3); \text{ etc.}$$

But what precisely are the intervals separating the successive levels? In other words, what precisely is duration itself? We have seen throughout this chapter that while all children determine duration by the flow of the liquid, the youngest have great difficulty in grasping the fact that one and the same duration can express motions of different velocity (slow drop of level from I_1 to I_2, etc., and rapid rise of level from II_1 to II_2, etc.). In other words, the child has no clear understanding of duration until he conceives it in terms of the correlation of motion and velocity. In the case of quantitative operations he would then obtain $t = s/v$ by transformation of $v = s/t$. However, since qualitative operations alone are involved, things are much simpler than that. If the child starts with, say, the flow $I_1 \, I_2$, he will argue that the distance s_1 between I_1 and I_2 measures both the duration and also the velocity v_1 of the motion. Next, he discovers that the distance between II_1 and II_2 or s_2 is greater than s_1 and, since $I_1 \, II_1$ and $I_2 \, II_2$ are simultaneous, he will conclude that the velocity $v_2 \, (II_1 \, II_2)$ is greater than the velocity $v_1 \, (I_1 \, I_2)$. If he now succeeds in equalizing the durations $(I_1 \, I_2)$ and $(II_1 \, II_2)$ it is because he considers that, as far as duration is concerned, the increase in distance $s'_1 \, (= s_2 - s_1)$ is offset by the increase in velocity $v'_1 \, (= v_2 - v_1)$. If this common duration is called α, we have

(5)
$$\alpha_{s_1 v_1} = \alpha_{s_2 v_2} \text{ because } (s'_1) \times (- v'_1) = 0$$

i.e. the duration α of a motion with velocity v_1 over the distance s_1 is identical to the duration α of a motion with velocity v_2 over the distance s_2. If the increase in distance corresponds (logical multiplication) to an increase in velocity with the same value (the latter being treated as negative because it annuls s'_1) the logical multiplication by the equivalent negative relation will correspond to the mathematical division s/v. It is therefore operation (5) which enables the child to equalize synchronous durations, i.e. to establish that $I_1 \, I_2 = II_1 \, II_2$; $I_2 \, I_3 = II_2 \, II_3$; etc.

Now if all intervals can be treated as distance covered at a given velocity (or as work done at a given rate) duration becomes a whole whose parts can be colligated as follows:

(6) $\qquad \alpha + \alpha' = \beta; \beta + \beta' = \gamma; \ldots$ etc.

where the terms α, α', β', etc., are defined as in (5), while corresponding to the intervals defined in (4) and (4a). This is the fundamental operation involved in the colligation of durations.

As for the operations involved in quantitative time, we saw that, in the early stages of their development, children fail to compare a given duration with an earlier or later one because they lack mental reversibility: the measurement of time therefore eludes them just as much as the equalization of synchronous durations (5), or the colligation of partial durations (6). At the final stage, however, they can compare successive durations because they have come to appreciate that the successive amounts of liquid run out are equal, a fact that can, moreover, be gathered directly from the equality of the levels in the cylindrical flask II. Now, since every difference in level $\mathrm{II}_1\, \mathrm{II}_2 = \mathrm{II}_2\, \mathrm{II}_3 = $ etc., is equal to the differences $\mathrm{I}_1\, \mathrm{I}_2$; $\mathrm{I}_2\, \mathrm{I}_3$, etc., the child obtains a system of units, $\mathrm{I}_1\, \mathrm{II}_1\, (\alpha)\, \mathrm{I}_2\, \mathrm{II}_2 = \mathrm{I}_2\, \mathrm{II}_2\, (\alpha')\, \mathrm{I}_3\, \mathrm{II}_3 = \mathrm{I}_3\, \mathrm{II}_3\, (\beta')\, \mathrm{I}_4\, \mathrm{II}_4 = $ etc., from which he then concludes that $\beta = 2\alpha$, $\gamma = 3\alpha$, etc.

Unlike qualitative operations, which are limited to the comparison of a partial duration to the total duration of which they form an element $(\alpha < \beta)$ or to the comparison of partial or total synchronous durations $(\alpha_1 = \alpha_2$ or $\beta_1 = \beta_2)$, quantitative operations involve the comparison of successive durations. To that purpose, they carry forward a unit α from the equalization $\alpha = \alpha' = \beta'$ etc., thus providing us with a means of counting the units involved in every total duration $\beta = 2\alpha$, $\gamma = 3\alpha$, etc., and hence of measuring time. The equalization of successive durations, therefore leads to the transformation of (6) into a system of quantitative colligations:

(7) $\qquad \alpha + \alpha = (\alpha') = 2\alpha\, (= \beta);$
$\qquad 2\alpha\, (= \beta) + \alpha\, (= \beta') = 3\alpha\, (= \gamma);$ etc.

where α, α', β, β', etc. stand for $\mathrm{I}_1\, \mathrm{II}_1\, (\alpha)\, \mathrm{I}_2\, \mathrm{II}_2$; $\mathrm{I}_2\, \mathrm{II}_2\, (\alpha')\, \mathrm{I}_3\, \mathrm{II}_3$; $\mathrm{I}_1\, \mathrm{II}_1\, (\beta)\, \mathrm{I}_3\, \mathrm{II}_3$; etc.

However, it must be stressed that, simple though these operations are in their final equilibrium form, they involve a highly complex elaboration.

In fact, the equalization of two successive durations $\alpha = \alpha'$ calls for more than the qualitative operation of synchronization (5) since, though the child performing that operation deduces that $\alpha s_1 v_1 = \alpha s_2 v_2$ from his correlation of the velocities with increases in the distance, he does so only because the two motions begin and end simultaneously. However, synchronization plays no part in the equalization of two *successive* durations α and α', which calls for one of two much more complex operations:

(1) If the durations α and α' can be associated with a given distance and velocity (by virtue of (5) and (6)) they may be equalized provided these distances and velocities are equal as well:

(8) $$\alpha_{sv} = \alpha'_{s'v'}, \text{ if } s = s' \text{ and } v = v'$$

This is what happens when our subjects discover that the difference in the levels II_1, II_2 is equal to the difference in the levels II_2, II_3, etc., i.e. that the liquid rises with a constant velocity. ($\alpha = \alpha'$ because $s = s'$ and $v = v'$).

(2) The durations α and α' will generally be equal if the work is done at a constant rate r, i.e.

(8a) $$\alpha_r = \alpha'_{r'}, \text{ if } r = r'$$

This equation applies whenever the subject does not simply measure the time by the distance between two successive levels but by the quantity of water displaced at a given velocity ($=$ displacement of a given weight at a given rate).

Now, we find that both cases involve measurements that play no part in operations (1) to (6): i.e. the quantification of either the distance traversed ($s_1 = s'_1$) or of the work done (quantity of water displaced) and, above all, the quantification of the velocity as a result of which the conservation of velocity can be treated as a particular case of uniform motion.

In short, much more even than qualitative time, quantitative time involves a system of geometry, a system of dynamics, and a system of mechanics all at once, since over and above the relation between the work and the rate at which it is done, it also introduces the constancy of the velocities under consideration (uniform rectilinear motion or regular periodicity). Time thus becomes an integral part of the structure of the universe. In fact, the four great categories of thought resulting from the use of infralogical operations, or operations in space-time, constitute an inseparable whole: object (or substance) and space; causality and time. For if it is true to say that there is no object without space, nor any space without objects, then it is also true to say that the interaction of objects defines causality, and that time is nothing other than the co-ordination of these interactions or motions. It is from causality that time derives its order of succession, because causes are necessarily anterior to effects, and it is causality which is expressed by duration, since duration is simply the qualitative or quantitative ratio of distance to velocity (or, which amounts to the same thing, of work to 'power').

PART II

Physical Time

In the first part of this study (Chapters One and Two), we looked at the psychological problem of the construction of time, and identified the elementary operations involved. In what follows, we shall examine each of these operations in turn, and vary the experimental situation accordingly.

In Chapters Three and Four, we shall be analysing the reactions of children to successions and simultaneities, while they observe rather than reconstruct them. Chapter Five deals with the equalization of synchronous durations; Chapter Six with the additive and associative composition of durations; Chapter Seven with the colligation of durations; and Chapter Eight with the measurement of quantitative time by clocks and sand-glasses.

PART II

Principles and

CHAPTER THREE

The Succession of Perceptible Events[1]

As we saw in Chapter One, children have great difficulty in reconstructing the correct succession of even so simple a series of events as the flow of a liquid. This is because two distinct problems are involved: (1) the reconstruction of the correct order after the event and (2) the correct perception of this order while the event is actually taking place.

We shall look at the second problem first. To that purpose, we could present the child with two bodies starting side by side, moving with the same speed, and stopping (a) successively and (b) simultaneously. At each of the three stages we have described, the child would have no difficulty in establishing the succession or simultaneity of the stopping points—since the two motions are similar and concurrent, they are no more complicated than a single motion. Now, in that case the temporal order remains undifferentiated from the spatial order so that what replies the child makes to our questions would bear on the geometrical course rather than on time as such. If, therefore, we wish to analyse the child's idea of temporal succession as such, we must introduce bodies moving at different velocities—as we saw, time is a system of co-displacements. To simplify the problem, we can retain the parallel tracks and start or stop the two bodies simultaneously. In putting the questions, it is important to ensure that the child makes a clear distinction between temporal and spatial succession.

Once these precautions are taken, we can go on to find out whether or not the child is capable of fitting motions at different velocities into a single space-time framework. This is what we shall now go on to do.

---

[1] In collaboration with Mlle Esther Bussmann.

§1. *Experimental methods and general results*

The two experimental arrangements we use in the analysis of the child's concept of succession (Chapter Three) and simultaneity (Chapter Four) as he perceives them, are extremely simple. The first, which is more concrete but less precise, serves as a simple introduction to the second, which gives far more accurate results. In the first, the experimenter and the child run through the laboratory together. The experimenter gives three raps as the signal for the simultaneous start of the runs, and stops before, after or at the same time as the child, but at a given distance from him. The child is then asked if the starting and finishing points of the two runs were simultaneous, or which one came first. Since, in this experiment, the child is spectator and actor all at once, his answers are generally biased. We accordingly use this question merely as an introduction to the second experiment.

Here we present the child with two small figures or mechanical snails moving across a table either at different but continuous velocities or else, and this is generally preferable, by fits and starts, each start being accompanied by a rap on the table. In this case there can be no failure to perceive the synchronism of the two runs or the order of succession or simultaneity of the final stopping points. We then ask the child:

(1) Whether one of the figures (II) was still moving when the other (I) had stopped (in practice this question is generally put last to make sure that the child has grasped the data; the reader will note that it does not necessarily bear on the child's grasp of time as such). Let A_1; B_1; C_1; etc. be points along the path of I, and A_2; B_2; C_2; etc. those along the path of II, with $A_1 B_1 = A_2 B_2$, $B_1 C_1 = B_2 C_2$, etc.; let I cover the distance $A_1 D_1$ while II covers the distance $A_2 B_2$, and let II subsequently cover the distance $B_2 C_2$ while I remains in D_1. The child will have no difficulty in grasping that when I stops in D_1, II keeps moving forward (from B_2 to C_2). However, we shall see that the child nevertheless fails to conclude that I stopped before II, and, in fact, will generally take the opposite view. Sometimes he will even go so far as to assert that the duration A_1–D_1 is greater than that of A_2–C_2, simply because D_1 is further from the starting point, etc. The question of whether I was still moving

when II had stopped, and *vice versa*, thus involves only one, clearly defined, aspect of time: what one might call perceptive time by contrast to the intellectual time which is constructed at the moment of perception and which alone concerns us in this book. Perceptive time, in effect, is exclusively involved in what can be directly distinguished as being successive or simultaneous, but involves no comprehension of these concepts, much as the ear can distinguish chords from single notes without the mind having to grasp that the chord consists of two or more elementary sounds.

(2) Let I proceed from A_1 to D_1 while II proceeds from A_2 to B_2. Next, let II proceed from B_2 to C_2 while I has stopped. The child is then asked which of the two figures has stopped 'first'. Now this question introduces a linguistic problem—in trying to present our subjects with the idea of a temporal as distinct from a spatial succession, we find that it lacks a word to distinguish the two. If we say 'which one stopped before the other?', the word 'before' may mean 'in front of' as well as 'earlier'. To avoid this pitfall we can explain that I stops at lunch-time and go on to ask if II stopped before or after lunch.

(3) We next ask the child if I and II moved for 'the same length of time', or if not, which of them moved 'longer'.

(4) Let I stop in C_1 when II stops in B_2, both having started simultaneously from A_1 and A_2. We now ask the child whether I and II stopped 'at the same time' or 'at the same moment', and if not, which one stopped first. The answers to this question considered in conjunction with the answers to question (3) will be examined in Chapter Four.

We can finally vary the questions by introducing different starts with simultaneous stops, or simultaneous starts from different points with simultaneous stops in the same point, etc.

The results of all these tests fit easily into the three stages we have been distinguishing. During stage I, successions and durations remain undifferentiated from distances: 'longer' is equivalent to further; 'first' may mean 'before' or 'after', and differences in speed are thought to preclude synchronous processes and lead to confused estimates of duration. During the second stage, the initial intuitions slowly become differentiated or articulated, either because 'before' and 'after' in time and space become differentiated from each other, or else because simultaneity becomes recognized independently of positions or velocities, or finally because duration is understood to be inversely proportional to velocity. However, the point at which intuition becomes articulated varies from one subject to the next, nor does the initial step lead to the immediate articulation of temporal relations in general. In other words, at stage II, intuitions, even if articulated, cannot yet be combined into a general grouping, whence the incoherent reactions of our subjects. Finally, at stage III, the subjects become capable of applying the technique of operational grouping to all the relations involved, and go on to construct a coherent system involving both durations and successions.

§2. *The first stage: Confusion of temporal with spatial successions*

During stages I and II, simple or even articulated intuitions of succession and duration give rise to constant contradictions—whence their continual re-adjustment and the fact that correct answers alternate quite arbitrarily with wrong ones. Let us nevertheless try to fit these answers into some sort of scale.

Here, first of all, are a few examples obtained at the lowest level:

HES (4; 5). The yellow figure (I) stops in D_1 while the blue figure (II) keeps moving on from B_2 to C_2: Did they stop at the same time? *No.* Which one stopped first? *The blue one* (II). Which moved longer? *The yellow one* (I). When (I) stopped it was lunch time, so did (II) stop before or after lunch? *Before lunch.* But which stopped first? *The yellow one* (I). No, it was the blue one, the yellow one (I) *went on longer.* Let's do it again. (The race is re-run.) *The yellow one* (I) *stopped first, the blue one was still moving, so the yellow one went on longer.* But did one stop before the other? *The blue one* (II).

REG (4; 6). Same arrangement: Did they stop at the same time? *No, the yellow one* (I) *stopped before the other one.* Which one stopped first? *The blue one.* Which one stopped earlier? *The blue one* (II). If the yellow one stops at lunch, when does the blue one stop? *Before lunch.* See for yourself. (The experiment is repeated.) *Yes, the yellow one* (I) *stopped first, it went on longer.* And the other one (II)? *It stopped before lunch.* Look carefully. (The experiment is repeated again.) *Yes, the yellow one* (I) *went on longer, it stopped here* (D₁) *so it stopped first.* But when it stopped, wasn't the other one still moving? *Yes.* So which one stopped first? *The blue one.*

COR (5; 6). Same arrangement: What did you see? *The yellow one* (I) *stopped and the other one* (II) *kept moving.* So which one stopped first? *The blue one* (II). Which one moved longer? *The yellow one* (I). Let's say that (I) stops at lunch. So when did this one (II) stop? *Before . . . no, at lunch.* By way of control, we now let the two figures run in opposite directions, both starting at A. When I reaches D₁ on the right, II reaches B₂ on the left and continues as far as C₂. This time the subject has no difficulty in grasping that I stopped first.

DOM (6; 6): Did they stop at the same time? *No.* (II) *stopped before, sooner, first,* etc. Which went on longer? *That one* (I) *because it went further.* When (I) stopped was (II) still moving? *Yes.* And when (II) stopped was (I) still moving? *No.* So which one went on longer? *The yellow one* (I). Why? *Because it was further away.* If (I) stopped at lunch, did this one (II) stop at lunch as well or before or after? *Before lunch.*

ARL (7 years): (II) *stopped before the other one* and (I) went on *longer because it was further.* But which went on for the most time? *That one* (II), *no, this one* (I). And which went on longest? (I). Which one stopped first? (II). If (I) stopped at lunch when did (II) stop? *Before lunch.* Why? *Because it stopped in front of that one* (points to the space separating the two figures).

It should be emphasized that these reactions are in no way due to errors of perception: all our subjects were agreed that when figure I had stopped, II kept on moving, and that when II stopped I had stopped moving as well. Why then do they obstinately assert that II stopped 'first', 'sooner' or 'before' I, etc.?

One might argue that the whole thing is purely a matter of words, that the child uses the words 'before' and 'after' in a spatial sense, that he fails to appreciate that our questions have any bearing on time. However, whenever we checked the answers by reversing the direction of the paths, we obtained (e.g. in Cor's final answer) the correct reply without hesitation, simply because, no longer able to compare the velocities, the child tries to co-ordinate the two displacements, and comes to look upon several of the motions as episodes in a single history. If, on the other hand, the two bodies I and II move in the same direction, the child confuses time, space and velocity, which demonstrates that his errors are of a logical and not of a verbal kind.[1] This becomes particularly obvious in the case of duration, for when our subjects assert that I goes on 'longer' because it finishes 'further', they couple verbal differentiation to a lack of a logical differentiation between time and space.

What precisely accounts for this lack of differentiation between time and space? As far as duration is concerned, the explanation is quite simple, and agrees with the one we gave in Chapter Two: the child simply confuses time with velocity. Its argument runs roughly as follows: (1) If you go more quickly you necessarily cover more space (i.e. velocity is proportional to distance); (2) if you cover more space, you need more time to do so (hence distance is proportional to time); and (3) if you go more quickly you need more time because you cover more space. Each of these three 'mores' entails the other two.

Once all these assumptions are granted, it follows that the child's confusion of temporal with spatial succession does not result from the fact that he bases his concepts of succession on those of duration or *vice versa*, but from the fact that he constructs both by the same logical methods. This emerges more clearly when we introduce the idea of lunch time. Having granted that the figure stops at lunch, the child will invariably go on to assert that, though II continues to move, it nevertheless stops before lunch. Why? The answer was given by Arl when he explained that II stopped 'before lunch' because 'it stopped in front of that one (I)'. In other words, since it is at noon that you generally come home for lunch, the fact that you have not reached home by then, far from implying that you are late, simply means that time itself cannot possibly have reached the hour of lunch. This is why children use the terms 'before', 'first', 'earlier', etc. arbitrarily in their spatial and temporal senses, and why they equate the failure to reach a place at the normal time with failure to reach the normal time itself. Now since the orders of spatial and temporal succession coincide in the case of a single body moving with uniform velocity, the child thinks that he can apply the same idea to the case of two bodies moving with distinct velocities. In other words, children at this stage apply the time-space framework of the single body to the joint motion of two bodies by egocentric assimilation, instead

[1] Cf. Chapter Nine §3 for a similar error with respect to age.

of decentring the temporal relations from the spatial order of each of the motions. As a result, they fail to construct a time scale common to the two displacements.

In brief, they are no more capable of reconstructing temporal successions than are the subjects examined in §2 of Chapter One, and for the same reason: to reconstruct the phases of a motion when it is no longer perceptible (seriation of drawings) or to co-ordinate two perceptible motions with different velocities, calls for the dissociation of time and space, i.e. for mental reversibility. In the first case, when the order of events is no longer visible, the child has to select the correct temporal order from two possible spatial orders; in the second case, he must connect the positions of the two bodies by a relation distinct from that of the spatial successions: in either case, he must construct a unique and homogeneous time scale. The study of the child's conception of succession as applied to directly perceptible processes is therefore of greater expository value than even the analysis presented in Chapter One.

§3. *The second stage: I*

Sub-stage II A: *Beginning of differentiation between temporal and spatial order and articulated intuitions of time*

Of the subjects whose answers differed from those obtained at stage I (incorrect order of succession) and also from those obtained at stage III (immediate grasp of all the relations involved), approximately 45 per cent were able to divorce temporal from spatial successions, but nevertheless failed to evaluate durations correctly (further = more time), another 45 per cent could evaluate durations but failed to grasp the correct temporal succession, and approximately 10 per cent were able to grasp both ideas. But even in the last group, one of the two conceptions was generally more highly developed than the other. This suggests that progress in grasping duration leads to progress in grasping succession and *vice versa*.

Here are some examples of the first type of reaction: progress in handling succession coupled to lesser progress (Dan) or no progress at all (Pail, Ios and Yva) in handling duration:

PAIL $(5\frac{1}{2})$. Experimental set-up as described in §2. I stops in D_1 as II reaches B_2 before continuing to C_2: Did they stop at the same time? *No.* Which stopped sooner? (II). Which stopped first? (II). Which went on longer? (I). Why? *Because it went further.* (The experiment is repeated.) Did they stop together? *No.* Which stopped before the other one did? (II). Which stopped earlier? (II). If (I) stopped at lunch, did (II) stop before or after lunch? *After lunch because it arrived later.* (correct) So which one moved for a longer time? (I).

Ios ($5\frac{1}{2}$). Same set-up: Which stopped earlier? (II). And which stopped first? (I). Why? *Because it went on longer.* (The experiment is repeated) Which stopped earlier? (II). Was (II) still moving when (I) had stopped? *Yes.* So which one went on longer? *This one* (II), *because it moved through a very small . . . No, it's* (I), *because it went further.* But which one stopped first? (II). Let's say that (I) stops at lunch, then what about (II)? *It stopped at four o'clock because it arrived after the other one.* Very well, so which one moved for a longer time? (I) *because it went further.*

Yva (6 years) says spontaneously before we have time to ask her any questions: *This one* (I) *went on longer because it started first* (= because it overtook (II)) Which one stopped first? *The bigger one* (I) *stopped first because it went on longer.* Which stopped earlier? (I). And which stopped before the other? (I). When (I) stopped was the other still moving? *Yes?* So which one went on longest? (I). We repeat the experiment but this time by moving II as far as D_2 where it stops while I continues from B_1 to C_1: Which stopped first? (I) (wrong). Which stopped earlier? (I) (wrong). And which one moved longer? (I) (correct).

Dan ($6\frac{1}{2}$). Same experimental set-up: Did the two stop at the same time? *No, one stopped before the other.* Which one? (II). Which stopped earlier? (II). Why? *Because it was here* (= less far). Which one went on longer? (I). Why? *Because it went further.* If it stopped at lunch, did (II) also stop at lunch or before or after? *After lunch because it went more slowly.* So which one went on for the longer time? *That one* (I). Which one stopped before the other one did? (I) (correct). When (I) stopped was (II) still going? *Yes.* So which one went on longer? (II). Why? *Because when* (I) *had stopped it was still moving.* (correct). How long would you say (I) kept moving? *For five minutes.* And (II)? *Three minutes.* Which moved longer? (I).

And now for examples of the second type of reaction (correct evaluation of duration by inversion of the ratio between time and speed (quicker = less time) but with no progress or less progress in the grasp of succession).

CHAR ($5\frac{1}{2}$): Did they stop at the same time? *No.* Which stopped earlier? (II). And which stopped first? (II). Which went on longer? *That one* (II) *because it went at medium speed.* (correct). Which moved for a shorter time? *That one* (I) *because it went at a great speed.* If (I) stopped at lunch, when did that one (II) stop? *Before lunch* (incorrect).

CHRI ($6\frac{1}{2}$): (II) *went on longer because it was left behind* (correct). So which one stopped first? *The yellow one* (I) *stopped first, the blue one* (II) *carried on* (correct). If the yellow one (I) stopped at lunch, did the blue one (II) stop at lunch as well, or before or after lunch? *The second one stopped at 10 o'clock.* Is that before or after lunch? *That's before lunch.* Why did it stop before lunch? *Because it was only here.*

MAR ($6\frac{1}{2}$): (II) *went on longer.* Did they start at the same time? *Yes.* Did they stop at the same time? *No.* Which stopped first? (II). And which stopped earlier? (II), etc.

Both types of reaction are of great psychological interest for they seem to suggest two contradictory attitudes.

Subjects of the first type argue, in effect, that II must stop after I because it is still moving when I has stopped: if I stops at lunch, II arrives 'after lunch'. However, they continue to think that I goes on for a longer time than II because it goes further. It would therefore seem that the intuitive grasp of time succession precedes that of duration. By contrast, the second group argues that II went on longer 'because it was slower' (Chri), or because it 'went at medium speed' (Char). Moreover, they all agree that II arrives before lunch and this precisely because, being slow, it appears before I to anyone looking *along* the direction of the track. It would therefore seem that, with these subjects, the correct intuitive grasp of duration precedes that of temporal succession.

In reality, both reactions are easily reconciled once we appreciate that neither has reached the operational level: what progress has been made in either group is purely intuitive and, as such, lacking in generality; hence it is only natural that the differentiation of time and space should be restricted to either succession or duration. If the differentiation were of an operational kind, on the other hand, it would lead directly to the general restructuring of both concepts.

What, then, is the precise nature of this intuitive differentiation, and in what sense are we entitled to compare it to a perceptive regulation? It is, in fact, a gradual decentration leading the subject from the idea that time is 'centred' on a particular action or a single motion, to 'decentred' time and finally to the construction of a coherent system of co-displacements.

In the case of succession, the subject begins by confusing the temporal with the spatial order of the race because he centres his intuition on the track and neglects differences in velocity. He accordingly takes the view that the body (I) which proceeds from A to D must necessarily stop 'after' the body (II) proceeding from B to C, since D comes after C along the track. As for those subjects (and there are many of these as well) who declare that I stops 'before' II, they too are not thinking in terms of time but use 'before' as a synonym for 'in front of'. Pail and Ios went slightly beyond this primitive viewpoint, centred on the trajectory alone, when they used the following argument: since I stops at lunch (defined by the point D_1) the point C_2 must necessarily represent 'before lunch', an argument that still fully accords with the primitive centration of time representations of the track itself. But Pail and Ios, no longer content with taking a static view of the relationship between II in C_2 and I in D_1, prolong the motion of II to D in their imagination, and thus decentre their representation by so keen a sense of anticipation that they speak of II as if it had in fact reached D_2: II arrived 'after lunch' Pail said because it arrived 'later' and at 'four o'clock' according to Ios, because it arrived 'after the other'. Extending the motion of II by means of a representative anticipation which may be called a true decentration of intuition, these subjects thus implicitly re-introduce differences in velocity and then judge the time succession by the arrival of the two figures at a single point (D). Yva used much the same approach as well. However, since the progress of all three subjects was merely of a representative kind (articulated intuition by decentration) they failed to apply their conclusions to the durations, which they continued to evaluate by the final position of the two bodies.

Conversely, the subjects in the second group managed to decentre their pimitive intuitions to the point of correcting their estimates of duration but failed to apply these corrections to the order of succession. As far as these children are concerned, II goes on longer than I, but not because, having started at the same time, it stops before I does, but simply because it moves more slowly. Thus Char contended that II stops 'sooner' etc. than I, but that it takes more time because 'it goes at a medium speed'. Chri's reaction was even more curious; according to him II moved for a longer time because it was left behind, which suggests an apparent co-ordination of duration with succession, and he even added that I was the first to stop. However, he added that if I stops at lunch, II stops at 10 a.m. Being left behind, therefore, simply means going slower. In short, these children simply content themselves with treating time as being inversely proportional to velocity, and completely ignore the relationship of duration and succession. Now, as we saw in Chapter Two (§2), in order to grasp the fact that 'less quickly = more time' irrespective of succession or order, the child need merely divorce his introspective idea of actions from the results of these actions: in that case, the slower motion is simply 'felt' to be of greater duration. Unlike subjects of the first type, who correct their inuitive ideas about succession by anticipative representation of the observed motions, those of the second type correct their intuitive ideas of duration by a representative reconstruction of these motions.

In brief, children at the beginning of stage II show clear progress due to a representative process comparable to perceptive decentration: in both cases the initial egocentric intuition (confusion of time with length of action and hence with the work done or the space traversed) is gradually decentred either by means of representative anticipation which extends the observed motions, or else by representative reconstruction which helps to divorce these motions from their results. In either case, the initial intuition is corrected by compensations akin to perceptive regulations. The resulting articulation does not, however, lead to an overall co-ordination of succession and duration, so that there is a measure of local progress in a given sector of the initial intuition, but no overall grouping of concepts.

§4. *The second stage: II*

Sub-stage II B: Beginning of operational co-ordination of articulated intuitions

How does the child advance from these differentiated or articulated, but still contradictory, intuitions to the general operations by which alone homogeneous time can be constructed? The answer will be provided by subjects between stages II and III (corresponding to sub-stage II B of Chapter One). Here are a few examples:

DEN ($6\frac{1}{2}$). Same experimental set-up: Did they stop at the same time? *No.* Which one stopped first? *That one.* (I: correct). Which stopped earlier? II (wrong). Which went on longer? *That one.* (II: correct). Why? *Because it kept going when the other one had stopped.* Which one took less time? (I: correct). Why? *Because it stopped first.* If (I) stopped at lunch, when did (II) stop? *After lunch, because it went on longer.*

LIL ($7\frac{1}{2}$): Which one stopped before the other? *That one.* (I: correct). Which one stopped first? (I). Which one went on longer? *This one* (I) *because it stopped first, oh, no, it's that one* (II) *because it stopped after the other one.* If this one (I) stopped at lunch, when did that one (II) stop? *After lunch, because it was behind.*

ROG ($8\frac{1}{2}$): Did they stop at the same time? *No.* Which one stopped first? *This one* (I) *stopped before that one.* (II: correct). Which one went on longer? *That one.* (I: wrong). Which took more time? (I). Why? *Because it was in front.* How long did (I) keep going for? *For five minutes.* And (II)? *For four minutes.* When (I) stopped was (II) still going? *Yes.* So which one of them went on longer? (I). If (I) had stopped at lunch, when would (II) have stopped? *After lunch.* (correct). Which one went on longer? (II: correct). Why? *Because it arrived after lunch.* So? *This one* (I) *took less time, and that one* (II) *took more time.* Why? *Because it was going more slowly* (points to II).

These answers represent a clear advance over those we have just been discussing. At stage II A, as the reader will remember from Chapter One, our subjects fail to see that the colligation of durations is necessarily bound up with the order of succession, and it is precisely this lack of co-ordination which characterizes the intuitive approach to time. At stage I, duration is simply evaluated in terms of action (work done, path traversed, etc.)

or of preparation for action (waiting, etc.). The reason why duration becomes dissociated from the results of activity at stage II A is due to the discovery (representative reconstruction) that a given job of work done slowly seems to take longer than another job of work done quickly. However, the resulting intuition that 'quicker = less time' still lacks any relation to succession. Conversely, the idea of succession at stage I is simply based on the intuitive grasp of successive positions along a single track. This intuition becomes dissociated from the purely spatial factors as soon as the child is able to use representative anticipation to extend the motion of one of two bodies travelling with distinct velocities to the point reached by the other, and hence to compare the two (sub-stage II A). Now this dissociation of the temporal from the spatial order remains intuitive as long as it ignores duration. The great innovation of sub-stage II B is precisely the appreciation that succession is necessarily based on duration and *vice versa*: it is this appreciation which accounts for the change from intuitive regulation to operation.

The case of Rog is particularly telling in this respect. After maintaining that I continues for a longer time than II 'because it was in front', he discovered that if I stopped at lunch and II stopped after lunch, II must necessarily go on for a longer time. Similarly Lil, after first asserting that I continues longer, changed that opinion spontaneously on the grounds that II 'stopped after the other one'. For Den, duration was a function of succession and *vice versa*: I took less time 'because it stopped first', and II stopped after lunch 'because it went on longer'. Since duration is thus deduced from succession, i.e. from the interval between two ordered events—succession, in its turn, can be deduced from duration, and this is why with these subjects, intuitive time gradually gives rise to operational time, thus ushering in stage III.

How can we explain this emergence of operations? We have seen that intuitive regulation, like perceptive regulation, consists in transcending centration by means of anticipation and representative reconstruction: it goes without saying, therefore, that these regulations must culminate in operations, since (as we saw in Chapters One and Two) temporal, like all other, operations are defined by their reversibility. As soon as the motions to be compared can be mentally extended in two directions, time becomes an operational entity. This is the point which children at stage II B reach by gradual regulation, and which those at stage III reach quite directly.

§5. *The third stage: Operational succession and duration. Conclusions*

Unlike our last subjects, who start with intuition and arrive at the correct answers gradually, those at stage III use the correct approach right from the start.

DANI ($6\frac{1}{2}$): Did they stop at the same time? *No.* (I) *stopped first.* Why? *Because when it stopped the other one was still going.* Which went on longer? (II). Why? *Because it kept going after the other one had stopped.*

GIN (7 years): Which one stopped first? (I). Why? *Because the other one went on longer.* If (I) stopped at lunch, when would the other one stop? *After lunch.* For how long did (I) keep going? *For five minutes.* And (II)? *For more than five minutes.* Why? *Because this one* (I) *stopped before the other one did.*

IAC ($8\frac{1}{2}$): (I) *stopped before* (II). Why? *Because when* (I) *stopped the other one was still going.* Which went on longer? (II). Why? *Because it went less quickly.*

We find that these subjects can deduce duration from succession and *vice versa* at will. Hence they must necessarily divorce temporal from spatial succession, and appreciate that duration is inversely proportional to velocity. Temporal relations for them, therefore, constitute a general system that is both autonomous and also coherent, and one whose 'groupings' constitute the co-ordination of co-displacements (see Chapters One and Two).

In conclusion, we may therefore say that the reactions described in this chapter have provided us with a genetic explanation of the operations involved in the elaboration of temporal successions.

Since operations are reversible actions, they do not appear abruptly in the course of mental development, but represent the final equilibrium of a long process beginning with sensory-motor mechanisms and continued by the kind of regulations which our recent study of perception has tried to define.[1] In that respect, the relationship between intuitive and perceptive regulation (see §3) strikes us as being particularly significant. In the sphere of perception, centration leads to the exaggeration of the importance of a particular figure or relation, but the initial error may be corrected by further centrations, leading to 'decentration' and hence to gradual regulation. As Auersperg has shown, perceptive decentration, due to real or virtual movements of the eye, involves the interplay of sensory-motor 'anticipations' and 'reconstructions'.[2] Now, in the case of representative intuition, we are dealing with much the same mechanisms but on a larger scale. Here, the initial intuitions are also centred on a given relation, which is privileged inasmuch as it is bound up with the original awareness of the action. This exaggeration of the importance of a relation due to privileged centration is what we have called the 'egocentrism of thought'. Then, by the use of representative anticipations and reconstructions, the various 'centred' relations become adjusted as the child tries to remove the contradictions—in other words, they become 'decentred', not yet by an operational mechanism but by simple intuitive regulations or general compensations. Now, once these representative anticipations and reconstructions are produced far enough to enable the subject to extend two motions as far as their common meeting point, and also back to their common origin (reversibility), the system of displacements becomes operational, and the resulting groupings engender temporal relationships.

[1] See Piaget, Lambercier, Boesch and V. Albertine, 'Introduction à l'étude des perceptions chez l'enfant', *Arch. Psychol.*, Vol. XXIX, pp. 1–107.
[2] A. Auersperg and Buhrmester, *Experimenteller Beitrag zur Frage des Bewegtsehens*, Zeitschr. f. Sinnespsychol. Vol. 66, pp. 274–309.

H

CHAPTER FOUR

Simultaneity[1]

We shall now look at the reactions of children when presented with the same experimental set-up but under the following new conditions: the two figures I and II are set off together from the same starting line (A_1 and A_2), move in the same direction and stop together, but I is moved more quickly than II, with the result that they come to rest at a distance of some 3 to 4 cm. from each other [I stops in C_1, while II stops in B_2].

By their answers, the subjects can be clearly fitted into the three stages we have described. At stage I, they fail to grasp the simultaneity of the end points (and often even that of the starting points) and also the fact that the two figures move for the same length of time. Moreover, they argue that I takes longer than II because it goes further or more quickly, and think that II stops 'first' because it covers a smaller distance. During sub-stage II A, they still deny the simultaneity and equality of the two synchronous durations, but contend that II goes on for a longer time because it moves less quickly, or else discover the simultaneity of the motions but still deny the equality of the synchronous durations; a very few subjects at this sub-stage may, however, under certain conditions, grasp both the equality of the synchronous durations and also the simultaneity of the starting and end points. At sub-stage II B, these various advances begin to become co-ordinated. At stage III, finally, simultaneity and the equality of synchronous durations are appreciated and correlated straightaway.

[1] In collaboration with Mlle Esther Bussmann.

§1. *The first stage: No simultaneity. Duration judged proportional to distance*

Here are a few examples:

MAR (4; 6). To make certain that the subject understands the questions we put to him, we begin with two equal runs, i.e. with I and II starting simultaneously from A_1 and A_2 and stopping simultaneously in B_1 and B_2: Did they start at the same time? *Yes.* Did they stop at the same time? *Yes.* Did one of them go on longer than the other? *No. It was the same for both.*

I proceeds from A_1 to C_1 while II proceeds from A_2 to B_2: Did they start at the same time? *Yes.* Did they stop at the same time? *No.* Did they stop at the same moment. *No.* Did they go on for the same amount of time? *No.* Which one went on longer? (I). Why? *Because it went further.*

We repeat the runs over the two equal distances $A_1 B_1$ and $A_2 B_2$: Did the two stop at the same time? *Yes.* And what about these two ($A_1 C_1$ and $A_2 B_2$.)? *No.* But didn't they start at the same time? *No.* Now look again. (Simultaneous departures from A_1 and A_2 and simultaneous arrivals in C_1 and B_1.) *No.* Which one started first? (I).

MIC (4; 9). We run with the child through the room, starting and stopping simultaneously but leaving the child some 1·50 metres behind us: Did we start together? *Yes.* Did we stop together? *Oh no.* Which one stopped first? *I did.* Did one stop before the other? *I did.* When you stopped was I still running? *No.* And when I stopped were you still running? *No.* So did we stop at the same time? *No.* Did we run for the same length of time? *No.* Who went on longer? *You did.*

PIE (5; 5) also runs with the experimenter who allows the child to overtake him: Did we start together? *Yes.* At the same time? *Yes.* Stop at the same time? *No.* Which one stopped first? *Oh, I did.* When you stopped, was I still running. *No.* And when I stopped were you still running? *No.* So did we stop at the same time? *No, we didn't.* Did we run for the same length of time? *No.* Who ran longer? *I did.*

The experimenter and the child start walking simultaneously towards each other from two opposite ends of the room, and stop simultaneously at the same point, the child having covered a longer distance:

Did we start together? *No.* But at the same moment? *No.* One of us before the other? *No.* So we started at the same moment? *No.* Did we stop at the same moment? *Yes.* Did we walk for the same amount of time? *No.* Who took longer? *I did.* What sort of run did I take? *A short one.* And you? *A long run.* Did we stop at the same moment? *No.* Did we walk for the same time? *No, I walked longer.* Why? *Because I took a longer run.*

LIL (5; 5). The experimenter passes the child: Did we start at the same time? *Yes.* Did we stop at the same time? *No.* Did one of us stop before the other? *Yes, you did.* When I stopped, were you still going? *No.* And when you stopped was I still going? *No.* So did we stop at the same time *No.* Did we walk for the same length of time? *No. You took longer because you went further.*

We then start from two other points, this time facing each other, and stop at the same spot but not simultaneously: Did we stop at the same time? *Yes.* (We start again but stop with an even greater time lag.) Did we stop at the same time? *No.*

LUC (5; 9). The child overtakes the experimenter, and both stop simultaneously on a given sound signal: Did we start at the same time? *Yes.* Did we stop at the same time? *No.* Who stopped first? *You stopped a little earlier.* Did we take the same time? *No. Because you were walking and I was running.* Who stopped before the other one? *You did, because you were walking* (and did not run).

DON (6 years): I is in C_1 and II in B_2: Did they start at the same time? *Yes.* And stop at the same time? *No.* Which one stopped first? *(II).* Did they take the same time? *No.* (I) *took longer.* Why? *It went further.*

ARL (7 years). Same answers: Why do you think that (I) and (II) did not stop at the same time? *Because this one* (I) *went further and the other one didn't go so far.*

To make doubly sure, we place two glasses in C_1 and B_2 which the two moving figures reach and strike simultaneously. The child is told that the figures are coming home for dinner and ring the bell as soon as they come to the door: Did they both reach home at the same time? *No.* Did they knock the glasses at the same time? *No.*

All these answers are characteristic. We can sum them up very simply as follows: when two moving bodies travelling with the same speed start out from, and end up in, the same spot, the simultaneity of their departures and arrivals is readily appreciated; when they start out simultaneously from two opposite points and arrive simultaneously at the same spot but travel with different speeds, the simultaneity of the departures may be denied (Pie) or not, but the simultaneity of their end points is quite generally affirmed. On the other hand, if the two bodies start from the same point and finish up simultaneously at differend points (different speeds on parallel tracks) the simultaneity of their arrivals is generally denied.[1] Now this may not happen if the child ignores the differences in speed and distance, but as soon as he pays heed to these factors it invariably does occur. What are the reasons for this confusion? Certainly not a lack of perception or rejection of the perceived facts: every one of the subjects was agreed that when I had stopped, II was no longer moving, and *vice versa*. Things are therefore very much the same as we found them to be in the case of succession: simultaneity is, so to speak, perceived but not yet intellectually grasped. Could this be due to a purely verbal failure, i.e. to a systematic confusion of the terms 'at the same time' or 'at the same moment' with 'in the same place', and of 'for the same length of time' with 'over the same distance'? Now this hypothesis, far from solving the problem, merely shifts it, since we would still have to explain why the child lacks words to express simultaneity at a distance when the velocities differ, while he is perfectly familiar with adult usage when it comes to the simultaneous or successive lighting of two lamps placed 2 metres apart (the distance between the figures I and II is only a few centimetres). Since, therefore, the child's answers are neither due to a lack of perception nor to verbal confusion, there remains only one possible interpretation of his failure: two motions at unequal velocities lack a common time, i.e. there is no single 'moment' which two bodies separated in space can share. Arl put all this very clearly when, having granted that I has stopped running when II had stopped and *vice versa*, he nevertheless denied that they stopped 'at the same time'. When asked for his reasons, he explained that 'this one (I) went further and the other one (II) didn't go so far'.

All this would seem quite incomprehensible, had not the analysis of succession accustomed us to this lack of differentiation between time and space. Now if 'before' and 'after' in time

---

[1] Sometimes even the simultaneity of the departures is denied, but this is by false analogy with the arrivals. Thus Ger (5; 4) believed that of two bodies starting simultaneously, the second set out before the other; this was because it quickly overtook the first.

are confused with spatial succession, and if duration is identified with distance, it goes without saying that simultaneity at a distance, or with different velocities, can have no meaning for the child: he cannot possibly grasp that bodies moving in different places with different velocities can be fitted into a unique and homogeneous time scale. This negation of simultaneity therefore explains better than all our previous findings the purely 'local' character of primitive time concepts: as long as it remains intuitive, the conception of time must, in fact, remain a subjective evaluation of every motion or action considered separately. As a result, simultaneity cannot possibly be grasped in the case of motions or actions proceeding at different speeds. This applies *a fortiori* to the equalization of synchronous durations.

§2. *The second stage: Differentiation of intuitive conceptions* (*Early appreciation of simultaneity.
Duration inversely proportional to distance*)

In our analysis of succession we saw that stage II A involves two quite distinct developments: either the articulation of duration precedes that of succession, or else the opposite happens. When it comes to the problems of simultaneity and the equalization of synchronous durations (which constitute two particular relations between succession and duration) the situation is more complicated still, and we find that there are three ways of articulating the initial intuition, none of which can be called a clear advance on the rest. In the first, neither simultaneity nor the equality of synchronous durations is grasped, and duration is judged to be inversely proportional to the distance traversed. It might seem that this reaction is necessarily more primitive than the second type, were it not that some subjects who have grasped the idea of simultaneity nevertheless consider duration as directly proportional to the distance traversed. The second type is characterized by the comprehension of simultaneity but failure to equalize synchronous durations; sometimes the inverse relationship between duration and velocity is understood and sometimes it is not. Subjects of the third type, finally, who form the exception, can produce an intuitive equalization of synchronous durations (in a general, vague way) but fail to appreciate the simultaneity of the end points and sometimes even of the starting points. Clearly, therefore, in the case of simultaneity even more than in that of succession, stage II, or at least sub-stage II A marks the emergence of a range of articulations or fragmentary differentiations of intuitions but not of general co-ordination. It is only at sub-stage II B that this co-ordination is ushered in, thus foreshadowing stage III.

Here are some examples from sub-stage II A, Type 1, i.e. of subjects who have not yet grasped simultaneity or the equality of synchronous duration, and who simply proceed on the assumption that duration is inversely proportional to the path traversed:

(PAI 5; 2): Did they start at the same time? *Yes.* And stop at the same time? *No.* When (I) had stopped, was (II) still moving? *No.* The opposite? *No.* So did they stop at the same time? *No.* Which one stopped first? (II). Why? *Because it didn't go as far as the other.* Did they keep going for the same amount of time? *No.* Did one go on longer than the other? *Yes.* Which one? (II), *because it went more slowly.*

MAR (5; 6) similarly denied simultaneity though he realized that each one of the two figures had stopped running when the other had come to rest: Did one stop earlier than the other? *Yes,* (II) *did because he stopped first.* Did they run for the same length of time? *No,* (II) *ran longer because he was dawdling.*

Here, now, are some examples of Type 2, i.e. of subjects who grasp the simultaneity of the end points, but deny the equality of synchronous durations and assume that duration is either directly or inversely proportional to the path traversed:

Ios (5; 6): Did they start at the same time? *Yes.* Did they stop at the same time? *Yes.* At the same moment? *Yes.* Why? *When this one* (I) *had stopped the other one had stopped as well.* Did they go on for the same time? *No.* Did they take the same time? *No.* Did one take longer than the other? *Yes.* Which one? (I), *because he went further.* Duration is therefore thought to be proportional to velocity, and this despite the fact that the child has grasped the idea of simultaneity.

TEA (5; 5): Did they start together? *Yes.* And arrive together? *Yes.* At the same moment? *Yes. Almost at the same moment.* Did they keep going for the same time? *No.* Why? *Because one went further than the other.* Which one took more time? *This one* (II), *because he went more slowly.*

Tea thus recognized the simultaneities, but denied the equality of synchronous durations and made duration inversely proportional to the velocity or to the space traversed.

And here, finally, is a case of Type 3, i.e. of equalization of synchronous durations with denial of the simultaneity of the end points:

AL (6 years): Did they start at the same time? *Yes.* And stop at the same time? *No.* At the same moment? *No.* One before the other? *Yes, this one* (II). Did they keep going for the same time? *Yes.* Why? *Both went for a short time.* So did they stop at the same time? *No.* But did they start at the same time? *Yes.* And did they keep going for the same time? *Yes.* And they didn't arrive at the same time? *No, one arrived before the other.*

As we see, it is impossible to consider any of these types as being more advanced than the rest. True, it is tempting to claim that subjects of Type 1, who deny both the simultaneity of the end points and the equality of the durations are 'inferior' to Types 2 and 3 who recognize both. However, the mere fact that they have grasped the inverse relationship between time and velocity, while some subjects of the second type have not, shows that it is impossible to establish any clear progression, nor can we do so with Types 2 and 3. In short, there is no real reason for describing these three types as successive sub-stages. Moreover, and this is the crux of the matter, all their answers are unstable: when we see these subjects again after a few days or even after a few hours, their answers may be quite different, a clear sign that all of them are still at the pre-operational stage, and so display all the fluctuations of thought characteristic of perceptive and egocentric intuition.

But though this state of affairs complicates our classification, it is nevertheless highly instructive. Thus all three types provide clear corroboration of what we have briefly said (Chapter Three) about the regulative 'decentrations' governing the progressive articulation of the initial intuitions. Thus Type 1 uses representative construction, based on retrospection inasmuch as it allows of a distinction between 'lived' duration and duration as evaluated by the results of the action. As for Type 2, it is comparable to those subjects mentioned in Chapter Three who managed to establish the correct order of succession before successfully evaluating the durations. We have tried to explain this development by speaking of representative anticipation, by which the slower of two bodies can be projected forward in thought, with the result that it can be said to have 'arrived later' (in time) instead of having 'stopped first' (in space). But in the case of simultaneous arrivals at a distance, this approach does not work. However, we are entitled to assume (and we shall return to this point in §4) that, after having denied simultaneity because he intuitively identifies himself with one of the two bodies moving at different velocities, a subject of Type 2 'decentres' this intuition by considering the two bodies in the light of a new relationship or a new motion: this he can easily do if the two bodies signal to each other as soon as they have arrived at their respective destinations (by a sound, a visual signal or even by a look), or once the observer himself can connect them by signs of his own. In either case, the final position becomes independent of the preceding motion and can thus be incorporated into a new perceptive or intuitive relationship. This raises the question of why this apparently simple procedure does not ensure the appreciation of simultaneity from the start, but as we shall see in §4, the relations involved are far from being straightforward, and call for a special kind of decentration, i.e. for disregard of the prior velocities.

As for Type 3, it is more difficult to explain why the equality of synchronous durations should be grasped before the idea of simultaneity. In the case of operations, we could simply say that the relations between simultaneous positions have been generalized all along the path, whence the idea of synchronism and the equalization of synchronous durations must occur quite naturally, but this is not, of course, the case here. We must therefore assume that after having denied simultaneity because of the differences in velocity, the child decentres his representation as soon as he is asked questions about duration, when he ceases to think of anything but the brief moment shared by the two moving bodies.

In all three cases, we can therefore say that the initial intuitive conception (stage I) is supplemented with new relations based on representative reconstructions or anticipations which 'decentre' the former and thus modify it in various ways. However, since these articulations are not yet co-ordinated and remain unstable as well as fragmentary, we are fully entitled to compare this process to perceptive regulation.

During sub-stage II B, on the other hand, all these articulations are gradually co-ordinated as the representative anticipations and reconstructions on which they are based become reversible and hence sufficiently generalized to give rise to deductive operations. Thus the subjects we are about to discuss, after first vacillating in the manner of our previous subjects, gradually establish a precise co-ordination, and thus represent a clear transition to stage III:

NET (6½) begins by denying simultaneity: I and II did not *stop at the same time*; II stopped 'first' and I *took a longer time because it went further*. However, when, after experiments dealing with succession [during which Net, beginning with similar answers, finally came up with the correct reply (sub-stage II B)] we put the same questions again, he declared that I and II *stopped at the same time.* And did they move for the same time? *Yes, they did because they stopped at the same moment.*

DAL (7 years): Did they stop at the same time? *No.* When (I) stopped was (II) still moving? *No.* (And *vice versa*)? *No.* Did they stop at the same moment? *Yes.* Why? *Because both of them stopped.* Did they move for the same time? *Yes.* Why? *Because the two of them were moving together and stopped at the same moment.* Look again. (The experiment is repeated.) For how long did (I) move? *For two minutes.* And (II)? *Also two minutes.* Did they stop at the same moment? *Yes.* Why? *Because when* (II) *stopped* (I) *had stopped as well.*

These cases throw a great deal of light on the transition from intuitive regulation to deductive operation. Let us note first of all that all the subjects (like those at sub-stage II B) begin by confusing time with space, but later correct their error in the light of a new fact. With Net, this happened during the questions about succession; with Dal, the correction was made once he realized that when I stops II stops also, and *vice versa*. The early reactions of these subjects are therefore analogous to those we encountered at sub-stage II A: decentration of the initial intuition by anticipation or reconstruction of the relations involved. However, sub-stage II B is marked by three closely connected advances over sub-stage II A:

(1) Once the subject discovers a new relation, he does not merely apply it to the privileged situation in which he discovered it, but also to all comparable situations. It is thus that Dal went

on from the simultaneity of the starting points to the discovery of synchronism in general, and to the equalization of synchronous durations. Instead of leaving it (as subjects at stage II A do) at fitting the end points of the runs into a new relation independent of the prior motion, Dal realized at once that this relation applies equally well to every other position and successive moment of the motion, whence he concluded that the two durations are identical: 'the two of them were moving together and stopped at the same moment'. On hearing this very simple explanation of the quality of synchronous durations, we cannot help being astonished by the fact that children must wait for stage II B to arrive at it, and even then only after a good many trials and errors. This becomes quite obvious, however, once we grant that before the child can grasp the idea that two bodies can 'move together' despite differences in speed, he must first decentre his attention from these speeds, then go on to the realization that they stopped at the same moment, and finally view the combined motions in the light of this new relationship. Hence there must be a differentiation based on representative decentration, followed by a generalization of the new relationship—in short, regulation must be transformed into operation.

(2) By virtue of this dual character of regulative decentration, the differentiation of time and space in a particular point may subsequently be applied to other points by a sort of interaction in time of the various representations (comparable to the interaction of perceptions). It was thus that Net, having first denied simultaneity and synchronism, finally succeeded in solving the problem of succession: when led back to the original questions, he produced the correct answers at once, applying the regulation of succession automatically to that of simultaneity.

(3) Finally, and quite generally, the moment these decentrations which, as the reader will remember, result from representative anticipations and reconstructions, have become reversible, i.e. can be applied to the total motion [cf. (1)] and, by transposition, from one motion to the next [cf. (2)], the co-ordination of all the relations can be effected. For this to happen, each of the relations need merely be kept constant by means of generalized decentration: their reversible composition then constitutes the grouping of temporal operations.

In general, we may therefore say that starting from egocentric intuition which leads to the confusion of temporal and spatial successions, the subject goes on to decentre this intuition by means of representative reconstructions and anticipations. Then, once these regulations have become permanent and hence reversible, their generalization becomes, *ipso facto*, a deductive process, and the resulting operations can be combined to produce an overall co-ordination of time.

§3. *Stage III: Direct co-ordination of simultaneity and synchronism*

The only difference between the general reactions at stage III and the final reactions at sub-stage II B is that the co-ordination of simultaneity and synchronism has become immediate and no longer involves a host of preliminary trials and errors. Here are some examples:

SIA ($7\frac{1}{2}$): Did they start at the same time? *Yes.* And stop at the same time? *Yes.* Did one go further than the other? *Yes.* (I). But did they stop at the same moment? *Yes.* How do you know. *Because when one stopped the other one stopped as well.* Didn't one stop after the other? *No.* Did they continue for as long as each other? *Yes.* Why? *Because they stopped at the same moment.*

TAC ($8\frac{1}{2}$): Did they start at the same time? *Yes.* And stop at the same time? *Yes.* How do you know? *I saw.* You saw what? *When one stopped the other didn't go any further.* For how long did (II) go on? *For three minutes.* And the other one? *For three minutes as well.* How so? *Because they stopped at the same time.*

This final stage in the development of the concept of simultaneity is therefore analogous to the final stage in the development of the concept of succession. This is only natural, seeing that simultaneity is a limiting case of (zero) succession. However, it is nevertheless interesting to note that what applies at the level of infralogical or physical operations (see Chapter One, §5) applies equally well at the psychological and genetic level: the idea of simultaneity cannot be grasped by primitive intuition except in the privileged case of spatial coincidence. In all other cases it must first be constructed from succession: in the case of two bodies moving at different speeds and coming to rest at a distance of a few centimetres from each other, the child begins by thinking that they stop successively, simply because he cannot distinguish the spatial from the temporal order. Then, by a gradual process of dissociation, he arrives at the idea of simultaneity, seen as the limiting case of the initial succession. Now, even when he recognizes simultaneity at a distance without hesitation (stage III), he nevertheless continues to construct, i.e. deduce rather than perceive, it, in the same way as he constructs succession.

In fact, much as succession, on the operational level, forms a distinct and complementary grouping based on differences in duration and *vice versa*, so simultaneity, even at very small distances, is deduced operationally from the equality of the two synchronous durations and *vice versa*. It is true that Tac explained his conclusion by saying 'I saw', which seems to suggest direct perception, but we must stress that it is not until the age of seven or eight that our subjects can, in fact, 'see' this simultaneity. That being the case, what precisely has our subject 'seen'? He 'saw' that 'when one (of the two moving bodies) stopped, the other didn't go any further'. Now if that was the whole problem, younger subjects would, in fact, be able to 'see' it equally well, since from stage I onwards they have no difficulties in this respect. Nevertheless they all fail to deduce the idea of simultaneity! 'To see' that I and II stop simultaneously is therefore to construct it; i.e. to deduce it from the fact that the two durations involved have not ceased being synchronous because of differences in velocity. This elementary discovery lacks a temporal significance at stage I, and while subjects at stage II A (for instance Ios, 5; 6) can apply it to simultaneity, their failure to equalize synchronous durations prevents them from going beyond an intuitive, and therefore fluctuating and unstable, regulation of simultaneity.

From the moment that synchronous durations are conceived as necessarily equal, however, the resulting idea of simultaneity becomes stabilized as well, because it is now deduced and not merely perceived. Conversely, the equality of synchronous duration and synchronism in general, which were denied while duration was still evaluated in terms of distance and velocity, are adopted the moment simultaneity can be *deduced* from succession. In brief, simultaneity and the equality of synchronous durations, like succession and duration in general, become two complementary operational groupings as soon as intuitive regulation has reached the stage of strict reversibility.

However, we have still to solve another problem. Since even the youngest of our subjects recognize that when the body I stops, II has stopped as well and *vice versa*, would it not be true to say that they have grasped simultaneity intuitively or, as it were, purely perceptively, and that all the rest is no more than a superstructure and, so to speak, an intellectualization of the temporal datum? One could argue in this way if the two planes— the perceptive and the intellectual—were, in fact, completely discontinuous or at least independent of each other. However, if we are right in thinking that the operational grouping of successions and durations represents the final equilibrium of a continuous process of organization beginning with the perception of time, the stages we have been describing can legitimately be considered essential steps in that general construction. We shall now examine whether this is, in fact, the case.

§4. The rôle of the subject's own movements: Ocular movements in the perceptive evaluation of simultaneity and succession

We have seen that the concept of physical time, in its simply qualitative form, results from a grouping of co-displacements. As soon as the subject is able to prolong motions in two directions, he necessarily supplements his spatial co-ordination with a co-ordination of the various co-positions and co-displacements, which is nothing other than time. But how do these operations originate? We saw that the child's initial conception of time involves a complete lack of differentiation between time and space, with the result that, in the case of two motions, he 'centres' his attention on the end points alone, and completely neglects the co-displacements. This is, *inter alia*, the reason why he will deny simultaneity at a distance. However, as soon as children begin to anticipate the future state of the motions or to reconstruct their past, they automatically 'decentre' their initial intuition, i.e. correct it in terms of the co-displacements.

All this poses a further problem. We have been comparing the child's exclusive attention to certain relations to perceptive 'centration', and its subsequent corrections to 'decentrations' analogous to perceptive regulations. Now such comparisons would be quite impermissible unless the very perception of time gave rise to spatial decentrations. Does this happen in fact, or does the perception of time rather emerge as a coherent whole, at the same time as, and obeying quite other laws than, the intelligent grasp of time?

In what follows, we shall show that the perception of time does, in fact, involve mechanisms similar to those we have described during our discussion of the child's grasp of succession and simultaneity. To that purpose we have devised an experiment involving successive or simultaneous light signals from stationary lamps placed at some distance from each other. Here, the displacements are no longer external, but consist of ocular movements: the subject must look across from one lamp to the other. Far from being a passive reading, this perception of the temporal order thus involves an organization of bodily movements, and this, as we shall see, raises much the same problems, in the perceptive sphere, as we encountered in the case of intuitive or operational co-ordination.

This is not the place to attempt a general solution of the problem of time perception (duration, etc.) nor even of the perception of time succession, because this would lead us to a discussion of techniques that fall beyond the framework of this work.[1] Here we shall merely look at the question of the relation between time as grasped by the intelligence and by perception during the organization of the ocular movements (fixation and displacement) that go into the observation of successive or simultaneous processes. What we are concerned with, therefore, is not perceptive time as such (a problem we shall ignore here in its entirety) but the observational conduct leading to the perception of temporal successions.

Our subjects are presented with a set-up (designed by M. Lambercier) in which two lamps, at varying distances, can be lit up simultaneously or at intervals of 0·1 or 0·2 seconds. The subjects are then asked whether the lamps came on at the same time or not and, in the second case, which of them was lit first. In the experiment itself, we vary not only the distances between the two lamps and their positions with respect to the subject, but

[1] See 'Recherches sur le développement des perceptions', *Arch. de Psychol.*, Vol. LXXIX *et. seq.*

also the direction in which the subject looks at them: the child is instructed to fix his gaze on one of the lamps only, on a point situated half-way between the two, or on whatever point he himself chooses—in the last case we can determine whether or not his spontaneous behaviour produces the best results.

Now, the experiment poses no intellectual problems, since the child is no longer required to observe bodies moving at different speeds; to discover whether two lamps are lit simultaneously or successively is something a baby could do if it could speak—provided only the time intervals between the two signals are not too short. However, the fact that they are does raise special difficulties, and we must now examine what precisely they are. To say that they are of a perceptive rather than an intellectual nature is merely to give them a name. In fact, though no external motions are involved, the child has nevertheless to co-ordinate his ocular movements if he is to answer our questions. To discover the correct reply, he must look properly, and to look properly he must be able to order the events in accordance with the shift or fixation of his gaze. Now it is quite possible that this problem is, in some respects, analogous to the intellectual problem of co-ordinating co-displacements, and this is precisely what we shall find to be the case. Even when the two lamps are lit simultaneously, the eye must nevertheless shift from one to the next and this displacement may give rise to the impression that the lightings are successive. To perceive their simultaneity would mean reducing the duration of this displacement to a minimum, and to do that, the subject must first be able to ignore the illusions caused by the fixation of his gaze on one of the elements only, or rather to correct them by immediate decentration. We are therefore fully entitled to ask, as we did at the beginning of this chapter, whether the regulations involved in such decentration are comparable to those we have examined in Chapters Three and Four.

To answer that question, we arrange the two lamps on a long table at right-angles to the subject and at a distance of one metre from each other. Half-way between the lamps we place a small box. The subject himself sits 50 cm. in front of this box so that he can see both lamps at one glance. In a first series of ten experiments, he is allowed to look about freely, and the lamps are lit at random, successively or simultaneously. In a second series of ten tests, he is asked to look at the box and the lamps are again lit at random. In a third series, the child is asked to look at the left lamp and the lamps are again lit at random. In the fourth series, finally, the subject is asked to look at the right lamp.

In another series of experiments, the two lamps are placed at a distance of two metres from each other on the same long table but the child is seated at one end of the table, 30 cm. from one of the lamps, thus looking at the other in depth. We then run three series of ten tests each: free gaze, gaze fixed on the near lamp, and gaze fixed on the far lamp (fixing the gaze on a half-way point has no meaning in this experiment).

(We also made a number of tests in which one of the lamps was placed at a higher level than the other, but did not pursue the matter further.)

The reactions of some ten children at different ages (with roughly 70 results per subject) are summed up in the following table, showing the mean errors in per cent.

Lamps arranged at right-angles to the subject

Ages	5 %	6 %	7 %	10–11 %
Free gaze	41	28	29	6
Gaze fixed at centre	33	13	12	11
Gaze fixed on one of the lamps	42	31	24	13

Lamps arranged in depth

Ages	5 %	6 %	7 %	10–11 %
Free gaze	40	23	9	3
Gaze fixed on one of the lamps	48	28	20	12

These results are highly instructive in two main respects. The first is that the perceptive evaluation of simultaneity and succession develops manifestly as a function of age. At all ages, moreover, the grasp of simultaneity is slightly better than that of succession. The second brings out the full significance of the first: it is only with older children that free gazing leads to a better evaluation of succession or simultaneity than the fixed gaze and, curiously enough, even than the gaze fixed on the point half-way between the two lamps.

113

The importance of these results is quite clear. Younger subjects cannot compare the two lightings with the desired mobility: their free gaze does not shift quickly enough from one lamp to the next. Older children, on the other hand, manage to correct these errors of fixation either by quick shuttling or else by centring their look on an intermediate point from which they can survey the two lightings at a single glance.

Now there is no need for a deep analysis to arrive at a very simple interpretation. The statistical survey of the various errors —random though the absolute values are—suffices to underline their relative significance: (1) When the two lamps were lit simultaneously, 80 per cent of the subjects allowed to gaze freely believed that the lamp on which they happened to focus their attention was lit first. There is therefore illusion due to centration of the free gaze on one of the elements. (2) When the two lamps are lit successively, and the lamp at which the child gazes is lit first, nearly 50 per cent of subjects between five and seven years come up with the wrong answer. Of 100 such errors, approximately 8 result from the attribution of anteriority to the opposite lamp, and approximately 92 from the belief that the two lamps were lit simultaneously: this is because, by the time the child has shifted his gaze from the lit lamp to the other, the other has become lit up as well so that there is apparent simultaneity. (3) If, on the other hand, we first light the lamp at which the child is not fixing his gaze, we find that only 5 per cent of the subjects are mistaken, simply because, attracted by the sudden light, the eye shifts spontaneously from the lamp on which it was fixed. Of these latter errors, 20 per cent were due to the attribution of anteriority to the lamp on which the eye was originally focused, and 80 per cent to the belief that the lamps were lit simultaneously. (4) With the lamps placed behind each other, most of the errors occurred with the non-fixated lamp, but anteriority was more frequently attributed to the lamp at which the child happened to be looking; (5) when (with either arrangement of the lamps) the child is asked to look at one of the two lamps, the results are the same: (a) there are roughly three times as many errors when the lamp at which the child is asked to look is lit first, and of these five-sixths are due to a mistaken belief in simultaneity for the reasons we have just explained; (b) when the lamps are lit simultaneously, the errors due to the mistaken belief that the lamp at which the child is looking is lit first are roughly 10 times as many as the opposite errors. (6) Finally, if the child is asked to look at the central box, the mistakes are naturally reduced in number but remain significant all the same: when the two lamps are lit simultaneously, the chief errors result from the attribution of anteriority to the side to which the gaze shifts momentarily; in the case of successive lightings, two-thirds of the errors are due to the belief that the lamps were lit simultaneously (same mechanism) and one-third to reversal of the actual order of the lighting.

All in all, therefore, we see that the errors are due, in the main, to centration: no matter whether the lamps are lit simultaneously or successively, the child will, on principle, attribute anteriority to that lamp on which it has fixed its gaze or at which it is preparing to look. Moreover, as they shift their gaze from the lit to the as yet unlit lamp, younger children forget the time factor and therefore think that the two lamps were lit simultaneously. Now it is obvious that all these facts are related to those which we have described in connection with the intellectual difficulties of grasping the ideas of simultaneity and succession in general. It is therefore worth while, by way of a conclusion to Chapters Three and Four, to recapitulate briefly the overall problem of the development of the concepts of succession and simultaneity, starting from perceptive centration and continuing by way of perceptive and representative regulation to operation.

§5. *The genesis of the concepts of succession and simultaneity*

No matter whether we are dealing with the perception of the temporal relations of two stationary processes, or conceive of temporal relations in all their generality, time is always a system of co-displacements. However, in the first case, the displacements involved are those of our own body, i.e. our head or eyes, and if the events suceed one another rapidly enough, as in the case of the lighting of the two lamps discussed in §4, the mechanism of the organization of perceptive time can be readily analysed. Let us therefore start from this, the genetically simplest case of the grasp of physical time.

In §4, we saw that the perception of successions and simultaneities is fraught with systematic errors, which decrease with age and with the ability to co-ordinate ocular movements with external events: in younger children, the particular order of the centration gives rise to illusions of anteriority, and, since the duration of the ocular displacement is generally neglected, the real order of events becomes reversed or completely annulled (illusion of simultaneity). In brief, much as temporal succession is not divorced from spatial succession before the ages of 7–8 years, so the perceptive temporal order is not divorced from the order of centration or from ocular movements: because he does not grasp the purely chronological connection between the lighting of the two lamps, the child fails to look at the two lamps in quick enough succession and keeps his gaze fixed on one of them. Only when that one is lit, does he start to shift his gaze to the other and then confuses the external order of his own movements.

How are such errors corrected and what is the adaptive mechanism involved in the perception of temporal successions? In general, whenever a perceptive error is due to privileged centration (and all errors of perception we have studied so far are due to this factor[1]) the appropriate correction is made by decentration. If A and B are two elements (two lines, etc.), then, if centration on A leads to an overestimate of A and an underestimate of B, centration on B will have the opposite effect, and the passage from one centration to the other, or decentration, will reduce the importance of either. Decentration thus constitutes regulation by definition, i.e. it tends either to decrease one error to the benefit of the opposite error, or else it leads to a state of equilibrium, a sort of compromise between the two and, at the limit, to their cancellation.

In our particular case it is clear that this is what happens: centration on one of the two lamps leads to one error, centration on the other leads to the converse error, but the passage from one centration to the other (or decentration), provided only it is rapid enough, leads to the diminution of both errors.

Nor is that all. Why do these errors diminish with age? Here again the observed facts agree with the general scheme of spatial

[1] 'Recherches sur le développement des perceptions', *Arch. de Pyschol.*, Vol. XXIV (1942), pp. 1–107, 173–254, and 255–308.

or geometrical illusions we have been able to construct. Real centrations and decentrations must, in fact, be distinguished from virtual centrations and decentrations which latter result from the interaction of perceptions. Now, these virtual decentrations naturally increase in importance with age and allow the subject to correct the effects of centrations even before real decentration occurs. This is why, when ordered to look at one of the two lamps, the mistakes of most of our 10–11-year-old subjects amounted to only 14 per cent (6 per cent when they were allowed to look freely) while 5-year-olds were mistaken in 42 per cent of the cases (41 per cent when they are allowed to look freely).

Now what precisely are these virtual decentrations? They are simply anticipations or reconstructions of possible centrations past or future, in such a way as to correlate them with the present centration. Here we agree with von Weizsäcker and Auersperg, who contend that perception presupposes a mechanism of continuous anticipations and reconstructions, and it is, in effect, only by means of this type of mechanism that we can explain why our own subjects can perceive the simultaneous lighting of two lamps when their gaze has to shift from one to the other: to establish that A and B are simultaneous, they must anticipate B while their eye is still resting on A and reconstruct A when their glance has shifted to B.

In brief, erroneous centrations and regulative decentrations are two poles of the perception of successions and simultaneities. Now before looking at the intuitive conception of time, we must first mention another fundamental factor ensuring the passage from perception to reconstruction: the time of sensory motor intelligence which we observe between the ages of 3–18 months has precisely the same beginnings as perceptive time. Thus, a baby smiling at its mother beside the cot, will follow her with its eyes as she leaves the room, and, as soon as the door is closed, will look for her in the original place beside the cot. What better proof is there that the succession of events is conceived as a function of successive actions? Being unable to construct the objective path of the moving body (mother), the baby believes that if it places itself into the privileged situation in which the action originally took place, the initial event will recur. Similarly, having found an object under a pillow on the left, a child of eight or nine months will look for it in the same place, even after seeing it being placed under the pillow on the right, thus behaving as if the object must reappear where the action of finding it succeeded in the first instance. Since trajectories and space in general are thus centred on action, temporal successions are reduced to 'subjective' or 'egocentric' sequences. In other words, the temporal order becomes abolished or reversed in terms of a privileged situation, with the result that time cannot constitute a homogeneous medium common to all objects, or characterize a universe apart from the ego.[1] Here we have a close parallel with the perceptive relations analysed in §4, except that there the order of succession was mistaken as a result of visual centration while here it is mistaken as a result of a kind of centration on momentary actions that is no longer purely perceptive but also involves emotional factors.

How then does sensory-motor intelligence isolate practical time from the initial egocentric sequences? It does so by a process of decentration comparable to perceptive decentration, a process by which objects are divorced from actions and endowed with autonomous motions. Now, while the co-ordination of successive actions (which involves practical anticipations and reconstructions) helps to turn external motions into a practical group of displacements, the organization of the successive motions of another body or of one's own leads to the construction of external space and of practical time, and hence of the order of succession appropriate to actions.

Perception and sensory-motor intelligence are followed by a third level of awareness: that of intuitive intelligence which arises with the emergence of language and thus superimposes thought upon action. Now, thought is not immediately logical, as this book has tried to show: while it transcends action by means of representations, primitive thought does no more than prolong action in the form of 'mental experiments', and that is precisely why we call its structure 'intuitive'. All that precedes it on the perceptive and sensory-motor plane should help to explain more fully what we have said about intuitive centrations and decentrations in the sphere of temporal succession. Egocentric ideas which condition the perceptive and sensory-motor construction of reality are not, in effect, limited to these

[1] See Le construction du Réel chez l'enfant, Chapter IV.

early levels, but reappear on the intuitive level as well, albeit in new guise: relations constructed by means of 'mental experiments' now become modified not merely by actions but also by awareness of these actions, and it is this new mechanism which now governs the egocentric character of intuitive thought and quite particularly the centrations involved in the earliest conceptions of time.

By progress in sensory-motor intelligence, the child is thus enabled to construct practical time successions in terms of orderly motions in space. But how does it become aware of these motions on the intuitive plane? Experiments have shown[1] that motion is originally conceived of as a function of the final position of the moving body, in other words as a function of the goal to be reached. We have seen elsewhere[2] that the child originally endows every motion with intentionality and finality: motion is thought to tend, in the Aristotelean manner, towards a fixed place and a final state of fulfilment and rest. In quantitative terms, all children will therefore evaluate the paths covered by two moving bodies by the spatial succession of the end points of their motions and not by the distances between their starting and finishing points. In qualitative terms, they will argue that it is further to go than to come back, to climb than to descend, etc., etc. In brief, they treat motion egocentrically as a function of an actual or intended action, which comes back to saying that they treat it by privileged centration on the end point.

It is this initial type of representative centration which explains the earliest intuitive conceptions of temporal succession and simultaneity. Even if, 'perceptively' speaking, a problem such as the race between two figures (Chapters Three and Four) does not present any special difficulties, and even if 'practically' speaking, our subjects can easily master it, it remains a fact that, as far as initial thought or representative intuition are concerned, 'before' and 'after' in time are originally conceived as functions of the spatial order, and we now understand why: since the motion itself serves as a clock, and since its duration is judged by its terminal point in space, temporal succession must needs be 'centred' on spatial succession. Simultaneity, too, will

---

[1] See our forthcoming *Les Notions de mouvement et de vitesse chez l'enfant*.
[2] *La representation du monde chez l'enfant* and *La Causalité physique chez l'enfant*, Alcan, 1927 and 1928.

have no meaning, and for the same reasons. In short, much as the order of succession is mistaken as a result of perceptive and later of sensory-motor centrations, so it is now invalidated by intuitive centrations.

We now understand the true nature of intuitive decentrations. Instead of judging motion simply by its end point in space, intuitive thought has come to take all the other positions into account as well. It does so by representative anticipations and reconstructions, prolonging the perceptive, sensory-motor and practical, anticipations and reconstructions, as soon as the errors have become too glaring. At this point the see-saw of regulations and counter-regulations leads to the reversal of the initial relations and to overall co-ordination. There is thus no need to introduce operations to account for these early advances: it is sufficient to assume that the exaggeration of an error causes its reversal (regulation); that this reversal consists in introducing new elements (decentration), and that this process gives rise to increasingly wide anticipations and reconstructions (articulation of intuition).

Once this process of regulative decentration has been initiated, it tends towards final equilibrium, in which all the elements involved are integrated. As a consequence, anticipations and reconstructions become quite general and hence reach the stage of full reversibility: the resulting operations and their groupings constitute a system of co-displacements and hence a co-ordinated system embracing both time and space.

CHAPTER FIVE

The Equalization of Synchronous Durations and the Transitivity of Equal Time Relations

Having looked at the subject of succession, we must now make a closer analysis of duration and of simultaneity, and quite particularly of the equalization of synchronous durations.

We have seen (Chapter Two, §2 and Chapter Four, §2) that even when the child appreciates that two bodies start and stop simultaneously, he does not necessarily conclude that their motions are of equal duration. Before trying to explain this strange behaviour, we must first show that it occurs quite generally. To do so, we shall use an experiment that is far more precise than those we have met in the earlier chapters of this book.

A large vessel (the reservoir) is allowed to empty through an inverted and tapering tube yielding two identical jets of water. The water is collected in small bottles or glasses of different shapes and dimensions. A single tap controls both branches of the Y-tube so that the water can clearly be seen to start and stop running simultaneously.[1] If the two bottles are of the same shape and dimensions, the water will obviously rise to the same level in both; in that case, the equality of the synchronous durations is invariably recognized. On the other hand, if the two bottles do not have the same shape, and equal quantities do not rise to the same level, children at the lower stages will deny the equality of the time of flow. We can then ask them a number of questions, not only about synchronization as such but also about the logical construction of the equality of durations, and about the relation between time and the amount of water run out.

---

[1] To make the simultaneity of the terminal points even more obvious, both bottles can be pulled away from under the taps at the same moment.

We begin by asking, before the tap is turned on, which of the two dissimilar bottles will be filled more quickly and if it would take more or less time to fill than the other one.

When the water in one of the bottles (which we shall call A, B, C, etc., in order of increasing size) has risen to A_1 (in the case of the smallest bottle the subscript 1 means full to the top) the water in the second bottle will have risen to B_1 (A_1 and B_1 represent equal quantities of water). We then put our next question (simultaneity): 'Did the water start and stop flowing at the same time from both tubes?'

Third question: 'Did the water take some time to go from here (A_0 = the bottom of A, empty) to there (A_1)? And did it take the same, or more or less time to go from B_0 to B_1?'

We next make quite certain that the child fully understands that the two flows are simultaneous by saying: 'As you can see, the water runs out the same way from both these taps, and we started it running into the two bottles at the same time, and stopped the flow in both at the same time.' Once this is agreed, we ask the fourth question: 'Is there the same amount (or the same water) in here (A_0–A_1) as there is in there (B_0–B_1) or is there more water in one of the bottles?' Then, to check the answer, we ask: 'If we poured that lot (A_1) into B' (= another vessel identical to B) how high would it rise? And if we poured that lot (B_1) into here (A') how high would that rise?' Finally we might add another question: 'If we poured this lot (A_1) into L (= an elongated tube) and that lot (B_1) into L' (L' = L) would it rise to the same height or not?'

Our fifth question (or rather set of questions) bears on the logical co-ordination of synchronous or colligated durations. We fill two vessels X and Y, of different shape, simultaneously to the top, so that X = Y. Now, if Y = Z, will the child be able to conclude that X = Z? And if $Z_2 > Y$, will it conclude that $X < Z_2$, i.e. that it takes longer to fill Z_2 than X?

Now the stages of development represented by the answers to these questions (and especially questions 3 and 4) are generally comparable to those described in Chapters One to Four. Hence we need not dwell too long on the results, and can concentrate instead on the construction of the concept of synchronous duration.

§1. *The first stage: Failure to grasp simultaneity and synchronization, and failure to quantify the flow*

Here, first of all, are a few reactions:

PER ($4\frac{1}{2}$): Question 1: Look at these two bottles (B and F.) We are going to put both under these two taps at the same time and remove them at the same time. How far will the water rise in both? *They'll be full at the same time.* Just look. (Experiment) *Only one is full.* Why? ...

Question 2: Did we start at the same time? *Yes.* Did we stop at the same time on both sides? *No.* Didn't we take the bottles from under the taps at the same time? *No.* (wrong) (The experiment is repeated.) Did we stop them together? *Yes.* So did we stop them at the same time? *No, because this bottle* (F) *is not full.* (We start again, counting this time.) 1 ..., 2 ..., 3. Did we stop at the same time? *No.*

Question 3: How long does it take from here to there (B_0 to B_1)? *Don't know.* A short time? *Yes.* And from here to there (F_0 to $F_1 = \frac{1}{3}$)? *Was it a short time as well?* The same time? *No, more for that bottle* (B) *because it was full.* (We now take a run together through the hall and stop together, but Per denies that we did so.) What was I doing while you were running? *You were walking.* The same time? *No. I took longer because I was running.* But wasn't I walking for the same time? *No.* (We go back to the bottles.) Did we stop the water at the same time? (We have been counting.) *No. ... Yes.* Did that one (B) take some time to fill? *Yes, a long time.* And how long did that one take to rise from here (F_0) to there (F_1)? *Not a long time.* Why? *Because that bottle* (B) *has lots of water.*

Question 4: If that were syrup, which bottle would you like? *The full one, because it's bigger.* (false: B is smaller than F) What happens if I pour the water in B into (the empty) F? *It would go right up to the top.* And if I pour (F_1) into (the empty) B? *Up to here.* (the same level, i.e. half of B!).

LUC ($4\frac{1}{2}$) also denies that we stopped the flow of water into C and G simultaneously: Why? *Because* (G) *is not quite full and* (C) *goes right to the top.* Did they take the same time? *No. That one* (C) *took more time.* Why? *Because it went very quickly at the end* (narrow neck). (Two figures are moved along the table and brought to a simultaneous halt.) *That one took less time because it didn't go so far and this one took more time because it went further.* (We return to the bottles C and G: Question 2): Same amount of water?

No, there's more water there (C) *because it's bigger.* (false: G is bigger than C) If I pour these two bottles into these (L and L' = two identical tubes) what happens? *There would be more with that one* (C). (We perform the experiment.) *Yes, just a tiny bit more, oh no, it's the same thing.* (We pour the water back into C and G.) So was it the same? *No, it's not the same amount of water.* But did we take the same time to fill them? *No.* Look, we're going to put a mark on the clock (ink marks at the start and the finish of the two fillings). Did it take the same time? *No, because that bottle* (C) *filled up very quickly and the hand went less quickly.* So? *It took a little longer with that one* (C). Why? *Because it's smaller* (= more quickly filled = more time).

JACK (5; 10) predicts (Question 1) that two bottles E and C (E visibly larger than C) *will fill up together.* (Experiment) How much time for C_1? *One minute.* And for E_1 (= $\frac{2}{3}$)? *1 second. That's less.* The same time for both? *No, that one* (C) *took more time.* Why? *Because it is small and the other one is bigger.* (Similarly with B and F): (B) *is fuller and smaller, it gets filled more quickly because it's smaller.* So does it take more or less time? *More time.* Question 4: the fuller one *contains more water, this one* (C) *will go higher* (in L) *than that one* (E). After observing that the levels in L and L' are equal, Jack nevertheless continues to think that if the contents of E were poured into C they would only fill it to $\frac{2}{3}$.

As for running in the hall, he fails to appreciate the simultaneity of the stopping points, and makes the time proportional to the speed and the distance.

These three subjects produced the most primitive reactions we obtained by this method, i.e. failure to grasp simultaneity and synchronization and above all, a complete inability to quantify the work done (the flow of the water).

As regards the first point, though all these children realized quite clearly that by shutting off the tap we stop the flow into either bottle, and that the two bottles were withdrawn together from underneath the jets of water, they were nevertheless almost unanimous in denying the simultaneity of the end of the flow. This fully confirms what we have said in Chapter Four, and Per shows us precisely why: ignoring the different dimensions and capacities of the two small bottles B or C and of the two larger bottles F or G, the child, aware that the two taps give off water at an equal rate, expects the two bottles to be filled simultaneously ('they will be full at the same time' as Per put it). Now, when he saw that one of the bottles was filled before the other, he simply concluded that the flow could not have stopped 'at the same time', simply '. . . because this (the other) bottle is not full'. Here we have yet another example of the fact that children conceive of time as the complete course of a single action and not as the relation between, or common frame of, different actions. Now since, in our experiment, the taps are obviously turned on at the same time, the child treats the beginning of the flow as a single, simultaneous action. However, since one of the bottles fills up more quickly than the other, in much the same way as one of the runners mentioned in Chapters Three and Four overtakes his competitor, the child now faces two quite distinct actions with seemingly distinct end points in time. More precisely, he fails to appreciate the simultaneity of the end points because he fails to attribute a common time to these separate actions—having predicted that the two bottles will be 'full at the same time', and seeing that one is filled before the other, the child simply denies that the flow has stopped 'at the same time', meaning that there is no such thing as the 'same time', and that times cannot be compared for lack of a common duration.

This explains our subjects' peculiar reaction to the synchronization of durations, i.e. their denial that the small bottle gets filled to the top in the same time that the big bottle gets filled to a third of its capacity, and their claim that it takes longer to fill the small bottle. According to Per, this happened because 'it was full'; according to Luc it took longer because 'it went very quickly (at the end)'; and Jack gave both reasons when he said 'It is fuller and smaller, it gets filled more quickly because it's smaller.' Luc summed it all up when he claimed that the small bottle 'took a little longer . . . because it's smaller'. In brief, we are back with the general idea that time is proportional to velocity, the greater the speed, the greater the work done (distance covered, etc.). In our particular experiment, there is the added complication that the small bottle seems to contain more liquid because it becomes filled to the brim.

This brings us to the third reaction characteristic of this stage: the fact that failure to grasp simultaneity goes hand in hand with failure to synchronize durations, simply because time is thought to belong to each action separately and because the child thinks that actions can only be co-ordinated by their results (the work done). Now, since the results cannot yet be quantified, they cannot serve the child as objective criteria.

In respect of question 1, we saw that our subjects completely overlooked the obvious differences in the size of the bottles B or E, F or G, and so predicted that all of them would be 'full at the same time' (Per). Here we have the old misconception about synchronous processes, i.e. the evaluation of duration by the results of the action alone joined to a rather subjective or ego-centric quantification of these results based, not on the actual work done, but on the final objective (filling the bottles to the top). This also explains the curious reactions to question 4: the full bottle, however small, is thought to contain more water than the unfilled bottle, however big. Per even combined this misconception to his erroneous views of duration, when he argued that it takes longer to fill B 'because the bottle has lots of water'; 'the full one is the bigger one'. Similarly, Luc declared that 'there's more water there (C) because it's bigger', and this despite the fact that he also claimed that (C) takes 'a little longer (to fill) because it's smaller'.

In brief, we are back with the same primitive intuition we met in previous chapters: duration is evaluated by the results of an action, and these results do not depend on the interval between the starting and finishing points, but on the finishing point alone. In the case of two runs, the latter was represented by a point in space, in the case of the flow of liquid, the amount of water run out is judged by the levels irrespective of the size of the bottles—even if the water is poured back into equal vessels before the children's very eyes, they stick to their old evaluations. As for the use of a watch, we saw from Luc's reaction that the motion of the hand is simply incorporated into the general system of interpretation.

§2. *The second stage. Sub-stage II A: Inverse relation between time and velocity and correct prediction of the filling rate as a function of the size of the bottle; simultaneity but neither synchronization of durations nor correct quantification of the flow of liquid*

Subjects at this sub-stage generally succeed in answering questions 1 and 2 correctly, but not questions 3 and 4 (nor, *a fortiori*, question 5). They are therefore of particularly great importance to the genetic analysis of time. Here are some examples:

WUT (5; 10). Question 1: Wut immediately applied the inverse proportion: *It will take longer to fill the bigger one* (G). *The little one* (C) *will be filled more quickly.* (Experiment) Did we start filling them at the same time? *Yes.* And stop at the same time? *Yes.* How much time to fill the little one (C)? *Two minutes.* And that one (G) up to there ($\frac{1}{3}$)? *One minute, because there's less water inside.* Was the same amount of water run into both? *No, more into the small one because it's full.*

BLAI (5$\frac{1}{2}$). Question 1: *It would take longer with that one* (G) *because it's bigger.* Which one will be filled more quickly? *The small one* (C). Questions 2–3: The bottles C and C ($\frac{1}{3}$) are filled simultaneously: *The little one is winning, I was right.* Did they start at the same time? *Yes.* And stop at the same time? *Yes.* How much time for (G) ($\frac{1}{3}$)? *One minute.* And for (C)? *Less than a minute* (because it was not filled to the brim). *Oh no, it took a minute for the little one, and less time for the big one because that one* (G) *is always bigger* (= because it is never quite filled). I see. But do these two (C$_0$ to C full and G$_0$ to G $\frac{1}{3}$) take the same time to fill? *I have no idea.* Think about it. *I can't tell, it's impossible.* Question 4: You see these two tubes (L and L')? If I pour (C) into (L) and (G) into (L'), how far will they go? *That one* (G) *up to there and this one* (C) *will go lower.* Why? *Because this one was less full than that one.*

PONS (5; 4). Question 1: *The small one* (C) *can be filled quickly; it takes longer to fill the big one.* Questions 2 and 3: *The flow started and stopped at the same time.* Take this watch, and make a mark where the hand is when I put the bottles under the tap, and another mark where the hand is when I take the bottles away. *The hand moved up to here.* Did it move just as far for the big bottle? *No, it went further because it was turning more quickly.* (Experiment with C and E.) How long did it take to fill (C)? *Five minutes.* And for (E) to come up to here ($\frac{1}{3}$)? *Ten minutes.* Question 4: Was the same amount of water run out from both sides? *No. There is more water in the big bottle.* If it were syrup, which one would you take? *The small bottle, because it's full.* Let us pour (C) into (L) and (G) into L'), how far will the water rise? *Higher with* (G) *because the bottle is bigger.* And if we pour (G) into (C)? *It will run over because there will be too much.* Is there as much to drink in both bottles? *No. I prefer the little bottle, it's full, so there'd be more to drink.*

CLAN (5$\frac{1}{2}$). Question 1: Correct answers. Question 2: *At the same time because you took the bottles away together.* Questions 3 to 4:

One minute for that one (C) *and less than a minute for this one* (G); *it has less water so it fills up more quickly.* What will happen if I poured this one (C) into here (L) and that one (G) into there (L')? *The water will be higher with that one* (C). And what if we pour (G) into (C)? (Points to the ⅔ mark). *Oh no, it's less.* (We pour the two into L and L'.) *It's the same height because they are the same glasses.* Same amount of water? *Yes, it's the same.* And if we poured (C) back into (G), would there be the same amount to drink? *No, because that one* (C) *is smaller. Oh no, there will be more water in* (C), *I'd prefer that one.*

We take two other bottles B and E, and ask the child to count while we pour. How much time for (B)? *Two minutes.* And for (E)? *Three minutes because it's bigger.* Watch (we pour B into L, E into B, and L into E). *Oh, it's the same thing. It took the same time for both of them.* Clan has therefore momentarily reached sub-stage II B, but what follows does not bear out his general progress.

Two new bottles, K_1 and K_2 of different shape but of the same capacity: Did we begin and finish at the same time? *Yes.* How much time for (K_1)? *Two minutes.* And for K_2? *Three minutes, the other one is smaller.* Did the water run the same way? *Yes.* So isn't there the same amount of water in both (K_1 and K_2)? *No, one bottle is bigger than the other* (i.e. the quantity of water depends on the size of the vessel). But look here. (We transfer the contents into L and L'). *Oh, it's the same thing.* And did it take the same time for both? *Oh yes, because we stopped at the same time.* Look and count (the experiment is repeated). *One, two three.* Same amount of water? ... How much time? *Four minutes for* (K_2) *and two minutes for* (K_1). But you said just now they took the same time? *Yes, but there's more water in here* (K_2). So? *Four minutes and two minutes. It takes longer here* (K_2).

At sub-stage II A, therefore, children recognize simultaneity, divorce time from velocity, and predict intuitively that the larger of two bottles will be filled less quickly and in more time. On the other hand, they fail to equalize or synchronize durations with simultaneous starting and finishing points, or to quantify the amounts of liquid run out.

As for their general progress, we saw in Chapter Two §2, that once the inverse ratio of time and velocity is understood by means of articulated intuition, retrospective reconstruction leads to the distinction between the results of an action (the sole criterion of time at stage (I) and its duration. Now as soon as this distinction is made, the child will necessarily react differently to question 1 (prediction of the time needed to fill two bottles of unequal size) from the way it does at stage I. At stage I, in effect, he expects that, with identical outflows, the two bottles will be filled at the same time, as if the final result depended exclusively on the rate of flow and not at all on the work to be done (size of the vessels). During stage II, on the other hand, thanks to the distinction which we have just mentioned, the child expects that the bigger of the two vessels will take more work to fill than the smaller one, and consequently that the latter will be 'filled more quickly' (more quickly in terms of velocity and also of time).

As for simultaneity, we saw in Chapter Four (§3, Type 2) that it, too, is recognized at sub-stage II A, once representative anticipations and reconstructions help the child to link the end points of a motion by a system of signals, etc. Now, in the present series of tests, these developments are particularly obvious. Subjects at stage I deny the simultaneity of the end points (withdrawal of bottles or shutting of tap) because they centre their attention exclusively on the rise of the water level in the two bottles. At stage II A, on the other hand, they take the simultaneous withdrawal of the two bottles into account as well as the rise in level, and the resulting decentration leads them straight to simultaneity (cf. Clan's 'at the same time because you took the bottles away together'). Now, as the grasp of this relation is much more highly intuitive than that of the simultaneous stopping of the two runners at some distance from each other, simultaneity is recognized not merely by a particular category of subjects at sub-stage II A (Type 2 in Chapter Four) but by the great majority.

Let us now look at the failure of subjects at this sub-stage to synchronize durations and to quantify the contents of two vessels. It may seem strange, that once simultaneity has been discovered, the equality of synchronous duration should not be deduced directly, but should lag almost further behind than in the case of the two runners. In fact, we found no subjects who, like those mentioned in Chapter Four, §3, arrived at equality before simultaneity. This is probably because the synchronization of duration is a more complex process than the recognition of the simultaneity of the starting and end points, because synchronization implies the simultaneity of *all* the corresponding instants between these two extremes. Thus, while the child can readily deduce the initial and terminal simultaneities of the flow from the fact that the two bottles are placed together under the jets of water and withdrawn together, there is nothing by which he can correlate the flows during the interval, with the result that he thinks of nothing but the unequal rate with which the bottles are being filled and hence denies the equality of the durations. In particular, if, at the moment of withdrawal, one of the bottles is full and the other only a third or a half full, the child generally thinks that the durations must be unequal: 'The little one is winning', Blai exclaimed, whence he concluded first of all that the smaller bottle took less time, later that it took more time, to fill, and finally that it was impossible to compare the durations.

True, the child might establish the equality of the durations independently of simultaneities and of synchronous durations by a simple reference to the fact that equal amounts of water are being run out at the same rate. In other words, since he succeeds in answering question 1 (time proportional to the size of the bottles) one might expect him to answer question 4 (equality of the quantities of water poured out) as well, and hence to deduce the equality of the durations. But, interestingly enough, all our subjects are influenced by yet another factor, and it is this factor which persuades them to deny the equality of the durations: the small bottle seems to contain more water because it is full to the brim (there is 'more' in the small one 'because it is full' Pons said, after vacillating between the two interpretations). Now, no matter whether we ask the child to evaluate the quantities of water by pouring the liquid back into two identical tubes or by transferring the contents of one bottle into the other, it invariably wavers between answers based on the size of the bottles and answers based on their relative fullness. The only point on which all subjects are agreed is that the filling time is directly proportional to the quantity of water run out. Since they have no means of estimating the latter, they deny that the amounts of water involved are equal.

But does the experiment not provide the child with a simple means of quantifying the amounts of liquid involved? After all, the water is run out through two identical taps and at the same rate, and this point is constantly brought home to the child during the experiment, so much so that all the subjects agree that 'the water runs the same way from both sides'. Seeing, therefore, that they are watching equal jets of water that start and stop running simultaneously, why do these children fail to conclude immediately and even intuitively that the quantities of water run out from either side are equal? It is precisely because, before they can recognize this equality *a priori*, they must first have acquired a conception of time that is structured enough to enable them to deduce the equality of synchronous durations from the simultaneity of their end points. Now, conversely, since the child looks upon duration simply as a function of the work done, he cannot establish this equality before he has developed a conception of quantity structured enough to suggest the equality of the two amounts of liquid run out, i.e. before he realizes that if these two amounts of liquid were poured into two identical vessels the levels in both would be identical.[1] There is therefore a vicious circle.

Now, this vicious circle holds the key to the operational construction of time. If we pose the problem in all its generality it becomes clear that the elaboration of time is identical with the quantification of the universe in its entirety and *vice versa*. While time represents the distance covered (or the work done) at a certain velocity, the distance covered represents the time during which a certain motion took place with a certain velocity, and the velocity represents the relationship between time and the space traversed. The measurement of time is therefore part and parcel of a 'group of transformations' which transforms the vicious circle on which it is based into a coherent and closed operational system. However, at the intuitive level (stages I and II), the child still faces an inextricable situation. On the one hand, his intuitive conception of time, even if articulated, does not allow him to deduce the synchronous nature of the durations from the perception of the simultaneities; on the other hand, his intuitive conception of space does not allow him to deduce the equality of the quantities of water run out, and to construct the latter he must first appreciate the synchronism of the two flows! We shall see how, in the course of stages II B and III, the situation becomes resolved to the point of transforming this vicious circle into 'groupings'.

[1] No child below the age of 7 can do this. See Piaget and Chelinska, *La Genèse du Nombre chez l'Enfant*, Chapters I and X.

§3. *Sub-stage II B: The empirical discovery of synchronization*

The last of the subjects discussed in the previous paragraph (Clan) showed a momentary grasp of synchronous duration when he postulated the equality of the quantities of liquid run out. The subjects we shall examine next also succeed in grasping the equality of synchronous durations and of the quantities of liquid run out, but only after a series of trials and errors. However, once this result has been achieved, they can apply it to all analogous situations: were it not that their constructions are still intuitive and empirical and, lacking generality, not yet operational, we might easily be misled into thinking that they had fully grasped the idea of synchronization.

Here are some examples; first of all a subject representing a transition from sub-stage II A to II B:

PAS (6; 4). Question 1 (C and G): *The bigger one* (G) *will be filled last. It takes more time.* (Experiment) Did they stop together? *Yes.* Did it take the same time (to reach C full and G ⅓ full)? *No. This one* (G) *took less time because it wasn't completely filled.* How much time? *One minute for* (C), *but less for* (G) *because there isn't so much water in it and it's bigger.* So did one take more time than the other? *Oh no! The same time, because both were being filled in the same time.* Why in the same time? *Because that one* (C) *is smaller and that one* (G) *is big, but it wasn't completely filled.* Very well. And if we pour (C) and (G) into these two tubes (L and L′)? *It'll take longer for the big one because there is less.* (Experiment) *Ah yes, it's the same, because they were being poured at the same time.*

DIUS (6; 8). Questions 1 and 2: correct answers. Experiments with C and E: *It* (C) *didn't take a minute, it only took a second.* And what about this one (E ⅔)? *Less time because it is taller.* Did we start together? *Yes.* Stop at the same time? *Yes.* Did you say that it took only a second with the smaller one? *Yes.* And with the big one? *Also a second, it's the same time.* And if I poured the water into (L) and (L′) how high would it rise? *Oh, the same amount.*

Look at these two other bottles. (Experiments with B and D.) How much time with this one (D, ⅔)? *One second.* And with that one (B, full)? *Two seconds, because it's taller.* And if we poured both into (L) and (L′)? *It wouldn't be the same thing, there is more in that one* (B). Did we start and stop at the same time? *Yes.*

How much time with (D)? *One second.* And with (B)? *Two seconds.* But if we begin at the same time and stop at the same time how is it that one takes one second and the other one two seconds? *Because one of the bottles is bigger.* I'm going to empty them both into (L) and (L'). *That won't be the same.* (Experiment) *Oh yes, it is the same.* How much time with (D)? *One second.* And with (B)? *One second as well.* Why? *Because the water is running out the same way.* And what does that mean? *That both took a second.* But you said the opposite. *Well, this bottle (B) is filled up to the top and that one only up to here (D, $\frac{2}{3}$) so it's the same thing.* The same as what? *There is the same amount.*

Two new bottles E and F which look similar: *They'll take the same amount of water because they are the same size.* (Experiment) *No, not the same amount.* The same time? *No, the bigger one took longer.* And if we poured both into these (L and L')? *Not the same thing.* (Experiment) *Oh, yes.* And what about the times? *Did it take the same time for both?* The same length of time? *Yes, it took the same length of time.*

MAG ($6\frac{1}{2}$). C and G ($\frac{1}{3}$) are filled while he counts: 1, 2, 3. What happened? *There is more water in here (C).* Did we start at the same time? *Yes.* And stop at the same time? *Yes.* How much time? *One minute for (C), half a minute for (G) because there is less in it.* What if we poured the contents into (L) and (L')? *The same time; I don't really know; no, it'll take less all the same because one is taller; no, it's going to take the same time because the other one is bigger.* And if we poured (C) into (G) and (G) into (C)? (Points out the levels correctly.) And what about the times? *One minute for both because (G) is bigger, but still it took the same time to fill both.* Why did you think otherwise before? *Because I thought there was less water.* With E and F: correct answers.

MAR (7 years). Question 1. Series of comparisons: the bigger bottle invariably takes longer to fill. Questions 2 to 4 (C and G): Were they filled together? *Yes.* Same time? *Oh no, longer here (G) because it's bigger.* When the water ran into (C) what was happening here (G)? *It rose up to there ($\frac{1}{3}$).* So did it take the same time? *No.* We shall now pour the water into (L) and (L'). *It'll take the same time.* Why? *Because there's the same amount of water.* How much time (for C and G)? *The same time.* Why? *Because we stop at the same time.* (Mar clearly has recourse to simultaneity but only after successful quantification.)

Bottles E and F: The same mistakes at first: We are going to pour the water into (L) and (L'). *It'll go lower with (F), but I don't really know. Oh, it'll be the same thing because that one is wider and this one is thinner* (and taller). And the time? *It'll take the same time because we stop at the same time.*

LIL (7; 1) also begins by denying the equality of the durations and quantities (with C and G), but discovering that the water reaches the same level in (L) and (L′), she exclaims: *The same amount of water.* Why? *Because you stopped at the same time with both bottles.* How much time? *Three minutes and three minutes again.*

These reactions throw a great deal of light on the child's construction of time, in that they bring out clearly the relationship between the discovery that the flow of liquid is synchronous and the recognition that the quantities of liquid are equal. However, it should be stressed at once that, though all these subjects (except the first, who was an intermediate case) made both these discoveries quite spontaneously, they did so in different order. Thus when Dius, after first declaring that E takes longer than C, discovered that the flow was synchronous, he immediately deduced the equality of the amounts of water in both bottles. However, the same child, when looking at B and D, discovered the second equality first (by correct prediction of the levels in L and L′) and then deduced the first from it. Mag discovered the equality of the two amounts of water first 'because that one is wider and this one is thinner', and then concluded that the two durations were synchronous, because it took the same time to fill both bottles. He also explained that the reason why he was originally mistaken about the durations was 'because I thought there was less (water)'. Mar, too, discovered the equality of the amounts of water first. He explained that the synchronism could be inferred from the simultaneity of the end points of the flow, but failed to draw this conclusion before he had quantified the amounts of liquid. Lil argued in much the same way. Pas, finally, deduced the synchronism from the simultaneities and then justified his deduction by reference to the equality of the amounts of water. These he subsequently denied again, but seeing that the levels in L and L′ were equal, he reverted to his original view, and this time justified it by the synchronism of the flow. We must therefore distinguish three types of reaction which can, moreover, co-exist in one and the same individual. In the first, the child deduces the equality of the synchronous durations from the observable fact that the flow starts and ends simultaneously and does so without explicit or implicit reference to the quantities of water run out (for example Dius at the beginning of the questioning, or Pas when he said: 'The same time because both were being filled at the same time'). This type of reaction is comparable to that described in Chapter Four in connection with the discovery of the equality of synchronous durations, based on the simultaneity of the starting and end points of two runs. Now the similarity of these two reactions is easily explained: by progressive decentration of his attention, which was originally focused on the end point only, the child gradually extends his intuitive conception of simultaneity to all corresponding intervals of the two processes and thus passes from simultaneity to synchronism ('the same time because they were both being filled in the same time,' as Par put it). However, because of its peculiar mode of formation, this kind of synchronization may lack generality, and hence retain a purely intuitive character instead of reaching the operational level. We shall see that this is so in Chapter Seven, §3: subjects at sub-stage II B can recognize the synchronism of two elementary durations $A_1 = A_2$ or $A'_1 = A'_2$, without recognizing that, if $A_1 + A'_1 = B_2$ and $A_2 + A'_2 = B_2$, it follows necessarily that the total duration $B_1 = B_2$.

In the second type of reaction, the child (for instance Mar and Lil) may base synchronization on the respective simultaneity of the beginning and end point of the flow, much like the previous subjects, but only after having recognized the equality of the quantities of water involved. In their case, synchronization is, therefore, based implicitly on the quantification of the work done, i.e., in the experiment under discussion, on the equality of the quantities of water run out.

In the third type of reaction—and this is the most frequent—the child begins with the discovery that the amounts of liquid run out are equal (quantification of the work done) and then deduces the equality and synchronism of the durations. But in that case, how does the child discover the equality of the quantities in the first place? He often does so by a purely spatial argument, i.e. by assuming that while one of the vessels is taller, the other one is wider, and that these differences cancel out. But even in that case, he bases his argument on the fact that both taps were opened and shut simultaneously: thus Mag, who used a purely spatial quantification to justify the equality of the quantities, added spontaneously that the amounts of water were the same because 'it took the same time to fill them'. In brief, no matter which path our subjects choose, they all clearly base synchronization on the equalization of the quantities of water and *vice versa*. The two discoveries are therefore inter-related, as we suggested at the end of §2, and this fact is of the greatest importance in the construction of the concept of time.

Time cannot, in fact, be conceived of as a medium common to different processes unless the latter are organized into a system of co-displacements in which the various motions or states are interrelated. Now such interrelations cannot be es-tablished without prior quantification of the motions them-selves, e.g. of the flow of water in our experiment. Thus there is good reason why our subjects should derive the synchronism of the durations from the equality of the two amounts of water run out, and hence from the quantification of the work done and the motions involved. It is true that this case is a particularly simple one, since the velocities of the two flows are equal. Now, in most other cases the velocities differ, so that the quantitative results of a synchronous transformation will differ. This is precisely what happens when, instead of thinking of the flow, the subject thinks only of the rise of level in two differently-shaped flasks (cf. Chapters Three and Four); but even then, the discovery of synchronism and of the equality of durations in-volves a quantification: that of the space traversed at a given velocity $\left(t = \dfrac{s}{v}\right)$. This applies equally well to psychological time, in which the motions reduce to actions and the velocities to the rate at which the work is done.

§4. *The third stage: Immediate synchronization and quantification*

We shall again begin with an intermediate case:

BAC (7; 6). Bottles C and G: *The smaller one* (C) *will be filled more quickly*. (Experiment) Did we start at the same time? *Yes.* And stop at the same time? *Yes.* How much time for (C)? *One minute.* And for ($\frac{1}{3}$ G)? *Also one minute.* Why? *Because they were done together.* Is there the same amount of water in both bottles? *Yes.*

136

What if we poured them into (L) and (L')? *The water will rise to the same height because there is the same amount of water in both.* And if we poured (C) into (G) and (G) into (C)? *It will go up to where it was before in both* (correct).

But with two new bottles B and E, after first saying that *it takes the same time because they stopped together*, Bac denies that the same amounts of water are involved: *There is more here* (E) *because the bottle is bigger.* However, he quickly corrects his error. With a third pair of bottles, he says straight away: *The same time because the same amount of water was run in from both sides.*

LET (7; 8). If bottles C and G ($\frac{1}{3}$) were poured into L and L' the water would rise *the same way in both.* Why? *Because one is bigger* (wider) *but the other one is taller.* But how long did it take to fill them up to here? *One minute for this one and one minute for that one.* Why? *Because they stopped together.*

NEUR (7; 10). C and G: What happened? *This one* (C) *went more quickly.* Why? *Because it's smaller.* How much time? *One minute.* And how long to fill that one ($\frac{1}{3}$ G)? *The same time.* Why? *Because it's the same amount.* If it were syrup, which one would you like to have? *It makes no difference.* And if we poured (C) into (G) and (G) into (C)? *It'll be the same as before.* Now look. (We fill C while looking at a clock.) And for that one ($\frac{1}{3}$ G)? *The hand will go to the same place.*

We see once again that the greater the grasp of synchronization the better the quantification. We also find the persistence of the two types of reactions introduced at sub-stages II B, except that they they have become a justification of, and no longer a means of discovering, new concepts. Some of our subjects, such as Bac and Let, base the equality of synchronous durations on the simultaneities, and hence go on to the equalization of the quantities of water, while for others, such as Neur, it is the second equality, also based on the simultaneities, which leads to the equalization of the first.

However, with children of the first type, i.e. those who justify the equality of synchronous durations by simultaneity alone and without reference to the quantification of the work done, we may well ask whether their reactions are in effect operational or whether they have remained intuitive. In fact, Bac represents an intermediate case between the intuitive mechanisms of sub-stage II B and the operational mechanisms of stage III: he failed to apply his results directly to all the pairs of bottles and was briefly mistaken with B and E: he continued to base synchronization on simultaneity without deducing the equalities of the quantities of water run out, thus demonstrating that this second quantification is essential to any real grasp of synchronous duration.

In what way, then, can we ascertain whether or not a given subject's reactions are truly operational? We can do so by means of Question 5 which we shall now examine more closely, incidentally demonstrating that Let succeeds in answering it while Bac fails to do so.

§5. Question 5: Transitivity of synchronous and equal flows

Whereas operationally constructed relations of time constitute 'groupings', intuitive relations of time cannot be 'grouped' together. To establish whether or not the equality of synchronous durations or of quantities of water run out are constructed by operational or intuitive means, we need therefore merely present our subjects with a problem involving the elementary composition (transitivity) of these equalities. This problem could, in fact, be solved by formal logic, i.e. independently of the contents of such concepts as time and quantity, but only if formal logic were constructed before the elaboration of the concepts which serve as its contents. Now, in the present case, as in all other cases we have been examining,[1] we have found that formal logic does not emerge until the concepts defining it are structured enough to lend themselves to 'grouping'. As a result, children up to the ages of 11 or 12 have no grasp of formal logic but work towards it by means of increasingly complex 'groupings', originally built up of 'concrete operations'.

Now, for Question 5: if C_1 takes the same time to fill as C_2 (two flasks of different shape but with the same capacity) and C_2 takes the same time to fill as C_3, does C_1 take as long to fill as C_3, and do they contain the same amounts of water? Now, it might seem that even those subjects who fail to grasp the temporal or quantitative relations involved could arrive at the correct solution by simple inference; however, their answers

---

[1] See particularly Piaget and Inhelder, *Le Développement des Quantités chez l'Enfant.*

show that, at the intuitive levels, they fail to appreciate that these relations are transitive, i.e. they fail to construct them operationally, and that it is not until they grasp both the equality of the synchronous durations and also that of the amounts of water run out that they appreciate that the equations $C_1 = C_2$ and $C_1 = C_3$ are transitive! Not a single one of our subjects could solve this problem ($C_1 = C_3$) before he was able to answer Questions 1 to 4 correctly; moreover some subjects who had apparently reached stage III because they could answer questions about synchronization and quantification involving simple pairs of bottles (for instance Bac) failed to grasp the transitivity of these relations directly.

Obviously, there is no point at all in putting Question 5 to children at stage I who cannot yet recognize simultaneities and therefore fail to grasp the very data involved. We shall therefore begin with a subject at sub-stage II A:

SAUT ($6\frac{1}{2}$). C_1 and C_2 are filled: *They were filled together.* Did they take the same time? *Yes.* And these two? (experiment with C_2 and C_3) *Yes, the same time, as well.* And if we filled C_1 and C_3 what would happen? *That one (C_3) would take less time and this one (C_1) would take more time.* Why? *It's bigger.* But wasn't that one (C_1) and this one (C_2) filled together? *Yes.* And these two (C_2 and C_3)? *Yes, also.* So what about them? *That one (C_1) would take longer.*

We can see that the problem of synchronization ceases to pose any difficulties, even at stage II A, once the two pairs of bottles are filled simultaneously to the top (here we have a confirmation of what we said in §1 and §2 about the importance of the end point in estimates of quantities and durations). Nevertheless, this intuitive grasp of synchronization does not lead the child to the idea of transitivity.

Here, now, two subjects at sub-stage II B:

PAS (6; 4). C_1 and C_2 are produced: What is going to happen? *It will take more time for (C_2) because it's bigger.* (Experiment) *No, it took the same time.* And these two (C_2 and C_3)? *This one will fill more quickly (C_3) so it will take less time.* No, they were full together. So what about these two (C_1 and C_2)? *Together.* And these two (C_2 and C_3)? *Together.* Then what about these two (C_1 and C_3)? *Not together.* Why? *That one (C_1) is bigger.*

LIL (7; 1). C_1 and C_2 are filled: *It took the same time.* Is there the same amount of water in both? *Yes.* What would happen if we poured them into (L) and (L′)? *It will be the same.* Why? *This one (C_1) is bigger and not so tall and the other one is smaller.* (C_2 and C_3 are filled) *Same amount of water.* And what about the time? *Three seconds for both.* Why? *This one is taller and not so big and that one is bigger and shorter.* And will these two become filled together (C_1 and C_2)? *Yes.* How much time? *Three seconds.* And these two (C_2 and C_3)? *Also.* And what would happen if we took these two (C_1 and C_3)? *This one (C_1) will be filled first because it's smaller.* The same amount of water? *I don't think so. . . .*

As for stage III, here, first of all, is an intermediate (not yet fully operational) case (see his reactions in §4):

Bac (7; 6): Do you think that the two bottles (C_1 and C_2) will be filled in the same time? *No, because when the smaller one is full the other one will only be half-full.* (Experiment) Well, how much time did it take to fill this one (C_1)? *One minute.* And that one (C_2)? *Also one minute.* And for these two (C_2 and C_3)? *They'll be filled in the same time.* (Experiment) How much time? *One minute for both.* And what about this one (C_1) and that one (C_3)? *The smaller one will be full when the other one is only half-full.* (Experiment) *Ah, the same time.* Could you have told in advance? *No.*

Look, we are now going to fill these two (D_1 and D_2). *The same time.* And what about these two (D_2 and D_3)? *Also.* And what if we used these (D_1 and D_3)? *It'll be the same.*

Here, finally, is a subject who gives the correct answers immediately:

Let (7; 8): (C_1 and C_2)? *Same time.* The same amount of water or not? *Yes.* Why? *One is thin and tall and the other is fat and short.* And what about these two (C_2 and C_3)? *Same time.* And what if we used these (C_1 and C_3)? *It'll be the same time as well.* Are you sure or are you just guessing. *Quite sure.* Is it possible to tell beforehand? *Yes.* And what about the amounts of water? *The same.*

Clearly therefore, there is a close correlation between the discovery of the transitivity of equalities and their very construction. However, since the subject of transitivity will crop up again during our discussion of the colligation of durations (Chapter Six), we shall not pursue it further at this stage.

The Colligation of Durations and the Transitivity of Unequal Time Relations[1]

At the end of the last chapter, we saw that as soon as the child discovers the equality of synchronous durations by quantification of the work done, he becomes capable of grasping the transitivity of equal durations or of equal quantities of water. He therefore realizes that, if A = B, and B = C, then A = C, and we must now go on to ask if he also realizes that if A < B, and B < C, then A < C, or more simply if he is able to construct the qualitative series A < B < C < . . . etc.

Now, a seriation of the durations A < B < C < . . . etc., provided it is not restricted to successive or completely synchronous durations, constitutes a more or less complex system of colligations similar to those we discovered in Chapter Two. It is therefore the colligation of durations in general that we shall be looking at in this chapter.

The experimental technique we have adopted is extremely simple and directly based on that described in the last chapter. We again present our subjects with a reservoir discharging water through a Y-tube and with ten bottles of increasing capacity, A, B, C, . . . J. These bottles are of various shapes so that it is impossible to judge their capacity and the time needed for filling them by eye alone. We choose two bottles at random and ask the subject (1) which of the two will be filled more quickly, (2) why, and (3) whether it will take more or less time to fill than the other. Having obtained the answers (and it is important to ask the same questions with each pair of bottles) we then present the child with two problems. (I) We ask him to arrange three or four bottles in increasing order of filling time (e.g. A < B < C or B < E < J, etc.). It should be stressed that whereas this operation would merely be an ordinary seriation if the child were asked

[1] In collaboration with Mlle Vroni Richli.

to arrange the bottles in the order in which they become filled, it constitutes a colligation when he is being asked to consider the filling times, since the duration of A is contained in that of B, etc. It follows that the series $A < B < C \ldots$ represents a series of inclusions or inequalities involving parts or wholes of increasing magnitude.[1] (II) We ask questions about the transitivity of the colligations: if $A < B$ and $B < C$ (as demonstrated by experiment) is $A < C$ or is $A > C$? If $C_1 = C_2$ and if $C_2 < D$, then is $C_1 < D$ or is $C_1 > D$, etc.

By their answers, all the subjects can be fitted into the three stages we have previously distinguished. At stage I, they are incapable of arranging three bottles by the method of comparing two at a time and, *a fortiori*, of making any logical deductions as to the durations. At stage II, they have learned to compare two bottles at a time, but fail to co-ordinate different pairs of bottles, contenting themselves, for instance, with establishing that $A < B$ and $B < C$. After having gradually mastered these problems at sub-stage II B, the subjects finally arrive at stage III, where they show themselves capable not only of constructing seriations or colligations but also of grasping the resulting transitivity.

SECTION I: THE COLLIGATION OF DURATIONS

For greater clarity, we shall look first at seriation alone, and defer the discussion of transitivity to Section II.

§1. *The first stage: Inability to compare two terms at a time*

The reader will recall that when presented with two runners, subjects at stage I are quite unable to appreciate the simultaneity of the end points, the synchronous durations of the runs, or the fact that time is inversely proportional to velocity. It is evident that, under these conditions, the colligation of durations is quite beyond them. We accordingly restrict our questions to the order

[1] At stage I, we merely tell the child to arrange the bottles in the order in which they become filled ('start with the one that was filled first') and not in the order of the time it took to fill them ('start with the one that took least time') because the child does not understand the data.

142

n which the bottles became filled, but even in that case our subjects are unable to go beyond the following elementary seriations, which they produce up to the age of 6–7 years:

CLAV (6; 10): Look at these two bottles (B and J). Will one of them get filled first? *Yes, (B) because it's much smaller and so it gets filled much more quickly.* Will it take more or less time to fill it? *More time.* And which of these two (B and D) will take less time? *That one (B).* The child is then asked to arrange E, F, and G in the order of their filling: Put the one which will be full first here, then the one which will be full next, and then the one which will be full last. He arranges them by height: $G < E < F$. Are you perfectly certain? *Yes.* Well, fill them then. He fills G and E only and then constructs $G < E < F$ and so sticks to his earlier opinion.

ALF (6; 11). When asked to arrange D, E, and F in the order of filling, he fills D and E and then F separately, and forms the series $F < D < E$: Is that right? *No.* (He changes the arrangement to $D < F < E$.) *This one (E) will get fuller than that one (F).* How do you know? *It's bigger, the other one is smaller* (he makes no attempt to check his answer).

And these (G, H, and J)? (He puts down $G < J < H$, then tries J with H and says): *This one (H) takes less water and that one (J) takes more* (then he fills G by itself and says): *That one takes more.* (He then constructs $H < J < G$.) How do you know that you are right? *Because the other one (G) is big.* Which one takes more time? (Points at J in the middle of his series! He then changes the arrangement to $J < G < H$.) Are you sure? *Yes.* When did you try it? *Just now.*

CHRI (7; 3) working with G and J, thinks that J will be *filled first because it's smaller.* When the experiment proves him wrong, he concludes that G takes *more time because here (J) the water runs more slowly, and there (G) it runs more quickly.* How far can we count while (G) is filling up? *Six.* And with (J)? *Five or four.* He is then asked to arrange D, E, and F, and after inspecting the empty bottles, constructs the series $E < D < F$. You can try for yourself, you know. (He tries filling F with E, and then puts down $E < F < D$ without trying D. He next fills D separately, i.e. without comparing it to the other two.)

CONS (7; 1) also constructs $B < D < C$ according to the heights of the bottles. He then tries B with D and re-arranges them without trying C. With D, E, and F, he puts down $F < D < E$: Can we be sure? *No.* So what must we do? *Measure them* (he fills E and F and puts down $E < D < F$ without filling D). No mistakes now?

No, because that one (F) *is correct and that one* (E) *is correct as well*
And what about this one (D)? *It takes less time.*

Such, in general, are the reactions at stage I. They would be
difficult to understand without our earlier discussion, which
showed us that such apparently simple terms as 'fills up first'
or 'fills up last' involve all the problems besetting the child's
grasp of duration, synchronous processes, simultaneity, and
succession.

This explains why we cannot usefully ask children at stage I
to do more than arrange the bottles in the order of their filling—
if we ask them to arrange the bottles by the time it takes to fill
them, they will simply use their idea that time is proportional
to velocity to start their series with the one 'least quickly filled'
and finish it with the one 'most quickly filled', which comes back
to the order of the fillings themselves. Again, if we asked them to
consider the velocities, their answers will be equivocal because
'quicker' to them can mean either 'more rapidly' or 'sooner'.
Finally, if we asked them to construct their series according to
the amounts of water run out, they will simply go by the heights
of the bottles. In brief, to make quite certain that we are being
understood we must base the seriation on the order of succession
of the fillings (the moments when each bottle is filled to the
brim). According to adult logic this is tantamount to a seriation
based on the colligation of the durations, but to the child at stage
I it is nothing of the kind, and this for the reasons we have just
explained. Now, since children at stage I fail to produce the
correct order of the fillings, it is clear that they will be even less
capable of seriating or colligating the durations themselves.

Why, in fact, do our subjects fail to arrange three bottles in
the order in which they are filled? Their reactions are remarkably
uniform: all of them compare two of the three bottles by filling
them together, and judge the third quite independently. Here
we have a characteristic feature of all early attempts at seriation,
be it of lengths, weights, or anything else.[1] Now, this type of
reaction shows clearly that the particular quality on which the
seriation is brought to bear is still treated as an absolute rather
than relative predicate. In our particular case, the reason for

---

[1] See *La Genèse du Nombre chez l'Enfant*, Chapters V and VI, and *Le
Développement des Quantités chez l'Enfant*, Chapter IX.

144

this behaviour is quite plain: the child, in fact, arranges the three bottles by their heights, which it can judge by eye before the experiments are started, and believes that the filling times must necessarily be proportional to these heights. When asked to check his opinions, he fills the bottles grudgingly and, moreover, rejects the results of the experiment when they contradict his predictions. In brief, we encounter much the same difficulties here as we found in the case of earlier seriations (Chapter One, §2): children at stage I fail to produce series because they cannot mentally reconstruct the general motion of which particular levels are so many phases. Now, their failure, in the present case, is clearly not the result of a general incapacity to form series, since they are perfectly capable of arranging the bottles (or, in Chapter One, the levels) by height, but reflects their inability to construct time series, i.e. to conceive of a unique time scale common to all the events that occur in it.

§2. *The second stage: Sub-stage II A: Comparison of two bottles at a time but failure to co-ordinate the resulting pairs*

Unlike children at stage I, those at stage II no longer judge the flow by looking at one bottle in isolation. However, what pairs they choose for comparison remain unco-ordinated.

Lou (7 years) thinks that B will be filled more quickly than D, and that one can count up to five while B is being filled and up to six for D: Try to arrange these three (E, F, G) by putting the one that takes least time to fill up here, then the one that takes a little longer, and finally the one that takes the longest time to fill. (He arranges E < G < F by eye.) Are you sure? *No, we'd have to put the two bottles under the taps at the same time.* (He tries E and G and then puts down E < F < G but changes this arrangement to E < G < F.) Why did you change them? *Because this one* (E) *takes less time than that one* (F). (He tries E and F and comes up again with E < G <F.)

BER (7; 10): Which of these two (D and G) will be filled first? *They'll both be filled at the same time.* Are you sure? *I'll have to try* (he does so). *This one* (D). More time or less? *Less.* Then arrange these three (D, E, F) by the time it takes to fill them. (He puts down D < F < E by eye.) Are you sure? *I'd have to try with the water.* (He tries D with F and puts them back in the same place.)

145

That's correct now. **And** what about this one (E)? *It takes more time because it's bigger.* (tries D with E and re-arranges them as before).

AN (7; 3) thinks that G will be filled before J because it is thinner but *it's better to try.* She verifies that she was right and concludes that (G) *takes less time.* Then arrange these three (E, F, G), putting the one that takes the least time to fill here, next the one that takes a little longer, and over here the one that takes longest to fill. (An wants to compare them three at a time, but finds that there are only two taps.) *Which ones should I take?* Whichever one you like. (Tries E and F and puts down E < G < F.) *What do I do next?* (Compares E and G and leaves E < G < F). Is it all correct now? *I don't know.* Might it be like this (E < F < G)? *I don't know.*

We produce G, H, and J. She arranges H < J < G by sight, compares G and J, and then puts down H < G < J. Is this correct? *I don't know* (tries H and G and then puts down G < H < J). All correct now? ...

TEA (7; 4) puts down D < E < F by eye and then tries D with E and puts down D < F < E: Why did you put F there? *It goes between the other two.* Are you sure? *Not entirely* (tries E and F and correctly puts down D < E < F). Try to fit in (C). (He tries D with E, then C with F, and puts down D < E < C < F.) Asked to arrange A, B, C, D, he tries D with A and says: (A) *comes first.* Then he tries C with B and puts down A < D < B < C. *Is this correct?* Not entirely. (Puts down first A < B < C < D and then changes it to B < A < C < D.)

These subjects have clearly made great progress over those at stage I: while the latter never compare more than two bottles out of three and judge the third one by sight or by filling it separately, the former check all their assumptions by working with pairs. As a result, there is an increasing appreciation of the relativity of durations, and this fits in with the other articulated intuitions we have encountered at this level.

But having reached this point, our subjects fail to co-ordinate the several pairs they have been comparing. Thus Lou, when arranging E, F, and G, compared E to G and then to F and put down E < G < F, without bothering about the relation between F and G, etc. The less advanced of these subjects therefore fail to arrange three bottles despite all their efforts to compare them by pairs. True, some of them succeed by a series of lucky guesses and with some prompting (e.g. An and Tea) but not a

ingle one was able to arrange four elements, even when aided
y our questions.

The reason for all these failures is very simple: as we said
t the end of §1, before he can seriate three events $A \to B \to C$
where the arrow signifies 'precedes'), or colligate the associ-
ted durations $\alpha < \beta < \gamma$, the child must be capable of conceiv-
ng of a unique time scale based on a system of co-displacements,
n which the durations associated with the various motions, no
natter whether synchronous as a whole (Chapter Five) or in
art only (the present experiments), can be correlated. Now, if
he three bottles presented to our subjects were of the same
hape and merely differed in height, the problem would be
educed to one of spatial seriation (increasing heights of level)
nd our subjects would have no difficulty in solving it (see
Chapter One, stage II). But in the case of three bottles of
lifferent shape, the water levels no longer provide a standard of
omparison, since the displacements take place in height, width
nd depth. As a result, the child is forced to seriate a complex
ystem involving increases in volume or in quantity. Now, since
ime is part and parcel of these complex co-displacements, they
an no longer be reconstructed by intuitive procedures. We have
hown that this is so in the case of synchronization, and it is
lear that synchronization and the colligation of durations are
losely interrelated: two unequal durations, α and β, of which
he first forms part of the second, are simply two synchronous
lurations α_1 and α_2 plus a difference α' such that $\beta = \alpha_2 + \alpha'$.
Hence the colligation of durations poses the same problems as
ynchronization: the reason why the child fails to correlate two
airs $x < y$ and $y < z$ is that, instead of constructing transitive
elations, he produces an incoherent system in which intuitive
deas about levels, capacity, velocity, etc. have become jumbled
ogether. Hence, once one pair of elements has been compared,
ts place in the overall series is not determined by the same kind
f comparison, but either by a preconceived system of perceptive
elations (for example, the heights of the bottles) or else quite
rbitrarily. In other words, time remains particularized or
eterogeneous, and its several parts can therefore not be
olligated.

§3. *Sub-stage II B: Empirical discovery of the correct sequence of three terms but failure with four terms*

Subjects at sub-stage II B differ from those described in the last § (An and Tea) in that they no longer need any prompting to verify the assumed relationships. Instead, they use successive but unsystematic trials and errors to discover that A < B < C. Here are some examples:

MAR (7; 3) (Previously mentioned in Chapter Five, 3). When asked to arrange D, E, and F, says spontaneously: *Oh well, I'll take these two* (F and E), *then I'll empty* (F) *and go on with* (F) *and* (D). He tries F with E, then F with D, and then puts down D < E < F (random choice) and ends up with E < D < F without measuring D against E.

With A, D, E, he establishes A < D and A < E, and puts down A < D < E, but seeing that the level of E is slightly lower than that of D, he changes them round to A < E < D. Which one got filled most quickly? (A). And most slowly? (D), *no* (E). *Oh, I'd like to try these two* (D and E). He does so and puts down A < D < E. When asked to fit in C, he puts down A < D < E < C, then tries A with C and replaces them as before; he next tries C with E and changes the arrangement to A < D < C < E. Then he says: *I think I should try these* (C and D) *again*. He ends up with A < C < D < E.

JAC (7; 11) (D, E and F) puts down by sight E < F < D, then tries F with E and F with D and puts down E < D < F. Which takes longest to fill? (F). Which takes the least time? (E) (tentatively). Are you sure? *No, we might change* (D) *and* (E) *round*. (Tries D with E and puts down D < E < F.)

PIE (8; 5) puts down E < D < F by sight, then tries E with D, replaces them, tries F with E, replaces them, tries E with D, and finally puts down D < E < F.

LIS (8; 6) puts down E < F < D by sight but adds: *I think* (F) *and* (E) *will get filled at the same time*. Tries D with F and puts down D < F < E; then tries E with D and puts down D < E < F. When asked if he is sure now, Lis replies, quite rightly: *I must still try* (E) *and* (F). After doing so he concludes: *Now I'm perfectly sure*.

We see that these subjects, unlike those at the last sub-stage, succeed in co-ordinating pairs of elements after comparing them among themselves. They do so by stages and empirically, and even if they proceed according to a plan, as Mar did, they fail to appreciate that the middle term of two pairs must necessarily be greater than the first and smaller than the last. However, they arrive at the correct result without any prompting, and this progress in seriation and colligation goes hand in hand with the construction of time—subjects at this sub-stage are able to use the same empirical methods to equalize synchronous durations (e.g. Mar, Chapter Five).

However, precisely because their success in ordering three terms results from trial and error, they fail to extend their discovery to four or *n* terms; though they occasionally manage to introduce a fourth term into a series (e.g. Mar) they are lost once the four terms are presented to them all at once.

PIE (8; 5). Presented with E, F, H, and J, immediately tries H with J, then says: *I'll take these two* (E and F) and puts down F < E < H < J. Next he compares E and H and puts down F < H < J < E, then tries F and J, and ends up with E < H < F < J. To fit in G, he tries G with J and obtains E < G < H < F < J, then compares G and H and ends up with E < G < H < F < J.

LIS (8; 6) compares H and J and puts down H < J, then compares E and F and puts down E < F, finally compares E and J and ends up with F < E < J < H. Which took longest? (H). Are you sure? *I can't remember very well*. Next he compares E and J, and E and F, and puts down E < F < J < H, then tries H and J again and obtains F < E < H < J. With A, B, C, D, he tries A and C, then B and D, and finally A and D and obtains B < A < D < C: Are you sure? *Yes*. There's still one mistake. *I shall try* (B) *and* (C). (After discovering that B < C, he puts down B < A < D < C, tries A and D once again and says): *They're all correct now*.

These tests confirm the empirical and intuitive character of the methods used at stage II B: when presented with four elements, the subjects either proceed by unco-ordinated pairs (a method they no longer use with three elements) or else they repeat earlier measurements as if these might yield fresh information. It follows that, at the intuitive level, the seriation of four elements is very much more difficult than that of only three. However, as we shall see below, once the child uses the operational method of searching out the mean term, he rapidly masters the problem of arranging four or more terms.

§4. *Stage III: Operational seriation and colligation*

We shall call operational all seriations and colligations based on the transitivity of inequalities or inclusions, and hence leading to the establishment of a mean term B between A and C such that $B > A$ and $B < C$. Here are some examples:

JAC (8; 3) when asked to arrange D, E and F says: *I can't tell beforehand.* He tries D with E then says: *I must still try these two* (F and E). Then puts down $D < E < F$: Can you be sure now? You haven't tried (D) with (F) yet? *But* (D) *comes before* (E) *because we filled* (D) *with* (E) *and* (E) *with* (F). . . . *I can't put it very well.* For A, C, D and E, he puts down $C < A < E < D$ by sight, then tries C with A, C with D and E with D and obtains $A < C < D < E$.

RIT (8; 9) presented with D, E, F, tries D with F and puts down $D < F$; then tries D with E, puts E aside, tries E with F and concludes with $D < E < F$.

With E, F, H, J, he tries H with J, puts J at one end and H at the other, then tries E with J and puts E in front of H; then tries F with J and puts F before E, then E with F, and concludes with $H < E < F < J$: Are you sure? *No* (he tries E and H and puts down $E < H < F < J$, then compares F and H and concludes with $E < F < H < J$. Now fit in this one (G). (He tries G first with J and then with H.) *It gets filled more quickly than these two. I'll try it with that one* (F). *Yes, that's it. We've already looked at this one* (E). (He ends up with $E < F < G < H < J$.)

REN (9 years). With D, E, F, tries D with F then puts down $D < F < E$ and says: *I believe that one* (E) *comes last but I'll have to try.* He does so and then puts down $D < E < F$, adding: *I still have to try these two* (D and E). For A, C, D, E, he tries D with E and says: *I shan't put this one* (D) *down first because I must try the others.* He discovers that A comes first, followed by C and D and ends up with the correct series.

The reader will have noticed the formal progress of these subjects over those at sub-stage II B: they either pick out the middle term for comparison by chance (e.g. Jac) and then see no point in comparing the end terms to each other, thus showing that they have grasped the idea of transitivity (of which Jac said: 'I can't put it very well'), or else they begin by comparing the two end terms (e.g. Ric and Ren) but realize that they cannot form the complete series without further comparison. In either case, they make use of transitivity.

Moreover, once they use transitivity when working with three elements, they very quickly apply the same methods—and this is a clear sign that they have reached the operational stage—to four or even five terms. Now these are, in fact, the subjects who also succeed in equalizing synchronous durations immediately (Chapter Five), and it is clear that this is no mere coincidence: synchronization is but a special case of the colligation of durations. In both cases, time is seen as a general flux embracing all phenomena, so that durations can be colligated as so many parts of a single whole. Now, it is precisely because they grasp this general flux, that our subjects conceive of the possibility of seriating several elements, and that they look for a middle term to prove the existence of such a series.

But might it not be argued instead that progress in seriation is simply due to an increasing aptitude for seriation in general, i.e. for the application of formal and operational techniques to all concepts, and hence to a general advance from perceptive intuition to reasoning? In fact, experience shows that it is generally not until after the age of 11 that the 'form' of thought becomes divorced from its content and can be applied to things in general: until then, form and content remain inseparably welded together in an overall organization of intuitive relations. It is only when relations have become reversible and hence operational, that their 'grouping' enables the child to proceed to —deductive constructions and adequate definitions. It follows that the idea of an increasing aptitude for seriation in general must be discarded.

This is what we shall also be able to demonstrate by the explicit analysis of the arguments on which all seriations or colligations are based implicitly, i.e. the transitivity of what temporal relations the child gradually constructs in the course of its development.

SECTION II: TRANSITIVITY OF UNEQUAL AND SYNCHRONOUS DURATIONS

At the end of Chapter Five, we mentioned the remarkable correlation between the child's ability to equalize synchronous durations and his ability to deduce that, if the durations α and β, and β and γ are equal, α and γ must necessarily be equal as well. We shall now go on to examine whether there is a similar correlation between the ability to colligate *unequal* durations and the grasp of their transitivity.

§5. *Stage I: No transitivity*

It is clear that all the characteristic features of stage I we have been describing bear witness to a complete failure to grasp transitivity. Now, we can, in fact, verify this in a way that, at one and the same time, corroborates our claim that the structuring of concepts is always anterior to the emergence of a formal logic. Here are some examples:

WEN (6; 8) thinks that of A and B, A will fill up *more quickly* and take *more time* to fill: Which one contains more water? (A). Why? *Because it gets full more quickly.* And these (B and C compared under the taps)? (B) *has more water.* Which gets filled more quickly? (B). And what about these (A and C compared by eye only)? *That one* (C) *will be filled more quickly.* And in which would there be more water? *In* (A).

CLAV (6; 10) concludes from the experiment that A gets filled more quickly than B and therefore takes *more time*. After watching the experiment with B and C, he states that B *goes faster*, but when asked to predict what will happen with A and C, he thinks that (C) *will fill more quickly*. Why? *Because the water runs more quickly.* With other pairs, Clav makes some false and some correct predictions, the latter purely by chance or else by relying on perception.

No long commentaries are needed to explain these reactions, since they are of a kind with those we have mentioned in §1: because these children use neither time nor speed in an unequivocal sense, they are quite incapable of arriving at any reasonable conclusions. Is this failure due to a formal lack of deductive powers, or does the latter spring from the former? The answer is that the two form part of a single whole, because formal deductions are simply explanations and 'groupings' of conceptual relations, and the latter cannot be organized coherently without an overall grouping.

152

§6. *The second stage: Non-transitivity (sub-stage II A) followed by the empirical discovery of transitivity (sub-stage II B)*

Despite their stabilization of the concept of simultaneity and of the inverse relation between time and velocity, subjects at stage II, like those at stage I, begin with a failure to grasp transitivity.

STUZ (6; 10). A and B_1: Which one will take longer to fill? *That one* (B_1) *because it is bigger* (experiment: correct). And these two (B_1 and B_2)? (Experiment) *At the same time.* Let's try these two (B_2 and C) (Experiment). (B_2) *takes less time because it is smaller.* Very well. (We put down A $< B_1 = B_2 <$ C.) And what about these (B_1 and B_2)? *Same thing.* And these (B_1 and C)? *Don't know.* Can't we tell from what we've seen before? *No, we'll have to try them, one can't tell.* And what about these (A and B_1)? *We've seen that this one* (B_1) *takes longer.* And these two (B_1 and B_2)? *Same time.* And these (A and B_2)? *We'll have to try them.* And these (A and B_1)? (B_1) *takes longer.* And these two (B_1 and C: experiment)? (C) *takes more time.* And these (A and C)? *I don't know.* (Experiment). (C) *takes longer.* Could you have told? *No.*

BEA (6; 11). We establish that A $<$ B, C $<$ D, and B $<$ C: Can you remember all that? (He points the order out correctly.) Well then, arrange them for me, by putting the one that took longest here, etc. (He puts down B $<$ A $<$ D $<$ C.) Do you remember what we have said? (He points to the pairs.) Can we tell which one took the longest time of all? *No, we can't tell.* And what of these two (A and B)? *It's* (B). And of these (B and C)? *It's* (C). And of these (A and C)? *I don't know.* But can we tell if (A $<$ B and B $<$ C)? *We'd have to try.*

CAT (7 years). A and B_1 (experiment): (A) *goes more quickly.* Which takes more time? (B_1). And of these (B_1 and B_2: experiment)? *They get filled up together.* And these (A and B_2)? *It's* (B_2) . . . *or* (A). Can't one tell? *No, one can't.* But do you remember (A) and (B_1)? *Yes,* (A) *went more quickly because it was smaller.* And (B_1) and (B_2)? *Same thing.* And (A) and (B_2)? *Maybe* (B_2) *goes more quickly.*

And these (A and B_1)? (A) *goes more quickly.* And these (B_1 and C; experiment)? (B_1) *gets filled more quickly.* And these (A and C)? *It ought to be* (C). Why? *It's smaller.*

FLEI (7 years). (Experiment with A and B): (B) *takes longer.* And what about these (B and C: experiment)? *It's* (C) *which takes more time.* And these (A and C)? *This one* (C) *will take longer; no, it's* (A); *no, it's* (C). What do you think? (A) *because it's the biggest.* Are you quite sure? *One can't tell without trying.*

MARG (8 years): A $<$ B$_1$, B$_1$ $=$ B$_2$, but A and B$_2$ fill up in *almost the same time.*

And now for some subjects at sub-stage II B, who start out in the same way but end up with the discovery of transitivity:

GAIL (7; 10) predicts that (A) *will take longer to fill than* (B) *because it's bigger* (Experiment). *Oh no, it's that one* (B). Why does it take longer? *It's a little bit bigger.* What if we emptied (A) into (B)? *It'll run over* (Experiment). *Oh no.* And which of these (B and C) will take longer? (B) (Experiment). Were you right? *No, it's* (C). And which of these two (A and C) will take longer? (A) *because it's bigger.* Do you remember which of these took longer (A and B)? (B). And of these (B and C)? (C). So what about these (A and C)? *Oh, yes,* (C) *will take longer than* (A). What if we emptied (A) into (C)? *It would go over the brim, oh no, it would go into here* (B!).

PIT (7; 11) discovers that A $<$ B and B $<$ C: And what about these (A and C)? He looks attentively and says: *That one* (C) *will take more time.* Why? *It's bigger.* If (A $<$ B and B $<$ C) can we be sure that (C) will take longer than (A)? *One can't be sure without trying.* But (A $<$ B)? *Yes.* And (B $<$ C)? *Yes.* So what about (A) and (C)? (C) *will take longer.* Can we tell in advance? *Not altogether.*

And what about these (B $=$ B$_2$: experiment)? *Same time.* And these (A and B$_1$)? (B$_1$) *more time, we saw that just now.* And these (A and B$_2$)? *Perhaps* (B$_2$) *will take longer as well.* Can we be sure without trying? *It would be better to try.* (Experiment). *I was right* (shows no astonishment).

It is interesting to note the resemblance between these reactions and those we described in connection with seriations and colligations at the corresponding stages.

In the same way that subjects at stage II A are unable to seriate three elements because they fail to discover a middle term B such that B $>$ A and B $<$ C, so they fail to appreciate that if A $<$ B and B $<$ C, then A $<$ C. Now, since this argument is a logical factor in the construction of series or colligations and since, conversely, it presupposes them, because series and colligations are simply 'groupings' of asymmetrical relations or inclusions whose transitivity is expressed by the argument $(A < B) + (B < C) = (A < C)$, we might ask ourselves if the two types of operations are not, in fact, psychologically identical. From the point of view of the non-operational psychology, a seriation does, indeed, seem to constitute a much more concrete, and hence a much simpler, construction than the deduction of a hidden relation from two given ones, no matter how concrete. However, the fact that subjects at stage II A produce the same reactions to both, shows clearly that, in psychological terms as well, the two problems are identical.

As for subjects at sub-stage II B, it is equally remarkable that their empirical procedures in establishing transitivity, closely recall those by which they establish the correct seriations and colligations. In both cases, they originally judge the relationship between A and C purely by eye, and without bothering about the relations $A < B$, $B < C$. However, once a series has been postulated, either concretely on the table or mentally by deduction, and compared with the previous data, it introduces quite new implications which, once verified, lead to successive corrections culminating in the correct result. But just as the final series is not recognized by the child until it has verified all the relations, including those that spring logically from the rest, so all arguments based on transitivity are given no more than semi-credence at this stage, a fact that Pit expressed quite clearly by saying: 'One can't be sure without trying.'

It should be noted how this failure to grasp transitivity at stages I and II A and the gradual construction of transitivity at sub-stage II B fit in with our interpretation (end of Chapter Four) of the transition from perceptive intuition to operations by a process of perceptive and later of intuitive decentration. Quite clearly, progress in handling the idea of transitivity goes hand in hand with the gradual decentration of successively centred intuitive relations. Now, if transitivity were, indeed, the thread running through all seriations and colligations, it should enable us to interpret the structuring of durations in the same way as we have interpreted the structuring of successions. That this is so, we shall show after first looking at a few stage III reactions.

§7. *The third stage: Correct deductions based on transitivity*

After the age of 7 and normally at 8, an increasing number of subjects succeed in solving all the problems we have been discussing and produce systematic and correct seriations and colligations at once:

Mos ($7\frac{1}{2}$). A and C: (A) *will take less time because* (C) *is bigger.* (Experiment) *Yes, because* (A) *gets filled more quickly.* And these (A and B: experiment)? *It's still* (A) *which comes first.* (He puts down A < B < C.) *Why do you put* (B) *in the middle? Because it takes more time than* (A) *and being smaller than* (C) *it takes less time than* (C). Which takes longer, (A) or (B)? (B). Which goes more quickly? (A). Which takes more water? (B). (We compare C and D). (D) *takes longer because it is bigger* (this is not apparent). And what about (D), (B) and (A)? (A) *and* (B) *go more quickly than* (D). Why? *Because we saw that* (D) *takes more time than* (C) *and that* (C) *takes more time than* (B) *and* (A), *so* (A) *and* (B) *must get filled more quickly than* (D). Which one holds most water? *That one* (D).

Bar (8; 6). B_1 and B_2 (prediction): (B_1) *will fill more quickly because* (B_2) *will take more time: more water will go into it.* (Experiment) *Ah, they take the same time.* How much? *One minute each.* Which takes more water? *They both take the same.* What about B_1 and C (experiment)? (C) *takes more time because* (B_1) *is thinner than* (C). And what about the water? *More goes into* (C) *and less into* (B_1). And what would happen with (B_2 and (C))? *More time for* (C). Why? *Because* (B_1) *and* (B_2) *are the same.* And the water? *More into* (C). And (C) and (A)? (C) *will take more time.* Which will get filled more quickly? (A).

Bon ($8\frac{1}{2}$). A < B (experiment): B takes *more time*, but A full and B $\frac{2}{3}$ full take *the same time*, and if B $\frac{2}{3}$ were poured into A: *It'll rise to the top, it'll just about fill it.* We establish next that B < C: And what about (A) and (C)? *It'll take longer for* (C) *because* (A) *takes the place of* (B). Bon thus clearly makes use of deductive substitution.

Once again there is a complete parallel between the use of arguments based on the transitivity of colligations or synchronizations and the operational construction of series with three or four elements.

Let us now try to account for the overall development

from stage I to stage III, by looking at the case of transitivity alone.

Why, in fact, do subjects at stages I and II A fail to grasp transitivity to the point that they completely forget relations they have acknowledged explicitly only a moment before? Clearly because their attitude, which is characteristic of intuitive, ego-centric thought, is a simple and natural extension of conduct at the perceptive and sensory-motor level: much as the last element in a series of perceptions drives all the rest out of the perceptive field, so each successive relation (A < B or B < C, etc.) drives all the preceding relations out of the field of attention; and just as in the visual field, a subject focusing on a central figure will exaggerate its importance *vis à vis* a peripheral phenomenon, so also, in a complex problem, he concentrates exclusively on a particular relation by intuitive centration, i.e. by monoideic attention. Non-transitivity is therefore the hallmark of intuitive centration. Thus when our subjects consider the relation A < C, they completely forget that they have already established the relations A < B, and B < C, and behave as if each pair AB, BC, AC, were an entirely new perceptive structure, one that automatically cancels all the previous ones (except that A < B suggests unconsciously that A < C, or C > B suggests that A > B, etc.).

At sub-stage II B, on the other hand, we see the emergence of a rudimentary correlation of successive relations, and this process, too, is analogous to a perceptive one, namely to decentration. In effect, at this stage there can as yet be no question of operations as such, since transitivity is not yet introduced by necessity, but merely as a probable or likely solution. What happens is that, in trying to determine the relations between A and C, the child simply recalls the relations A < B and B < C, not for the purposes of correlation, but as if the very act of recalling them was enough to confer an inferior value (<) upon A and a superior value (>) upon C, whence it becomes plausible that A < C. In other words, just as, with growing mental ability, successive perceptions interact increasingly in time and space, and just as the resulting decentration serves to reduce over-estimates or increase under-estimates[1] so relations successively centred by intuitive thought eventually come to affect one

[1] See *Arch. Psychol.*, Vol. XXIX, 1942.

another by a kind of transposition, and it is this intuitive de-centration which leads to pre-regulative, and not yet fully logical, corrections.

Finally, at stage III, decentrations and regulative transpositions become fully reversible: when thinking of A and C, the subject is capable of recalling the relations $A < B$ and $B < C$ with the same facility with which he originally established them: as a result, the relations $A < B < C$ can be just as easily constructed from $(A < B) + (B < C) = (A < C)$ as they can be broken down into $(A < C) - (B < C) = (A < B)$ or $(A < C) - (A < B) = (B < C)$. This decentration, which has become absolute because it is completely reversible, is, by definition, no longer a simple regulation, but has become an operation. Transitivity, or rather the reversible construction characteristic of the latter, is therefore nothing else than complete freedom to pass from one relation to the next by a process of complete decentration, i.e. by a process that, ridding the mind of perceptive centrations, helps to supplant the static and limited equilibrium of intuitive thought with the dynamic and unrestricted equilibrium of deductive intelligence.

Now, if this is, indeed, the true explanation of transitivity, it also explains the construction of the seriations and colligations we discussed in §§1–4: while the piecemeal evaluations of durations or of velocities characteristic of stage I reflect the predominance of primitive centrations, the construction of unco-ordinated pairs at sub-stage II A marks a clear shift towards decentration (comparable to the 'perceptive comparisons' the author has been investigating with Marc Lambercier[1]). With the empirical discovery of the 'middle term' at sub-stage II B, and its methodical use at stage III, finally, decentration becomes transformed into operation and the construction of series is readily mastered. We might point out that the application of the intellect to the seriation of diverse elements calls for the type of attention that has been called 'synthetic' in contrast to the 'monoideic' attention characteristic of lower levels of intelligence (Ribot). While the latter is based on intuitive centration and ignores whatever is not directly to hand, the former is identical with the very effort of construction involved in decentred thought. It follows that the equilibrium reached at stage III

[1] *Arch. Psychol.*, Vol. XXIX, 1942, pp. 173–253.

cannot be anything but a 'grouping of operations', since the consistent use of decentrations is tantamount to the co-ordination of relations that were previously considered one at a time.

In general, the organization of durations and successions therefore proceeds along parallel paths. While it is at first confused with the space traversed due to centration on the point of arrival, duration acquires a structure in the form of synchronizations that go hand in hand with decentrations, and of colligations which, in their turn, result from the same kind of decentrations as are involved in the grouping of successions.

CHAPTER SEVEN

The Additive and Associative Composition of Durations

Our discussion of the concept of synchronous durations (Chapter Five) led us to the problem of the evaluation of durations in general (Chapter Six). This evaluation, in fact, invariably rests, be it directly or indirectly, on the concept of synchronism: comparing two durations is tantamount to judging them equal or unequal, either in terms of their synchronous parts or else in terms of a third duration 'successively synchronous' to both. In the first case, we have a qualitative colligation; in the second, we introduce quantitative time, whose genesis we shall be examining in the next chapter. As for qualitative colligations, their analysis is by no means completed by the description of simple inclusions of the type $A < B < C$ we have given in the last chapter.

If such colligations are, in fact, governed by the laws of 'grouping', as we suggested in Chapter Two, they must fulfil at least two conditions: (1) they must explicitly obey the principle of additive composition (which we assumed implicitly in Chapter Six): if the child is capable of colligating durations into a series $A < B < C \ldots$ etc. he must also be able to combine two partial durations A and A' into a whole $A + A' = B$, such that $B > A$ and $B > A'$, and then combine B and B' into a whole $B + B' = C$ such that $C > B$ and $C > B'$, etc. In short, he must recognize that the addition of two durations still constitutes a duration and one, moreover, that is clearly defined. (2) He must also, and this is essential in the case of a 'grouping', introduce an 'associative' principle which ensures the conservation of the whole independent of the arrangement of its parts; i.e. he must be able to construct the equality $(A + A') + B' = A + (A' + B')$, and hence arrive at the same total duration $A + A' + B'$

= C, irrespective of whether the operations leading to it start from $(A + A') + B'$ or from $A + (A' + B')$.

§1. *Experimental methods and general results*

The child is told that two figures, one large (I) and one small (II) will run a race by stages and at different speeds. (Normally the bigger figure is moved more quickly but with subjects of 4–6 who like the smaller figure to win the race, the order can be reversed.) The two figures are started off from a common point 0 and run at right angles to each other, I covering a distance of 10 cm. in the same time that II covers a distance of approximately 5 cm. (the time A_2 = the time A_1). The two figures then start off again, and I covers approximately 20 cm. in the time A'_1 while II covers 10 cm. in equal time ($A'_2 = A'_1$). Finally, I makes a third run of, say, 8 cm. in the time (B'_1) while II again covers a smaller distance in equal time ($B'_2 = B'_1$). The end points of each partial run are carefully marked out, for example by blue counters for I at 10, 30 and 38 cm., and by yellow counters for II at 5, 15 and 19 cm. from 0, which is clearly marked as well. It may prove useful to draw out the two paths in advance.

During this, the first part of the experiment, our questions are intended to establish the following facts: (1) Does the subject appreciate that the synchronous durations ($A_1 = A_2$) are equal? If he does not, it is pointless to continue, except to suggest this relationship to him in some way or another, but in that case the question of additive composition can rarely be pursued. (2) Does the subject also assume that $A'_1 = A'_2$ and $B'_1 = B'_2$? (This question cannot, of course, be put before the second run.) (3) If the subject recognizes all these equalities ($A_1 = A_2$; $A'_1 = A'_2$ and $B'_1 = B'_2$) he is asked a question about the addition of time: do I and II take the same time to proceed from 0 to the end of their total runs? If the child denies this, we recall (but without special prompting, and as if it were merely a change of question) the synchronism of the elementary duration, and then repeat the original question.[1]

Once the subject has recognized or denied the equality of the total duration, we then pass to the problem of associativity: the child is told that the two figures are again going to start from

[1] We shall call this total equality $C_1 = C_2$.

the common point 0, but that this time they will not stop at the same time. We stipulate, and this is, of course, essential, that both of them are going to run at the same relative speeds as they did in the first experiment. We then start the two figures off from 0, but when II stops at his first reference point (5 cm.) we let I pass through his first reference point (10 cm.) and continue to his second reference point. In other words, II stops after a time A_2 while I runs for a time $B_1 = A_1 + A'_1$ (where $A_1 = A_2$). We then ask the child which of the two ran for the longer time, thus ascertaining that the facts are clearly understood. Then I and II are set off again simultaneously, but when I arrives and stops at the end of its itinerary, II continues until it, too, finishes the race. In other words, during this second part of the race, I runs for a time B'_1 while II runs for a time $(A'_2 + B'_2)$. We now ask the child which of the two has run for the longer time. Once the correct answer has been obtained, we go on to ask a question about associativity: Is the total time $(B_1 + B'_1)$ of the run of I equal to the total time $A_2 + (A'_2 + B'_2)$ of the run of II; in other words, is $C_1 = C_2$?

We can, of course, make things simpler for the child by choosing equal elementary runs (and hence equal durations ($A_1 = A'_1 = B'_1 = A_2 = A'_2 = B'_2$)). Conversely, we could complicate the problem even further by having the two figures cover different partial distances in each of the two experiments.

One might object that once the child has recognized the equality of the total times ($C_1 = C_2$) in the first part of the experiment, he could apply this fact to the total times of the second run quite automatically, i.e. without bothering to reflect about the new compositions $(A_1 + A'_1) + B'_1 = A_2 + (A'_2 + B'_2)$. However, experiments show clearly that this objection is invalid, inasmuch as it only applies to subjects who have a highly developed conception of duration, and not to those who are still in the process of constructing it (subjects up to the ages of 8 or 9). In effect, the two main difficulties of 4–8-year-old children are (1) the transformation of distances into durations when the velocities involved are unequal, and (2) the combination of partial durations into a total duration. Hence, having laboriously (by virtue of the first of the two difficulties) worked out the equality of the partial durations $A_1 = A_2$; $A'_1 = A'_2$; $B'_1 = B'_2$, the child does not simply take the equality of the total durations $C_1 = C_2$ for granted, but needs a great deal of reasoning to establish it. When he then goes on to compare the unequal durations B_1 and A_2, and B'_1 and $(A'_2 + B'_2)$, the experiment shows that he needs fresh reasoning to rediscover that $C_1 = C_2$, and that he does not simply rely on the associative composition of the paths. Moreover, other investigations[1] have shown us that, even in the case of lengths, weights, and volumes, small children have systematic difficulties in recognizing that the conservation of the whole is independent of the arrangement of its parts. We may take it, therefore, that the additive and associative compositions of durations constitute two distinct psychological problems, even though, as we shall see, their solutions coincide in a most remarkable way.

In fact, the results we have obtained throw a great deal of light on the structure of the particular 'grouping' that is represented by the evaluation of durations. We saw that the grasp of associativity, far from lagging behind that of additivity, which might easily have happened because of the greater intuitive difficulties involved in our second experiment, goes hand in hand with it. During an early phase, corresponding to stages I and II A, the child proves unable to synchronize the partial durations $A_1 = A_2$; $A'_1 = A'_2$, and $B'_1 = B'_2$. Consequently he can neither synchronize the total durations $C_1 = C_2$ nor grasp the idea of associative composition. During a second phase, corresponding to stage II B, the child does succeed in equalizing the synchronous part durations A, A' and B', but not yet in equalizing the total durations $C_1 = C_2$, thus confirming what we said in Chapter Five about the difference between intuitive and operational synchronization. Moreover, the child also fails to grasp the idea of associative composition. During a third phase (= stage III), finally, he is able to make use of both additive and also of associative composition.

In all the more than thirty subjects we have examined, we found that the grasp of additivity goes hand in hand with that of associativity, save for one exception, who assumed the first with hesitation, but denied the second.

---

[1] See Piaget and Inhelder, *Le Développement des Quantités chez l'Enfant*, Chapters I to VI.

§2. *Stages I and II A: Inability to synchronize elementary durations and failure to effect additive and associative compositions*

We shall merely look at one subject at stage I, during which children, even when prompted, fail to grasp the equality of elementary durations and consequently even to follow the trend of our questions:

PASC (6; 8). A_1 and A_2: Did the two figures start at the same time? *Yes.* Did they stop at the same time? *No. One of them stopped first.* Did he stop before the other one? *No, but he won!* Did they take the same time? *No.* If they started together and stopped together, would they take the same time to finish their runs? *No.* Under further questioning Pasc kept denying the equality of the total durations, and the associativity of the partial durations. He did the same with distances, denying that the segments x, y, z of a single line can be composed such that $x + (y + z) = (x + y) + z$.

By contrast, the analysis of the reactions of subjects at stage II A proves most fruitful because, while they, too, start out by denying the synchronism of the elementary durations, they allow themselves to be prompted. However, though in the end they come to accept the synchronism step by step, they obstinately deny the equality of the total durations and refuse to accept associativity:

GUIL (7; 11). First run I (A_1) and II (A_2): Did they start at the same time? *Yes.* And stop at the same time? *Yes.* Did they run for the same length of time? *One of them took longer* (II), *he lost because he was smaller.* But did they run for the same time? *No.* (The experiment is repeated.) Look at this stop-watch. How long did the first figure take? *Five minutes; no, four and a half minutes.* And the other? *Also four and a half minutes.* Did they take the same time then? *Yes, but one of them was dawdling.* And now (second run)? *It's still the same one who keeps running more slowly.* But did he take the same time (by the watch)? *Yes.* Third run: *idem.*

Now listen carefully. It took them some time to run through this bit, that bit and the third bit, didn't it? Now, let's think of the time it took them to cover the lot (C_1: the entire run is indicated by a gesture) and that lot (C_2: another gesture). Did it take the same time or not? *This one* (II) *took longer than that one* (I). Why? *Because this one* (II) *lost and the other one won.*

And now watch this (I covers B_1 and II covers B_2). *That one* (I) *ran for a longer time* (correct). And what about these (I covers B'_2 while II covers $A'_2 + B'_2$)? *That one* (II) *took longer* (correct). And what about this whole lot (we retrace $B_1 + B'_2$ and $A_2 + [A'_2 + B'_2]$)? *This one* (I) *took longer because he had to run a longer way.*

FLA (7; 11) says straightaway of the first run: *One of them took longer.* Did they stop at the same time? *Yes, but the first one was running faster.* And was he running longer or for the same time as the other? *Ah, yes, they both took the same time.* And what about this (second run)? Did they start together? *Yes.* Did they stop together? *Yes.* Did they run for the same time? *No.* Think of what you told me before. *Ah, yes, the same time.* Third run: *idem.*

Well then. Did (I) take the same time to make this whole trip (we move I through his three runs) as it took to make that one (*idem* for II)? *No, it took longer here* (I) *because it was a longer way.*

Look carefully now (B_1 and A_2)? *This one* (I) *took more time because he went further* (correct). And here (B'_1 and $A'_2 + B'_2$)? *This one* (II) *took longer* (correct). And the two trips together ($B_1 + B'_1$) and $A_2 + [A'_2 + B'_2]$)? *It took him* (I) *longer because he went further.*

DIS (7; 10), the same reactions. At the end of the questioning, when this subject came round to accepting the fact that the elementary durations, but not the total durations were synchronous, we tried unsuccessfully to persuade him of the additivity of even two durations: (A_1 and A_2)? *Same time.* And those (A'_1 and A'_2)? *Also the same time.* And these two together (B_1) and those two together (B_2)? (II) *took less time than* (I). But what about these (A_1 and A_2)? *The same.* And these (A'_1 and A'_2)? *Also.* So what about the two together (B_1 and B_2)? *No,* (I) *went further, so it took him longer.*

These reactions are interesting for a number of reasons. First of all, they show that the equality of synchronous elementary durations can be denied, even when the simultaneities of the starting and end points are recognized. The only way to convince the subjects of this equality, is to use a stop-watch or else to shout as soon as the two figures come to a common halt (sometimes with great conviction in our voice!). Now if these children have great difficulty in grasping that the partial durations are synchronous, they will quite understandably continue to deny the synchronism of the total durations. Their inability to master additive composition is quite easily explained: tempted as they are to deny the synchronism of elementary runs over unequal distances, they will deny it, *a fortiori*, in the case of the total runs, where the distances differ even more. Their failure in the sphere of additive composition is necessarily accompanied by failure in that of associative composition. It should, however, be stressed that the inequalities considered in additive composition are not necessarily the same as those considered in associative composition, and that the child uses two distinct types of reasoning in respect of them: thus Guil assumed (a) that II takes longer on the grounds that it runs more slowly, and (b) that I takes longer because it has to cover a larger distance.

§3. *Sub-stage II B: Synchronization of elementary durations but failure in additive and associative composition*

The subjects we shall now examine react much more strangely than the last in evaluating durations: though convinced from the start that the synchronous elementary runs are of equal durations, they nevertheless refuse to admit the equality of the combined runs (C_1 and C_2) or their associativity:

COL (7; 1). To simplify matters we begin with equal runs (5 cms.). Col naturally admits the synchronism of the partial durations: And now what about that lot (total run of I) and that lot (total run of II)? Did they take the same time as well? *Yes, because it's the same length on either side.* As for associativity: *It's the same thing, because they're the same length.*

But the moment we introduce unequal distances, the reactions change completely. First run: *Same time.* Second run: *Same time, as well.* Third run: *Same time again.* Now look, does this whole lot (C_1) take the same time as that lot (C_2)? *No.* (I) *took more time because he went further.*

What about here (B_1 and A_2)? *That one* (I) *took longer* (correct). And here (B'_1 and $A'_2 + B'_2$)? *It's the other one* (II) *which took longer* (correct). And these two together ($B_1 + B'_1$) with these two together (A_2) + ($A'_2 + B'_2$)? (I) *took longer.*

CHAT (7; 3) also gave the correct answers in the case of equal runs (approximately 3 cms.); with unequal runs, he admitted that the partial runs (A_1, A_2; A'_1, A'_2; etc.) were of equal duration but not the total runs: Did all these runs together (the three runs of I) take the same time as all these together (the runs of II)? *No.* Why not? *This one took longer* (I). Look here, we are going to repeat the experiment while you count. (I and II are moved forward and the table rapped loudly at every stop. At the first stop we ask): Did they take the same time? *Yes.* (We continue while he counts 1, 2, 3, ...) Well, didn't it take the same time (for C_1 and C_2)? *No.* How much time did this one take (I)? *Seven.* And that one (II)? *I didn't count!*

Associativity: same reaction.

These reactions clearly bring out the distinction between the intuitive and the operational grasp of synchronous durations: with the former, synchronization is applied to the partial durations only, with the latter it is applied to the total duration as well.

Since we do not wish to return to this topic, we must stress here that the reason why additivity and associativity are so much simpler to understand in the case of elementary runs over equal distances, at equal speeds and in equal time, is that the evaluation of durations coincides with that of the distances and can therefore remain purely intuitive. No wonder, therefore, that even subjects at stage II A give the correct answers to problems of this kind (we have deliberately deferred mention of this fact until this stage, where we can contrast the positive with the more negative reactions).

Now, as soon as I and II move forward at unequal speeds (and over unequal elementary paths), the evaluation of the durations can no longer be deduced intuitively. The question then arises why children recognize the synchronism of the partial durations associated with the elementary runs, and yet fail to recognize it in the case of the combined durations. This is, in fact, the true problem of the additive composition of durations, i.e. of the operational as distinct from the intuitive conception of durations.

The answer is quite simple: failure to apply the synchronism of elementary durations to the general case of total durations is due to the fact that the grasp of durations has remained semi-intuitive. We saw in Chapter Five how children at stage II B arrive at the discovery of synchronous durations empirically by focusing attention on the simultaneous starting or finishing points. The same is true here. Since the two figures keep starting and stopping simultaneously, our subjects, torn between the wish to deny the idea of synchronism because of the differences in speed, and the wish to adopt it because of the simultaneities, simply allow themselves to be influenced by the perceptive situation (displacements of equilibrium). In the case of small distances (a few centimetres) they will accept the fact that the durations are synchronous, but as soon as the distances are combined, their differences become too great, with the result that there is a 'displacement of intuitive equilibrium' and the synchronism is denied. These reactions therefore represent an intermediate stage comparable to that which we encountered in our study of the conservation of quantities, substance, weight and volume:[1] with small deformations, the conservation is accepted, but with greater deformation it is denied. It is clear that such subjects will not be able to make additive and associative compositions: their minds do not yet stretch to any but intuitive compositions representing a half-way stage between compositions based on the laws of statistical and irreversible (perceptive) equilibrium and those based on operational and reversible laws. It is highly interesting to note that additivity and associativity once again go hand in hand: both are rejected for the same reason, i.e. failure to grasp that the whole is equal to the sum of its parts, and it is this fundamental failure which attests to the fact that intuitive thought is intermediate to perceptive and operational thought.

The correlation between additivity and associativity is achieved by slightly more advanced subjects, whom we must place half-way between stages II B and III because they do not arrive at the additive and associative composition of durations directly, but only after some hesitation:

Dza (8;1). Run 1: Did they start at the same time? *Yes.* And stop at the same time? *Yes.* Did they run for the same time? *No, because this one* (I) *went more quickly; oh no, I was wrong, it must have been for the same time because they stopped at the same time.* (Second and third runs): *The same time.* Now look, did it take them the same time to make these three runs . . .? *No. Here* (total path of I) *it took longer because it was further.* (I) *moved more quickly.* But each of them stopped at the same time? *Yes.* So didn't the three runs of (I) and the three runs of (II) take the same time? *No.*

[1] *Le Développement des Quantités chez l'Enfant*, Chapters I to III.

(With a stop-watch) B_1 and A_2: *Not the same time. This one* (I) *took a longer run* (correct). $(B'_1$ and $A'_2 + B'_2)$? *Now that one took longer* (correct). And what about these two paths $(B_1 + B'_1)$ and those two $(A_2 + [A'_2 + B'_2])$? *The bigger one* (I) *took longer.*

We resume our questions on additivity, once again using a stopwatch to measure the elementary durations, which are recognized as synchronous without hesitation. As for the three combined runs of I and II: *The times are not the same. This one* (I) *took the longest run. Oh no, the times are the same! This one* (C_1: he points to the entire run of I) *and that one* (C_2) *are the same thing!*

We now return to associativity: And these two together $(B_1 + B_2$, etc.)? *They didn't take the same time. Oh yes, they did, because the smaller one stopped first and the other one went on, but the next time it was the bigger one who stopped and the little one who went on. So it's the same time.*

SAIN (8; 4) also hesitates as to the synchronous duration of corresponding elementary runs but then grasps it quite spontaneously: And for the three runs together? *This one* (II) *took more time because he didn't have so far to go.* How is that? *Ah no. The same time because both kept starting and stopping at the same time.*

Associativity: *That one* (total run of I) *took longer because it was further. Ah, no. That one* (II) *because he went less quickly. . . . Oh no. They took the same time because there was one side where the one didn't stop and then the same thing happened on the other side.*

As we see, these subjects, after some vacillation characteristic of the 'displacements of equilibrium' we have mentioned, do finally succeed in equalizing total durations, and they do so as soon as the necessary regulations have reached the level of operational reversibility. The arguments they use to justify associativity are highly significant: the total durations are equated on the grounds that, though one of the figures stopped first in his first run, the second stopped first in his second run. Now, this compensation (regulation) cannot be based on synchronization of the elementary runs (because these are not, in fact, synchronous), but represents the fusion of two partial inequalities into one overall equality, and hence an operational calculation that goes clearly beyond intuitive regulation, in that it involves the reversibility of relations. More simply, associativity appears as the necessary complement of additivity as soon as, instead of thinking about partial and total durations separately, the child begins to see the latter as the necessary results of the former. How precisely this comes about we shall discover during our discussion of the reactions at the third and last stage.

§4. *The third stage: Immediate grasp of additivity and associativity*

Here are a few examples of the correct reactions: the first not quite immediate, but the other two fully typical of stage III:

QUI (8; 3). Elementary runs: *It took the same time because they started at the same time and stopped at the same time.* And the three together here (I) and there (II)? *This one* (I) *took longer because he went further. . . . Oh no, they kept starting and stopping together, so it must have taken them the same time.*

Associativity: What about these two together (B₁ + B′₁, etc.)? *It's the same.* Why? *Because one of them went further the first time and the other one the second time.*

IAG (8; 11). Elementary durations: *It's the same thing.* And the three together here (I) and there (II)? *Also the same time.* Why? *Because this one* (A₁) *and that* (A₂) *took the same time,* etc.

Associativity: And the two together? (Hesitates): *It's the same thing.* Why? *Because this one* (I) *took longer the first time and that one* (II) *took longer the second time.* If we looked at a watch, how long would it take for this one (B₁)? *Two minutes.* And for that one (A₂)? *One minute.* And for that one (B′₁)? *One minute.* And that one (A′₂ + B′₂)? *Two minutes.*

Iag has therefore grasped the idea of associative composition.

STOH (9; 4). Elementary durations: *Same thing.* And the three together? *It's the same time, because one went more slowly than the other but they both started at the same time and stopped at the same time.*

Associativity: *It's the same thing, because they went almost the same way as they did the first time, but one stopped first and the other one stopped later.*

We can see in what respects these reactions differ from those we have been describing. In the first place, the subjects are able to effect additive compositions by means of an argument that is astonishingly simple when compared with all the complicated developments that preceded it: total durations are equal because they are composed of equal parts (see Iag)! And how do these subjects arrive at this conclusion? As Qui and Stoh put it, simply because the two figures kept 'starting and stopping at the same time'.

Now this equality of partial durations was already appreciated by subjects at sub-stage II B. Why then did they fail to conclude that the equality of the parts necessarily implies the equality of the whole? The entire problem of the difference between perceptive or intuitive and operational compositions is involved in this question. To intuitive and perceptive thought, the whole is not equal to the sum of its parts, simply because transformations are not reversible and because, with each change of external data, there arise new 'displacements of equilibrium', i.e. transformations that have not been compensated, or that have only been partly compensated, by decentration or regulations. Perceptive equilibrium and, to a lesser degree, intuitive equilibrium are thus comparable to a statistical system in which random combinations (in our case, those aspects of reality that give rise to perceptive or intuitive centration) constantly modify the total system, which, for that very reason, cannot be constructed by additive composition. On the other hand, once regulative decentration is complete, the resulting reversibility brings additivity in its train, i.e. leads to the recognition that the whole is simply the sum of its parts and no more. Now, additive composition, far from excluding organization as Gestalt psychology tends to assume, constitutes a new type of organization, and one that is more highly developed than those preceding it, because it consists of 'groupings' and hence permits of indefinite deduction.

The proof that this is so, is that as soon as the additive composition of synchronous partial durations into synchronous total durations is mastered, associativity is mastered as well. Now, associativity simply means that every whole remains unchanged by the re-arrangement of its parts, and this is why the discovery of the additivity of partial durations leads quite naturally to the discovery of associativity: without the latter, the whole would become unstable and hence cease to be additive.

We can, moreover, distinguish two cases of associative and of additive composition. In the first, the whole is independent of the order of its parts (commutativity). For instance, a lump of clay is formed of a certain quantity of matter, none of whose parts can be called successive to the rest. Associativity, in that case, is part and parcel of what we have called the problem of 'conservation' in an earlier work.[1] But sometimes, as in the case of time, the whole can consist of a combination of what are clearly successive parts. This does not mean that the addition of durations ceases to be commutative, but simply that it must necessarily ignore the order of events. If durations are not considered apart from the events, the whole will conserve the order of its parts. In that case, associativity leads to the same whole by two distinct compositions conserving the same order. That is why, in the case of durations, we had to look at associativity separately, i.e. as confirmation that additive composition implies the conservation of wholes.

[1] *Le Développement des Quantités chez l'Enfant.*

CHAPTER EIGHT

The Measurement of Time and the Isochronism of Successive Durations[1]

So far, we have been looking at qualitative physical time, whose progressive structuring into 'groupings' (seriations and colligations) is a prerequisite of the construction of quantitative time. What, precisely, is the latter? Quantitative time, like number,[2] results from qualitative groupings, but with this difference: in the case of time the groupings are infra-logical, and the colligation of durations (addition of the parts of a single object) takes the place of the colligation of classes (or sets of objects); the displacement of durations, which is an operation generating time, replaces logical seriation (which is independent of the space-time order), and the operational synthesis of partitive addition and displacement is a measurement and no longer a system of abstract numbers.

The reader may recall how numbers are constructed. Once the child is able to fit objects into a system of colligated classes or into ordered series, he can disregard the qualities of these objects and transform each one into a unit that can be substituted for any other within its class or series, the former becoming transformed into cardinal numbers and the latter into ordinal numbers. The two are inseparable because, as soon as their qualities are eliminated, classes and series are based on one and the same operation.

Now, precisely the same thing happens in respect of quantitative time. The qualitative colligation of durations, once achieved, constitutes a clearly defined system, but one in which each duration, qualitatively defined by the events constituting it, has to stay in its place; only the mind can introduce mobility

[1] In collaboration with Mlle Edith Meyer.
[2] Cf. *La Genèse du Nombre chez l'Enfant.*

into such a system, and 'decolligate' or 'recolligate' what moments in time it pleases. In other words, the system itself has become reversible, but the instants composing it cannot be interchanged. Moreover, the seriation of events, for its part, also constitutes a system of placements that cannot be interchanged, but that the mind can trace out in two directions (operational reversibility). These two 'groupings' are therefore of a kind, but do not fuse while they remain qualitative: durations are nothing other than the intervals between instantaneous events in time and that is why we can deduce the colligation of durations from the order of succession of events and *vice versa*. However, while the addition of two intervals is commutative ($A + A' = A' + A = B$), that of ordered relations is not, which shows the fundamental duality of the two groupings. This difference can be expressed as follows: if we say that the intervals A and A' are two parts of the interval B (and qualitatively equivalent inasmuch as they belong to B), we disregard their successive character; if we say that their limiting events succeed one another and go on to seriate them, we are no longer adding intervals but successions. It follows that this double qualitative system prevents the comparison of two durations when one of them is not synchronous to a part or the whole of the other. True, we can always say of two durations $A + A' = B$, that the total duration B is greater than either A or A', and we can, moreover, treat two synchronous durations A and A' as being equal, but we can say nothing about the quantitative relations of A and A' when they are successive instead of being synchronous. No matter whether $A > A'$, $A < A'$ or $A = A'$, the qualitative colligation $A + A' = B$ remains unchanged. Hence, if we wish to compare successive durations, we must first construct quantitative time, i.e. time from which the purely qualitative aspects have been eliminated.

Let us first of all suppose that we disregard the qualitative character of a duration A, in the way we do when we say 'a moment' without defining which precise moment we have in mind. How can we transform this duration into a 'unit' of time that can be equated to successive durations (A', B', etc.) in the form $A = A' = B' = \ldots$, and that can hence be treated as a quantitative system $A = 1$; $B = A + A = 2$; $C = A + A + A = 3$; etc.? To do so, we must, of course, be able to remove the duration A from its fixed place in the temporal framework, i.e. we must establish a mobile unit that lends itself to repeated application (iteration) and to substitution for any other unit in the series. Now, how precisely can this be done?

We have repeatedly referred to time as a system of co-displacements. A duration A can therefore be said to correspond to the partial motions α_1; α_2; etc., a duration A' to the partial motions α'_1; α'_2; etc.; the total duration B to their sums β_1; β_2; etc.; and the following duration B' to the successive motions β'_1; β'_2; etc. Now, these co-ordinated motions engender the synchronizations and colligations of durations, or the order of successions and seriations. To displace a duration A in order to equate it to the successive durations A', B', etc., is therefore tantamount to repeating the motion α_1 (or α_2, etc.) and to synchronizing it successively with α'_1; β'_1; etc.—much as we measure time by the repetitive movements of the hands of a clock or the flow of sand in a sand-glass.

In that way, we obtain a mobile and iterable duration A such that B = 2A; C = 3A; etc. Now, since that duration can be substituted for any other, it loses its distinctive quality. But as soon as it comes to distinguishing any two A's (for example two different hours) we are forced to reintroduce their general succession in the form of the precise order in which the identical motion α was repeated. The quantitative addition of two equal durations 1A + 1A = 2A is therefore both commutative (because one can change the order of the addends) and serial (because by changing the order of the motions we necessarily come back to a first and second A). The possible substitution of the units thus generalizes the operation of colligation, and their possible displacement generalizes the operation of 'placement' or of seriation, the two operations becoming fused, by virtue of these very generalizations, into a single whole during the 'arithmetization' of time or the 'measurement' of durations. It is in this sense that quantitative time combines into a single 'group' what are two distinct groupings on the qualitative plane.

But though this operational mechanism may be clear in its formal aspects, we have still to discover its practical and psychological construction. We came across an early example of that construction in Chapter Two, where we saw that, as soon as children at stage III succeed in seriating the levels and in

175

colligating the durations of the intervals, they also grasp that each equal difference in level corresponds to a unit of duration, and thus pass spontaneously from the qualitative correlation $A + A' = B$ to the quantitative addition $A + A' = 2A$. Now, if this reaction were typical, stage III would not be succeeded by a special stage representing the construction of quantitative time (or stage IV): as soon as qualitative time has been constructed, quantitative time is derived from it by virtue of the very organization of the operations involved.

We shall now look at this question in the light of the preceding remarks. Since it is exceedingly difficult to get children to make spontaneous measurements of time, we have devised a different experiment from the one used in Chapter Two. This has, in fact, proved highly instructive and has thrown quite unexpected new light on the connection between our earlier determinations and the use of watches, or sand-glasses in the measurement of time. It appeared that, at stages I and II, during which the comprehension of qualitative time remains incoherent, the child is at a complete loss with both instruments, at first (stage I) because he believes that their motions vary with the actions to be timed, and later (stage II) because he fails to synchronize these motions with those to be compared. At stage III, on the other hand, the problem is fully grasped thanks to the qualitative operations the child has learned to perform.

This brings us up to the essential problems of time measurement and, to begin with, to the problem of isochronism. In effect, the fundamental postulate on which all time measurement is based is the existence of motions that take the same time to recur under the same conditions. This interpretation of the isochronism of repeated actions involves a vicious circle[1] since, in order to ascertain the isochronism of a given motion, we have to measure its duration by means of other motions whose isochronism depends, in turn, on measurements which postulate it. But the vicious circle becomes 'opened up' as the coherence and range of the results increases and as the postulate of isochronism becomes transformed into a principle of conservation of velocities, and thus comes to rest on the very bases of inductive

[1] For the vicious circle involved in the physical measurement of time, see G. Juvet, *La Structure des nouvelles théories physiques*, Paris (Alcan), 1935.

thought: the permanence of natural laws, identifiable by the possibility of constructing 'groups' of transformations.

That being the case, it is perfectly normal that the young child, whose incoherent conception of time, as we saw, is bound up with his difficulties in quantifying concepts in the physical universe in general, should set out without any assumptions about the conservation of velocities and hence fail to grasp the isochronism of watches, etc. In what follows, we shall examine the manner in which he succeeds in overcoming this failure.

§1. *Isochronism and conservation of velocity in clocks*

Let us begin with a very simple test: we give the child a large sand-glass, 45 cm. high, and such that successive sand levels are readily distinguished. The lower part of the sand-glass (in which the sand collects) is masked so as to obviate any kind of equivocation. The upper part bears three gradations: a white line ($\frac{3}{4}$ way up), a green line ($\frac{1}{2}$ way up) and a blue line ($\frac{1}{4}$ way up) corresponding to equal and successive moments. We introduce the child to the principle of time measurement by asking him to correlate various stages in his own work (e.g. transferring small marbles from one jar to another) with the arrival of the sand at the white, green and blue lines. Next, we ask him to compare his work or movements at different speeds with the flow of the sand.

Now from the reactions at stage I, we discovered that the child thinks the sand runs more or less rapidly according to the speed of the work or motion whose duration he is asked to time. In order to establish whether these illusions persist with other instruments, we used a laboratory stop-watch whose hand turns through a large circle every minute, and then put the same questions.

Here are some reactions at stage I:

FRAN (5 years) transfers his marbles while the sand runs down to the green line, and then continues as far as the blue: Which took longer, the blue or the green? *The blue* (correct). And now once again as far as the blue, but work more slowly. (He does so.) How did the sand run? *Slowly.* And once again as far as the blue, but work very quickly. (He does so.) And how did the sand run now?

177

N

Quickly. Doesn't it run at the same speed if you work slowly or quickly? *No.*

Now walk round the table until the sand has run out completely. (He does so, looking continuously at the sand level.) And now again, but more quickly. (He does so.) How did the sand run? *Slowly.* And before? *Also slowly.* It is the same thing then? *No, a little more slowly.* When? *When I was walking slowly.* But did the sand run at the same speed both times? *No.* How come? You walked quickly first and slowly the second time. Did the sand go quickly and slowly as well or did it go the same way? *It wasn't the same way.*

And now keep moving your leg slowly until the sand has run down. (He does so.) (*Id.*) now quickly. (He does so.) Did the sand run at the same rate both times? *No.* How did it run when you were moving your leg slowly? *Slowly.* And when you moved quickly? *Quickly.*

Walk round the table again and look carefully. (He does so.) And now do so very quickly. (He does so.) How did the sand run? *Slowly.* Always at the same speed? *Yes, it's always the same* (he reflects). *No, it went a bit more slowly before.* But you just told me it always runs at the same speed? *Before it went at the same speed but then it went more quickly.*

We start off two miniature cars, one at high speed and the other more slowly: And how did the sand run this time? *It ran fast and the car went slowly.* And for the other car? *The sand went slowly and the car quickly.* But doesn't the sand run out the same way? *No, once it went quickly and once it went slowly.* And what if a car in the road goes quickly at first and then slowly? *The sand will run slowly and then quickly.*

GEO (5 years) is asked to rap on the table until the sand has completely run out: Do it again, but more quickly this time. (He does so until the sand has gone.) How does the sand run when you rap slowly? *It goes less quickly.* And if you rap quickly? *It goes more quickly.* But does the sand take the same time to run out? *Sometimes it takes long and sometimes it takes less long.*

With the stop-watch: Rap gently as far as here ($\frac{1}{4}$ of the dial). And now rap quickly (*idem*). Did the hand go as quickly, less quickly or more quickly? *Less quickly when I rapped quickly.* And when you rapped more quickly? *It went more quickly.* Didn't it go at the same speed? *No, it didn't.* Let's have a look again. You know, one of your friends said it went at the same speed (we repeat the experiment). *More quickly when I rap more quickly.*

LEA (5 years): And now rap quickly until the clock is at the same

178

place, and watch carefully to see if the hand goes at the same speed. (He does so.) The same time? *No.* What happened when you rapped quickly? *It took less time.* And when you rapped slowly? *It took more time.* Did it go at the same speed? *No.* When you were rapping quickly, how did it go? *More quickly.* Are you sure? Let's have a look again (he raps slowly then quickly, watching the hand). Does it go as quickly? *No.* When you rap quickly? *It goes less quickly.* And when you rap slowly? *More quickly.*

MARA (5½): Did you look at the sand? Did it run for the same length of time? *No, longer when I rapped more quickly.* And did it run at the same speed? *It ran slowly when I rapped slowly.* Let's have a look again and watch carefully what happens (experiment). Did it go at the same speed? *No, very slowly when I rapped quickly.*

GREF (6; 1): Move these marbles across here one by one until the hand reaches there (experiment). Do it again but more quickly and watch the hand again (*idem.*). Did the hand move for the same length of time? *No, the first time it went more slowly and now it goes more quickly.* But didn't it take the same length of time? *No, it didn't, because it went fast first and then not so fast.* New experiment with a metronome, beating slowly first and then more quickly: Did the hand (of the clock) move at the same speed? *No, quickly when the beat was quick and slower when the beat was slower.* With the sand-glass, the sand runs *more slowly the first time and more quickly the second time.*[1]

Let us now look at subjects at stage II, who intuitively assume the conservation of velocity of the clock.

MAP (6½): Did the sand run as quickly or more quickly? *More quickly. . . . No, the same way. . . . No. . . .* As quickly or more

---

[1] It is interesting to compare these results with those of an experiment during which one of our subjects, Syl (6; 5), was asked to compare the progress of a car with that of a cyclist travelling at half the car's speed: When did they start? *At six o'clock in the morning.* And when did they stop? *At six o'clock in the evening.* How long did the car run? *12 hours.* And the cyclist? *Ten hours.* But they started together? *Yes.* And both of them stopped at six? *Yes.* So they kept going for the same length of time? *No, not the same time, one went for ten hours and the other for eleven.* Similarly, Clan (7; 11) contended that the cyclist took ten hours and the car *eleven hours, because it was so far ahead.* But they both started at six o'clock in the morning? *Yes.* And stopped at the same time? *At six o'clock in the evening.* I see. So how many hours was the cyclist on the road? *11 hours, no, 12 hours.* Very well. And the car? *For 12 hours too, no, for 13 hours because it was ahead.*

quickly? *As quickly.* Why did you think more quickly? *It just slipped out, but it's because I myself was going more quickly.* And the clock? *Always the same way.* It goes for the same time no matter whether you go quickly or slowly? *The same time.*

ROB (7; 2). The sand: *Always as quickly.* Why? *Because it makes no difference whether you go quickly or slowly.* And the clock: *Always the same time.* Why? *Because it runs at the same speed.*

These replies show clearly that children at stage I, unlike those at stage II, believe that the speed of the measuring motion is affected by the motion they have been asked to time. But we must still ask ourselves on what sort of error this illusion is based: verbal confusion, perceptive failure or error of judgement?

We might easily come down in favour of verbal confusion. Since the child is asked to work at different rates or to look at cars travelling at different speeds, he concentrates on these differences and, relying exclusively on his sense of inner duration, concludes that time must vary with the speed of the actions under consideration. He accordingly expressed both in the same words. However, if this interpretation were correct, i.e. if he began with an intuitive evaluation of the velocity and the duration of the measured process (relying on the work done, the end point of the run and, above all, on his subjective assessment of the effort and acceleration) he would apply the same reasoning to the measuring process, the more so as he keeps his eyes fixed on the sand-glass or on the clock throughout the experiment. Now, as we saw, certain subjects conclude directly and others (the great majority) after a few questions, that the two relations are inversely proportional, i.e. that the sand and the hand run more slowly when the motions to be timed are speeded up: this illusion (see Fran, Lea and Mara) is therefore manifestly of a perceptive nature, and hence not based on verbal confusion.

Now such perceptive misjudgements are not at all uncommon in adults either: when we look at a sand-glass while making a boring telephone call it seems to run much more slowly than it does during, say, an interesting lecture. Only, as we know perfectly well that the flow of the sand is constant, we pay no heed to the purely perspective aspects, and at best smile at our own subjectivity. The fact that the child should labour under the same illusions, is therefore perfectly natural, and there should be little difficulty in establishing a statistical table of the causes of positive illusions (flow varies with speed of action, etc.), negative illusions (flow varies inversely with the speed of action) and null illusions (flow constant). But we are not so much interested in this correlation as in discovering why the child at stage I, far from considering his subjective impressions as perceptive illusions, should insist on their objective validity.

In point of fact, his reactions represent errors of judgements and not simply errors of perception. We might call these superposed errors of judgement, inasmuch as they are based on errors of perception: while purely perceptive illusions occur with greater or lesser intensity at all stages, subjects at stage I have implicit faith in their perceptions and refuse to correct them by reason. Now, this is precisely what egocentric intuition is all about, and the present discussion thus throws further light on its true nature. Intuitive thought, or perceptive intuition, must not be confused with perception itself, since identical perceptive data are interpreted differently at different stages, depending on whether the judgements brought to bear upon them have become operational or remain intuitive: unlike operational thought which corrects its data by logical co-ordination, perceptive intuition not only accepts them uncritically but supports them with false arguments.[1] Now, since it accepts rather than corrects perceptive data, intuitive thought is necessarily egocentric: it subordinates judgements of reality to subjective estimates and refuses to decentre the latter in favour of a co-ordinated system of relations in which the perceptive appearances are fitted into the objective universe.

Moreover, these stage I reactions help us to appreciate the precise part intuitive centration plays in prolonging perceptive centration (cf. Chapters Four and Six). At first sight, they suggest that many of our subjects behave as if they thought the speed of the clock were affected by external motions, and could be measured in that way. It goes without saying that this interpretation is improbable since, if children were capable of introducing this kind of subtlety, they would also be able to

---

[1] It is thus that, in the clay experiment (*Le Développement des Quantités chez l'Enfant*, Chapters I–III) we gained the impression that children of all ages think that weight changes with form, even when reason tells them otherwise.

distinguish the questions and hence to affirm the invariance of the absolute motion. But there are, in fact, two kinds of relativity: the 'relativity' of perceptions by which, for example, we judge relative bitterness or sweetness, coldness or heat, etc., in terms of a preceding sense impression (mechanism of illusions and Weber's law); and the relativity of judgements which treats such concepts as left and right, high and low, etc., as relations, and not as absolute predicates. Now, while the first type prevents any kind of objectivity (everything is relative), the second is a necessary condition of objectivity. What then is their precise difference, and hence the precise difference between egocentric intuition and operational thought? The answer is that, while perceptive or intuitive relativity leads to the common deformation of the terms to be correlated, operational relativity conserves the absolute value of the related elements. Now the deformation characteristic of the first of the two relativities is nothing other than centration: once attention has been centred on the motion to be measured, that of the sand or hand of the clock will appear to vary as well, and it suffices that the two centrations be sufficiently close in time or in space for them to re-inforce each other—and hence to prevent decentration.[1] Operations, on the other hand, enable one to compare a motion with velocity x to one with velocity y (e.g. x/y) without the values of x and y being altered in any way. Hence there is no contradiction when we claim that intuitive or egocentric thought is characterized both by the deformations inherent in the first of the two relativities (centration effect) and also by failure to grasp the second (adherence to absolute errors as a result of failure to use operational relations): the two are but different aspects of one and the same thing.

We must still explain why subjects at stage I fail to grasp the idea of isochronism and the conservation of velocities, and how those of stage II succeed in doing so. Of the thirty-two 5–7-year-old subjects we have examined, twenty-five failed to answer our questions correctly, while eighteen out of twenty-five 7–9-year-olds were able to do so. At the age of about 7–8 years, conditions must, therefore, be ripe for the necessary operational groupings and quantifications. But this problem falls outside the province

[1] Cf. my 'Interprétation probabiliste de la loi de Weber et de celle des centrations relatives', *Arch. Psychol.*, Vol. III, 1944.

of time as such, for it involves that of motion in general. We shall, therefore, discuss it in a separate work. As for the concept of time itself, we need only state here that once the idea of the conservation of a motion with a given velocity has been grasped at stage II, the child readily proceeds to the equalization of two successive durations corresponding to equal distances traversed successively by one and the same moving body. But though this elementary isochronism constitutes a necessary condition for the measurement of time, we shall see that it is not a sufficient condition, and that it must still be combined with a grasp of synchronous durations and of transitivity.

§2. *Isochronism and synchronism*

Let us first of all give a schematic description of the previous experiment, the better to explain the one that now follows. Let A be the duration of a motion of the measuring apparatus (sand-glass or clock) and A′ that of the next isochronous motion; let B be the duration of the work done during A, and B′ the duration of the work done at a different speed in the same time. The experiment described in §1 then involves the following equivalences (where we designate by = the equality or isochronism of successive durations and by < = > the equality of synchronous durations):

$$A < = > B; A = A'; A' < = > B'; B = B'$$

So as not to make our questions unnecessarily complicated, and to lay the full stress on the problem of isochronism of the clock itself, we base our preliminary questions exclusively on the equality $A = A'$, and neglect $A < = > B$; $A' < = > B'$; and also $B = B'$. Now, it is evident that in order to measure time, the subject must also appreciate these other equalities and hence be able to combine isochronism with synchronism, and above all to deduce ($B = B'$) from the other equalities and hence to compose them transitively. However, as we shall now see (and this in full accord with what we have said in Chapter Five), though the child assumes the conservation of the velocity of the clock at stage II, it is not until stage III that he succeeds in combining his elementary conception of isochronism with that of synchronism, since the latter does not appear before that stage.

Now, seeing that the isochronism of the successive motions of a single moving body (e.g. the sand-glass or the hand of the clock) does not, in itself, constitute a measurement of time (since measuring time means comparing at least two motions or co-displacements), it follows that time measurements cannot be constructed before stage III.

When it comes to the equalities $A < = > B$; $A' < = > B'$ and $B = B'$, however, we can no longer vary the rate of the subject's work, since, if we do so, the child has no means of verifying that $B = B'$ other than reasoning about it. We accordingly use the following procedure. We let the sand in the glass run for a time A_1, while the subject performs a clearly set task B, e.g. drawing a horizontal stroke across one square on the paper with every beat of a metronome, the combined strokes forming a straight line. Let us say the subject draws 30 strokes in A_1 ($A_1 < = > B$). We then produce a stop-watch to time the motion of the sand-glass by $30''$ intervals and draw the child's attention to the simultaneity of the beginning and end of these two motions. To simplify things further, we also mention the synchronism of A_1 and the duration indicated by the stop-watch, which we shall call A_2. (We therefore have $A_1 < = > A_2$.) Finally, we produce the squared paper once again and, using the stop-watch only, ask the child how long a line he thinks he would be able to draw under the same conditions as before (a stroke per square with each beat of the metronome) while the hand of the stop-watch advances from 0 to $30''$. We thus have:

$$A_1 < = > B; A_1 < = > A_2; (A_1 = A'_1 \text{ and } A_2 = A'_2)$$
$$\text{and hence } A'_2 = B$$

(where A'_1 and A'_2 are the durations of the motions of the sand-glass and the stop-watch respectively).

We see that, in both experiments, the isochronism ($A_1 = A'_1$ and $A_2 = A'_2$) is assumed implicitly, so that all our questions can bear on the transitivity of the successive synchronous durations, i.e. (1) on the time it takes for the sand to run down [(A_1) = a line of 30 strokes (B)]; (2) on the time needed for the sand to run down [(A_1) = $30''$ on the stop-watch (A_2)]; (3) on the child's realization that (1) must be equal to (2).

Now, as we have said, subjects before stage III are unable to deduce (3) (composition of synchronism and isochronism). Thus subjects at stage II, though appreciating the conservation of velocities, are unable to apply it to more than one moving body. There is no point in quoting subjects at stage I, since their reactions, as described in §1, show that they cannot possibly grasp the present problem. We accordingly begin with reactions at stage II.

These fall into several types, in the first of which the child refuses to make any predictions on the grounds that it is impossible to do so.

PAK (8; 8): Well, how far would the line stretch if we worked with the clock instead of the sand-glass? *One can't tell.* Why? *We must make an experiment first.* But the sand-glass ran up to where? *Up to here.* And aren't the sand-glass and this point (30″) on the watch the same thing? *Yes.* So if you worked at the same speed, how far would the clock go? *One can't really tell.*

PIC (9; 6): How far would the line go? *Perhaps further. . . . One can't really tell, we'd have to try.* (We perform the experiment.) *It's the same thing.* Why? *I don't know. One can't tell in advance.*

In the second type of reaction, the subjects predict that the work (the line of strokes) will be longer with the stop-watch because its hand moves more quickly:

RIC (8; 3): *The line will go further.* Why? *Because the watch goes more quickly.* Well? *That means it will go further.* After the experiment: *It's the same thing because the watch goes as fast as the sand-glass; both of them go at the same speed.*

MARG (9; 10): *It will go further because the watch goes more quickly than the sand.*

Closely related are reactions of Type 2a:

BAT (8; 4): *Less far.* Why? *Because the hand of the watch goes less quickly than the sand.*

In the third type of reaction, the child believes that the line will be longer because the watch goes more slowly and hence leaves more time for drawing strokes. Here are a few examples, beginning with a subject who vacillates between Types 2 and 3:

MON (8; 7): If I were to ask you to keep working until the hand stops here, how far would the line reach? *Further.* Why? *Because the hand does not go so quickly.* But why can you do more work

185

with the watch? *Because the watch goes more quickly than the sand* (Type 2!). The actual experiment astonishes him, but he continues to predict that the line will go further: Would you like me to start the experiment all over again? *Yes.* (The experiment is repeated.) Were you right? *No.* Well, what happened? *There were as many beats on the metronome* (one beat to each stroke).

NAUC (8; 3): *It would go further because the watch goes less quickly than the sand.*

ISO (8; 11): *The line would go a little bit further.* Why? *Because it took longer with the watch.* Why? *It went more slowly than the sand.* The experiment is performed, but he still predicts that *the line would be a little bit longer, but not much.* Why? *Because the sand drops down more quickly than the watch runs.* So? *I would have more time.*

Closely related are subjects of Type 3a who invert the relation:

IAC (9; 10): *I should be making fewer strokes.* Why? *Because the watch goes more quickly than the sand,* which would leave him *less time.*

In the fourth type of reaction, finally, the path of the hand is compared with the change in sand level:

DUH (8; 11): *More strokes.* Why? *Because the hand of the watch goes further than the sand.*

And the converse (4a):

MAD (9; 6): The line of strokes will go *less far.* Why? *Because the watch doesn't go as far as the sand.*

SUD (9; 9): *The line would go half as far.* Why? *Because the watch is only going at half the rate.* And in order to draw the same line with the sand-glass? *The watch would have to complete two halves.*

We see that these measurements completely stump subjects from 8 to $9\frac{1}{2}$, although they are in daily contact with watches and clocks. According to them, a job which takes 30″ by the sand-glass (A_1) does not take the same time by the watch (A_2), even though they have just seen that $A_2 = A_1$. At the age when he has already grasped the fact that the hand of a clock moves uniformly and that its successive periods are isochronous, the child is, therefore, still incapable of grasping the equality of time of two different clocks, even though he admits it verbally by affirming the simultaneity of the starting and stopping points of the sand-glass and stop-watch.

186

This lack of logic—or this pre-logical behaviour—would be incomprehensible had we not seen in Chapter Five that children have to wait until the age of 8–9 years before they will admit the idea of synchronous durations. Before then, they think that the time of the sand-glass has nothing in common with that of the watch, simply because the two motions are heterogeneous and proceed at different velocities.

This explains the four types of reactions we have just been describing. The first ('we can't tell') simply expresses the failure to grasp that the sand-glass and the watch share a common time. In the second, the work done is simply judged by the respective velocities of the hand and the sand. This type of reaction is reminiscent of the belief that time varies with velocity, though it seems probable that our present subjects do not think in terms of time at all. The third type of reaction, by contrast, introduces time explicitly but naturally ignores synchronization: since the hand of the watch moves more (or less) slowly than the sand, it leaves more (or less) time for the drawing of the strokes. As for children of the fourth (rare) type, they simply rely on the distance covered by the hand of the watch and the strokes, thus arguing much like those of the second type. What is common to all four types of reaction is the denial of synchronism, with the result that the isochronism of each measuring process, taken separately, cannot apparently serve any other purpose than the determination of its own time!

In order to discover whether these reactions remain unchanged if the subject is presented with two identical measuring processes, differing only in the velocity of their motions, we used our stop-watch in conjunction with another one which turns through a full circle while the first describes a semi-circle. The reactions proved identical:

Type 1. NAD (9 years): *I don't know. One can't tell.*

Type 2. EL (9 years): *That would let me draw more strokes, because the hand (2) goes more quickly.* Why more strokes? *Because it goes further* (transition to Type 4). But what difference does it make if the hand goes more quickly? *Oh, well, then I can make many more strokes.*

Type 3. TEN (8; 8): *Less far, because the other hand goes more quickly.* Why? *You do less work, because if it goes more quickly you have less time.*

187

Type 4. Pie (7; 10): *Further, because the watch (2) makes more turns and therefore goes further.*

Let us now examine the reactions of children at stage III to the first test (sand-glass and stop-watch):

Ani (8; 2): *The same line.* Why? *Because the sand runs to the bottom while the watch goes as far as here.* And with the two stop-watches: *Just as far, because this hand goes more quickly but in the end it comes to the same thing.*

Pers (8; 10): *The same, because the sand-glass and the watch stop together.*

Ir (9; 2): *The same thing, because the hand of this watch is here when the other one is there.*

In brief, these subjects have a clear grasp of the necessary condition of time measurement, because once they have assumed the idea of synchronism (cf. Pers), the isochronism of the measuring process enables them to compare the successive measurements.

§3. *Isochronism and the construction of time units*

So far we have been analysing the two basic conditions of time measurement: the grasp that the two measuring motions are isochronous, and the application of these motions to the motions to be measured by means of synchronization. We must now look at the third condition: the division of durations into units that can be repeated at will and applied to whatever processes one wishes to measure. This involves understanding the following three arguments: (1) that the clock does not change its velocity and therefore tells equal times; (2) that the time of the clock is identical with that of the motions or actions to be timed; (3) that the distance covered by the sand or the hand, etc., can be divided into units which, when related to the velocity of the clock, constitute successively equal units of time (by virtue of (1) and that these units can be used to determine the duration of other motions (by virtue of (2)).

Now, some prudence is needed in deciding at which precise stage the child becomes capable of grasping these facts. As we saw in Chapter Two, though subjects at stage II are perfectly capable of understanding that two successive and equal divisions of a cylindrical flask correspond to two equal durations (iso-chronism), it is not until stage III that they learn to transform these units into true units of time by synchronization with the levels in the non-cylindrical flask. Similarly, in the case of clocks, subjects at stage II realize perfectly well that equal divisions of the dial correspond to isochronous durations (we have seen why), but these units are not transformed into units of time until the clock is used to time motions at different speeds, and until time is distinguished from velocity.

In order to clarify this point we can put a question to the child that does not, in fact, involve units of time though it appears to do so: the child is told to count (with the metronome) until the stop-watch A_1 reaches 15″, and is then asked about the position of the hand of a stop-watch A_2, going at twice the rate. The answers at stage I are quite arbitrary—these children do not grasp the conservation of velocity—and there is no point in dis-cussing them. On the other hand, subjects at stage II do prove capable of giving consistent answers:

BEL (7; 3): *It would stop here* (30″). Why? *It goes much more quickly.*

DUN (8; 2): *Here* (30″). Why? *Because the other watch goes more slowly.*

IAGT (8; 11): *Here* (30″) *because it goes twice as fast.*

AEB (9 years): *There* (30″), *because it goes quickly, and so it covers an extra quarter*, etc.

But what these children are establishing, in fact, is a simple relation between the distances traversed and the velocities—time is not introduced as duration but simply as the simultaneity of the number 15 (counted with the metronome), the point 15″ on A_1 and the point 30″ on A_2. The gradations of the dials A_1 and A_2 are, therefore, not treated as units of time but simply as measurements of the velocity of two moving bodies (hands).

Next, we present the same subjects with another problem which, on the surface, seems analogous to the preceding one since, formally, it is based on the same relations. We again ask the child to count up to 15 in unison with the metronome while looking at the hand of a stop-watch (which advances from 0 to 15″ in the same time). Next, we mask the stop-watch and ask the child to count up to 15 once again but this time 'more quickly' (the metronome is set to beat more quickly) or 'twice as quickly' (the beat of the metronome is kept unchanged but the child is told to count two to every beat). He is then asked to predict how far the hand of the stop-watch will have travelled during the more rapid count.

Now, interestingly enough, children at stage II, who have no difficulty in solving the earlier problem fail to solve the second one, and this for the following reason: in the first problem, the time is left constant and the child need simply consider the relation between the velocities of, and the distances covered by, the measuring instruments; in the second problem, the work remains constant but its velocity and duration are varied in such a way that the child has to deduce the distance covered by the measuring apparatus from the duration alone. This results in two types of error at stage II: unable to synchronize the duration of the work done by himself (the count of 15) with that of the hand, the child will either compare the two velocities as such, or else the work done as such. Here are some examples of the first type of error:

BEL (7; 3) points to 25": *It would get to here because I'm counting quickly.*[1]

DUN (8; 2): *As far as here* (25"). Why? *Because I was counting quickly.* Does counting quickly take more or less time than counting slowly? *More time. . . . Oh, no, less time.* So? *Perhaps as far as here* (20").

IAGT (8; 11): How far will the hand go? *Up to here* (about 25"). Why? *Because I'm counting more quickly.* So what happens then? *The hand goes more quickly.* Does the clock go more quickly at one time and more slowly at another? *No, it always goes at the same speed.* So if you count slowly it goes as fast as if you count quickly?

Yes. Well, what did you mean when you said it goes more quickly? *That it goes further.*

The experiment is performed: *Oh, it doesn't go so far: when I go more quickly it goes more slowly than myself.*

AEB (9 years): *Here* (30"), *because the metronome goes twice as fast.* What does that mean? *It counts more quickly so it goes up to here.*

---

[1] It should be noted that the present questions were generally put before those mentioned at the beginning of this §.

ΊΕ (8 ; 8): *Up to here* (30″), *because when I count fast the watch goes more slowly* [than I do]. (Pie, like Iagt, appreciates that the velocity is constant.)

ΈR (8 ; 2): *Up to here* (30″). Which takes longer, counting quickly or slowly? *Slowly.* So if you count quickly, how far will the watch go? *To here* (30″).

When we checked these results with a sand-glass, we obtained the following reactions:

MOR (8 ; 6): Count slowly. Where will the sand stop? *There* ($\frac{1}{2}$). Count quickly. Now guess where the sand is. *It'll have gone down further because I've been counting more quickly.* Does the sand always run at the same speed or not? *Yes.* Are you sure? *Not altogether.*

DES (8 ; 7): *Up to here* ($\frac{3}{4}$). Why? *More sand runs out when I count quickly.* We perform the experiment, but instead of changing his mind, Des prefers to deny the constancy of the sand flow: *I think the sand must have slowed down. It's not running at the same speed as before.* There is therefore a momentary regression to stage I!

And here are some examples of the second type of error, starting with a subject who changes from the first to the second type in the course of the examination:

SCHNE (9 ; 4): *Up to here* (30″). Why? *Because the watch goes more slowly than the machine* (the metronome). Does the watch go slowly at one stage and then go more quickly? *No, it's always the same.* What takes more time, counting quickly or counting slowly? *Slowly.* And where was the watch when you were counting quickly? *Here* (30″). Why? *Because the machine went quickly and so the watch was behind.* So the watch went further? *I don't know.* If you count quickly, where does the hand go to? *Also up to here* (15″). Why? *Because the machine goes more quickly than the watch, so it can't catch up.* But why up to here (15″)? *Because the watch takes the same time when the machine goes more slowly.*

ΕΝ (8 ; 4): *Up to here* (15″). Why? *Because the hand goes slowly.* Does it always go at the same speed? *Oh yes, but when I count quickly it goes more slowly than I do, and when I count slowly it goes at the same speed as me.* So? *When I counted slowly the hand was here* (15″) *and now I'm counting quickly so the hand goes more slowly. When I am at 15 it'll be here* (15″), *the same as before.*

GOY (8 ; 5): *Up to here* (15″) *just as far as before.* Why? *Because I have counted up to 15 just as before.* But before you counted slowly

and now you counted quickly, does that make no difference? *No,
it makes no difference.* Why? *It's the same thing, so it's the same
time.*

ROUL (8; 5) thought at first that the hand would stop at 30" and
then changed his mind *because if you count quickly it's the same thing
as if you count slowly.* What takes longer, counting slowly or
quickly? *Slowly.* Are you sure? *No, I just think so.* So where
would the hand be? *Here* (15"). Why? *It's the same thing as
before.*

DUR (9; 10): *Here* (15") *because the watch goes as quickly as before.*
And you? *Faster.* So? *The watch can get up to here* (15") *while
I am counting. Before, I counted more slowly than the watch and now
I am counting more quickly than the watch, but the watch is going at
the same speed.*

Both types of reaction are of great interest in that they show
that these children, unable to synchronize durations, completely
fail to grasp the idea of a unit of time (this is in full accord with
what we have said in Chapter Five and in §2 of the present
chapter): when measuring time by the advance of the hands of
the watch, they are in fact, simply translating the equal or
greater velocity of the work done (counting up to 15) into an
equal or greater advance of the hand. In either case, they do not
bother about duration as such, and this because, as we have shown
at some length, children at stage II do not yet ascribe a unique
unit of time or a common duration to motions at different
velocities.

At first sight, we might tend to think that this failure is a direct
result of their failure to grasp the idea of isochronism or the
fact that time is inversely proportional to velocity. Now, it is
quite true that these two ideas have not yet taken full root in
these children. Thus Mor, and above all Des, were ready to
abandon the idea of constant velocities the moment things became at all complicated, and Dun, before correcting himself,
claimed that 'more quickly' was equivalent to 'more time'. However, we saw that, as a general rule, children at stage II show by
their answers to our questions that they have a grasp of both
these relations (Chapters Three to Four and in §1 of this chapter). It must, however, be stressed that showing one's grasp of
the fact that time is inversely proportional to velocity in the case
of two visible motions, where one can see that one is quicker

192

and therefore takes less time than the other, is something quite different from deducing the advance of a clock from the speed of a synchronous action.

The mistakes of these children are thus much simpler to explain than would seem at first sight. Unable to synchronize the rapid action of counting with the invisible motion of the hand or of the sand (because the simultaneity of the end points can no longer be perceived), the child simply neglects the durations. Hence he believes that if he counts more quickly the hand must necessarily advance further, because 'more quickly = further' (see, for example, Iagt), or because counting up to 15 in both cases 'that's the same thing = the same time' (Goy). In other words, duration is measured in the first case by the distance covered and in the second case by the work done, two criteria characteristic of this stage.

It might be objected that these generalizations are unjustified, and that the problems under discussion are simply the results of the particular experimental situation we have chosen, and quite especially of the particular divisions of the stop-watch. To meet such objections, we have used the following control experiment: four small cars are set in motion at different speeds so that they cover distances in the ratio 1 : 2 : 3 : 4 in the same time. We divide our sand-glass into 4 equal sectors and simply ask the child to tell us what mark on the sand-glass (which we remove) will correspond to the arrival of a particular car at its final destination. Now the results we obtained by this experiment were fully comparable to those obtained by the last. At stage I, the replies were quite arbitrary because even when the subjects were allowed to watch both car and sand, they failed to appreciate that the latter poured out at a constant rate (see §1, case of Fran). At stage II, most of our subjects produced the first type of reaction we mentioned a moment ago: they thought that the speed of the sand varies with that of the car, even though they appreciated that the sand ran out at a constant rate. Here are two examples:

KEN (7; 1): Where will the sand be when this car (the fastest) arrives at the end of its run? *Here* ($\frac{3}{4}$). And when this one (the slowest) arrives at the end of its run? *Here* ($\frac{1}{4}$). Just watch. *Oh no, I was wrong.* Can you explain why? . . . Let's start again. Where will the sand be for this car (medium speed)? *In the middle.* And when that one (the slowest) arrives at the end of its run? *There* ($\frac{1}{4}$). And

that one (the fastest)? *Down to the bottom.* Look for yourself
Oh no, here ($\frac{1}{4}$). Why? ...

ARM (8; 1): Now the brown (fast) car has arrived at the end of it
run. Guess where the sand will be? *Here* ($\frac{3}{4}$). And where will i
be for the yellow (medium speed) car? *There* ($\frac{1}{2}$). Which goes more
quickly? *The brown one.* So where will the sand be for the yellow
one? *Here* ($\frac{1}{2}$), *and there* ($\frac{3}{4}$) *for the brown one.* And what about the
very slow one? *Here* ($\frac{1}{4}$).

We also find the second type of reaction, i.e. the assertion that
the sand will always stop at the same time, no matter what the
speed of the car (over the same distance).

ALB (8 years): Where will the sand be when the brown (fast) ca
arrives at the end of its run? *Here* ($\frac{1}{2}$). And how does that one
(the yellow car) travel? *More slowly.* Where will the sand be
Also here ($\frac{1}{2}$). And for that one there (the slowest car)? *Also here*
($\frac{1}{2}$). Is it always the same? *Yes.* Why? *I don't know.* Wha
makes you think that it's the same thing? *Because all the cars stop
in the same place.*

Now for an example of the correct answers, given by
children from 7 years onwards, and more generally from 8
years onwards:

ALD (7; 6): Where will the sand be with the red (slow) car? *Here*
($\frac{3}{4}$). Why? *Because it goes slowly.* And for that one (a faster car)
Here ($\frac{1}{2}$). And for the one that goes very fast? *Here* ($\frac{1}{4}$). And
for the one that goes very slowly? *Right at the bottom.* Why
The sand has time to run out during its run.

All these reactions show clearly that, at stage II, children still
fail to transform the dial or sand-glass into distinct units o
time. On the other hand, as soon as synchronization has been
achieved (stage III), the synthesis of synchronous and isochronous durations engenders quantitative time, i.e. the operationa
fusion of the partitive addition of durations and the displace
ment in time of time-generating motions. Let us now examine
some stage III reactions (stop-watch experiment):

BLAN (8 years). With the metronome going at a faster rate: *The hand
will come to here* (10"). Why? *Because the metronome went more
quickly.* So what does that mean? *The hand had less time.* (Grasp
of synchronization.) And if you count twice as quickly (experiment)
It will go to there (points to between 7 and 8).

194

RIC (8 ; 3): *Up to here* (10″). Why? *Because I went more quickly than the watch, so it could only get to there.* Why did the watch go more slowly? *It went the same way as before* (isochronism) *but I was counting faster* (synchronism). And if you count twice as quickly as before? *It would go to there* (½ of 15″).

MON (8 ; 7): *Here* (10″), *because the metronome was going quickly, so the hand could not get to here* (15″) *in that amount of time* (synchronism). Why? *It always goes the same way* (isochronism). And if you counted twice as fast? *It would go to there* (½ of 15″). And twice as slowly? *There* (15″). No, I mean twice as slowly as the first time? *There* (30″).

The difference between these reactions and those at the preceding stage are most striking: combining isochronism with synchronization, subjects at stage III succeed in transforming the spatial units of the dial into time units proper, i.e. into units that can be applied to the measuring and to the measured processes alike. As we saw, the idea of isochronous durations was already grasped at stage II (§1 and §2), but for lack of synchronization, it could not be applied to more than one motion at a time. At best, therefore, these subjects went beyond stage I in that they endowed every body moving with a uniform velocity with a regular time (in respect of succession). However, the moment the idea of synchronization is combined with that of isochronous durations (stage III), the child is able to construct a time scale that is both homogeneous and uniform, with the result that units of distance traversed at a constant velocity become transformed into units of time. Quantitative time is therefore simply the operational synthesis of the colligation of durations (synchronism) with the equalization of successive durations (isochronism).

PART III

Age and Inner Time

In the first two parts of this work we have tried to discover how the child succeeds in organizing the time of external events, at first intuitively and then by a set of qualitative or quantitative operations. We can sum up our results by saying that at the intuitive level the child, in accordance with the general egocentric laws characteristic of that level, judges physical time as if it were inner time, i.e. as if it contracted and expanded with the contents of the actions that have to be timed. As a result, he fails to grasp the idea of a homogeneous time, common to all phenomena. Must we, therefore, seek the sources of time in the child's inner life, as a famous school of philosophers invites us to do, and consider that every temporal concept is based on this intuitive prototype? Does inner time, which is said to be 'pure' because it is divorced from external time, in fact, constitute true time, while physical time is no more than the product of spatialization and hence of an impoverishing abstraction? In this part of our book we shall try to show that nothing could be more erroneous than this Bergsonian interpretation of the psychological genesis of temporal relations.

In fact, all Bergson has done is to carry to its extremes a tendency of the old introspective school of psychology, based on the adult view that inner time can be grasped by introspection, while external time must first be constructed. However, here as elsewhere, introspection, which is a form of derived conduct, gives us nothing but incomplete and deceptive information: being utilitarian, it can tell us something about the products of our mental operations but nothing about their mechanics. Now, depending on its level, psychological, like physical, time must either be constructed by true operations [qualitative comparisons, seriations and colligations or quantitative operations such

197

as are used in music and poetry (time and metre)], or else by intuitive regulations. In the second case—in which the sense of durations appears to be 'immediate'—adult psychological time fully preserves the structure of infantile time in that it fails to apply intellectual, moral or aesthetic norms. However, before we can base an entire metaphysics of psychological duration and intuition on this fact, we must first establish whether these infantile and hence primitive notions are, in fact, of inner origin, and whether they are really untouched by external influences.

Now, contrary to a widespread misconception, there is no reason at all for assuming either that primitive time is of purely internal origin or that duration is constructed, let alone 'given', independently of the objects of one's actions.

True, we have seen that the physical time of young children is at first nothing other than 'egocentric' time, i.e. the projection of inner time into external objects. But this in no way implies that the child has an inborn sense of time which it subsequently attaches to things by means of a sort of 'induction' (analogous to that by which Maine de Biran tried to explain the transition from inner, primitive causality to outer, physical causality). If we have used the term 'egocentric' rather than 'subjective' to describe the essential character of the child's conception of time (and of all infantile categories), it was simply to stress the fact that there is a difference between the unconscious adaptation of things to activity, and the reading of ready-made inner data. Egocentrism is, in effect, characterized by a lack of differentiation between the subject and the external world, and not by precise self-understanding: far from leading to introspection or self-reflection, infantile egocentrism is a type of ignorance of the inner life and a deformation of the self coupled to a misconception of objective relationships. Just as the child endows objects with a set of qualities based on action (animism, artificialism, finalism, etc.), so he reifies his ego and thinks of his own activity as an inseparable function of these physical and spatial data.[1] Hence, though he conceives of physical time as a generalized form of psychological duration applied to the entire universe, it does not at all follow that he has an independent and primitive inner conception of time: on the contrary, to elaborate the

[1] See *La Représentation du monde chez l'enfant*, *La Causalité physique chez l'enfant*, and *La Construction du Réel chez l'enfant*.

various relations between inner duration and the time it takes to perform actions, he must first rid himself of his undifferentiated intuitions and elaborate the same system of qualitative (and partly quantitative) operations that goes into the construction of physical time.

Which brings us to the second point: if primitive time is neither internal nor even purely endogenous, but results from a lack of differentiation between the time of objects and that of the subject himself, inner duration must necessarily be constructed by a continual reference to objects. At all stages, as we shall see, psychological time is based on physical time and *vice versa*. At the intuitive level the two remain undifferentiated and hence become deformed; at the operational level, on the other hand, they become differentiated and their organization results in their ultimate correlation. Inner duration is, in fact, nothing other than the time of action (by action, we simply refer to the relation between the acting subject and the objects on which he acts). From the emergence of sensory-motor time, during the first year of life, the objectives pursued and the actions leading to them constitute a single framework of succession and duration. If the lack of differentiation at the early stage is egocentric and if, by contrast, we can speak of an objectivation of physical time at a later stage (we have previously[1] described its first sensory-motor manifestations and have followed its subsequent progress in the first two parts of this present work), it must nevertheless be added that this objectivation goes hand in hand with the 'subjectivation' of psychological time, by which we mean the internal and representative co-ordination of the subject's actions, past, present and future: this objectivation and subjectivation, far from remaining independent, are in constant intercommunication simply because the ego is the action, and, let us repeat, action cannot be creative unless it rejoins its objects. Thus 'pure duration' must be a complete myth; duration is the product of that constructive intelligence which is as necessary for the organization of the ego itself, in daily life, as it is for the elaboration of the universe.

In trying to come to grips with the workings of operational intelligence in the structuring of psychological time, we have thought of two types of situation in which it might be possible

[1] See *La Construction du Réel chez l'Enfant.*

to decide between the hypothesis that time is grasped by direct intuition and the hypothesis that psychological time is constructed by the intelligence at the same time as physical time. In the first place, we can analyse the time of action and ask ourselves if the time 'lived' during an action is judged by peripheral factors (effort, speed, the material results of the action, etc.) or by central factors (pure awareness of time). This is what we shall be doing in Chapter Ten. But we can also look at the concept of 'age', which involves ideas of biological growth and also of total duration. It is with the second problem that we shall begin our examination.

CHAPTER NINE

The Concept of Age[1]

The analysis of children's ideas of age raises a number of important questions. Does the child look upon ageing as a continuous process in time? Is this time the same for all individuals? And, above all, does he associate age differences with the order of births? These questions will be discussed in §3, §4 and §5 of this chapter.

The child's idea of age has been the subject of a highly evocative study by O. Decroly[2] who, after observing the spontaneous reactions of his daughter S. between the ages of 4 and 6, concluded that young children tend to confuse age with height—as if ageing were tantamount to growing. Moreover, when he asked several groups of children how old they were last year, how old they would be next year, and how old they were at birth, he discovered that 75 per cent of his subjects below the age of 7 failed to give the correct answers to questions 1 and 2, and that question 3 eluded even older children—not surprisingly when we consider that it is of a metric rather than qualitative kind. From the answers elicited by Decroly, it would also appear that young children fail to grasp the relation between age and the order of succession of births. The most typical reactions were those of Claire, aged 4, who 'no longer remembered' her age at birth—'it was much too long ago'; and of Jacqueline (5; 6): 'I can't remember. . . . Oh yes, I was two months old!' In what follows we, too, shall find clear signs of this initial lack of co-ordination between the ideas of duration and succession.

[1] In collaboration with Mlle Myriam Van Remoortel.
[2] O. Decroly, *Etudes de psychogenèse*, Brussels 1932, Chapter V.

§1. *The age of persons*

I. The first stage

All our studies of the development of the concept of physical time have shown us that young children behave as if duration varied as the distance covered by moving bodies and as their velocity, i.e. as if physical time were heterogeneous. This brings us to our first two questions, namely whether children realize that age differences are preserved throughout life or whether they rather believe that, as people grow older and bigger they catch up with their elders; and secondly whether young children grasp the connexion between age and the order of birth. As we saw in our discussion of physical time, the second question impinges upon the relation between duration and succession, though with the added difficulty that, since the idea of age is more frequently discussed in the home and among informed acquaintances, than any other temporal concept, few children will give unprejudiced answers. For that reason, we have thought it best to question them on the age of plants and animals rather than on their own age and that of their near relatives. Nevertheless, we have found that, by dwelling upon personal age differences, we can bring to light a number of systematic difficulties, and so discover agreement between the results obtained in this field and in those we have already covered.

One thing in particular strikes one directly, namely the essentially static and almost discontinuous character of the child's idea of age. To him, ageing is not a perpetual and continuous process, but rather a process of change tending towards certain states; time ceases to flow once these states are attained. That is precisely why young children equate ageing with growing up: when growing stops, time apparently ceases to operate. Their conception is reminiscent of the ancient Greeks' idea of 'becoming', and this similarity is yet another indication that childish thought resembles the static, and relatively unoperational, approach of the Ancients.

We can distinguish three stages in the development of the child's conception of age. During the first, age is independent of the order of birth, and age differences are thought to become modified with time conceived as a heterogeneous flux. During the second stage, the child believes either that, though age differences are not maintained throughout life, age depends on the order of births, or else that age differences are maintained but do not depend on the order of births. In the third stage, finally, duration and succession have become co-ordinated, and their relations are preserved by virtue of this very fact.

We shall now look at a few examples from stage I:

ROM (4; 6) does not know her birthday. She has a small sister called Erica: How old is she? *Don't know.* Is she a baby? *No, she can walk.* Who is the older of you two? *Me.* Why? *Because I'm the bigger one.* Who will be older when she starts going to school? *Don't know.* When you are grown up, will one of you be older than the other? *Yes.* Which one? *Don't know.* Is your mother older than you? *Yes.* Is your Granny older than your mother? *No.* Are they the same age? *I think so.* Isn't she older than your mother? *Oh no.* Does your Granny grow older every year? *She stays the same.* And your mother? *She stays the same as well.* And you? *No, I get older.* And your little sister? *Yes!* (categorically).

Who was born first, Erica or you? *Don't know.* Is there a way of finding out? *No.* Who is younger, Erica or you? *Erica.* So which one was born first? *Don't know.* How many years older are you than Erica? . . . One year? *No.* Two years? *More.* Three years? *Yes.* When you are a lady will you still be three years older than Erica? *Don't think so.* Were you alive when your little sister came? *Yes.* And who was born first, your mother or you? *Mummy.* Your Granny or your mother? *Don't know.* Your father or your little sister? *Don't know.* Your father or you? *Can't say.*

JEAR (4; 9): Have you any brothers? *Yes, Charles and Eric.* Are they older or younger than you? *They are young* (1 and 3 years). Were you born before or after Eric (1 year)? *We were born at the same time. All three of us were born before the Escalade* (Geneva festival). Are they the same age? *No.* Or the same age as you? *No.* Who is the oldest of you three? . . . And the youngest? *Eric.* Is your mother older than you? *She is young.* And do you get a little older every year? *No, I stay young.* Will you be the same age next year? *No, I'll have my birthday and I'm getting skates. I'll be 5½.* Have you got a granny? *Yes, she's older than Mummy.* Was she born before or after your mother? *Don't know.* What do you think? *I don't know.* And your grandfather—is he older than your father? *Oh yes.* Why? *My Daddy is younger.* Who was born first? *I don't know. My grandfather was old right away.* Are you older than Eric? *Oh yes.* Older than Charles? *Yes.* Who is the oldest? *Me. I'll stay young and so will they.* Who was the first to go to (nursery) school? *Me.* And who will be the first to go to the big school? *Me.* And who will be the first to be a man? *Don't know.*

BOR (4; 9): *I have two brothers, Philippe and Robert.* Are they older or younger than you? *Older than me.* Much older? *Yes.* How old are they? *I don't know.* Do they go to the big school? *Yes, both of them.* Is one older than the other? *No, both of them are the same age* (wrong). Were they born on the same day? *Yes* (wrong). Are they twins? *No.* But they are the same age all the same? *Yes, the same age as myself.* Who was born first then? *Philippe and then Robert* (correct). Who was born first, Philippe or you? *I* (wrong). So who is the oldest of you three? *Nobody.* You told me you were born before Philippe, so you must have been there when Philippe was born? *Oh sure, I was there* (this seems quite evident to him . . .). Who was born first in your whole family? *No one. Philippe came second, then Robert, and I was the fourth because I am four years old.*

PTI (4; 9): How old are you? *4½.* Is it a long time since your birthday? *It hasn't been yet, it will be in June.* How old will you be? *8 years.* Come, come! *No, 5 years.* Have you any brothers or sisters? *I have a big brother. He goes to the school in Secheron* (the 'big school'). Were you born before or after him? *Before.* So who is older? *My brother, because he is bigger.* When he was small, how many years older was he than you? *Two years.* And now? *Four years.* Can the difference change? *No. . . . Yes. If I eat a lot of soup I shall grow bigger than him.* How can one tell which one is the older? *The one who is bigger.* Who is older your father or your grandfather? *They're both the same age.* Why? *Because they are as big as each other.*

Pierre and Paul are two brothers. Pierre was born first. Can you tell which one is the elder? *It's Pierre.* But look, Pierre is the smaller of the two. *Then Paul is the older: the older one is the one who dies first.*

MYR (5 years): *I have a sister.* Is she older or younger than you? *Older.* And when you grow up to be a lady, will she still be older than you? *I don't know. She'll be a lady.* Can one tell if your sister will always remain older than you? *Yes, one can tell, but I can't myself.* Who is older, your mother or yourself? *I don't know, because both of us are young.* Was your mother born before you or after you? *I can't remember.* Who is the oldest in your family? *Papa, because he has a tanned face and he can work.* Who is the youngest? *I don't know.* But your sister is older? *I don't know if we are the same age because she is still at Secheron* (primary school).

AUD (6 years) has a friend: Is he older or younger than you? *He's bigger.* Was he born before or after you? *After.* Is your father older or younger than you? *Older.* Was he born before or after you? *I don't know.* Who came first, you or him? *Me.* Are you going to stay the same age all the time or will you grow older? *I shall grow older.* And your father? *He'll remain the same age.* And will your mother grow older? *No.* Why? *Because she is old already.*

These stage I reactions are in remarkable agreement with those of the corresponding stage in the child's conception of physical time: failure to grasp the ideas of succession and duration operationally, and inability to co-ordinate pre-operational intuitions with respect to them.

As regards the idea of succession, it is surprising to find that children not only fail to affirm that they were born after their parents, but that many of them claim anteriority—one might almost say priority, with all the value judgements that term implies. While the more prudent subjects, e.g. Rom and Myr (*It's possible to tell, but I myself don't know*) confess their ignorance, the more audacious are uncompromising, and, like Aud, insist that they preceded their father into the world. Such replies would be incomprehensible had we not learned (Chapters Three and Four) that these children fail to grasp temporal succession whenever the starting and end points of a process do not coincide in space. Hence the children who reply 'I don't know' when asked about the order of births in their family, are speaking the truth: the problem has no meaning for them. As for those who attribute anteriority to themselves, they stress another kind of truth: from their point of view, time, and hence the existence of older people, begins with the dawn of their own memory. This explains why Myr could not 'remember' whether her mother was born before her, or why Bor, asked about the birth of his older brother, declared: 'Oh sure, I was there'—and, indeed, for as far as his memory stretched back he was always 'there' to record his brother's presence. Here we have a temporal egocentrism that clearly reflects the incoherent nature of the untuitive and pre-operational idea of temporal succession.

Now the best proof that this egocentric conception of intuitive time in no way reflects the predominance of the inner life over the organization of spatial objects, but that it represents a lack of differentiation between subject and object, is that our subjects' ideas about duration (age itself) are based on a confusion between time and the spatial or physical data serving as its content: age is equated with size, so that age differences can be annulled or reversed by growth in height. That was why Rom thought that her mother was the same age as her grandmother, and that neither grew any older. By contrast, she herself and her sister were still growing older, but at different rates. Jear will always stay young, while his grandfather was born 'old straight away', and though he appreciates that he himself is older than his juniors, he is not at all certain that he will grow up into a man before them (here temporal egocentrism goes hand in hand with emotional insecurity or feelings of inferiority, which seems paradoxical until we remember that this attitude is based on a lack of intellectual, and not of moral, differentiation). Pti believes that his older brother used to be his senior by two years, that the difference has now increased to four years, but that he himself will grow older than his brother if only he eats enough soup. Myr did not know if she would always remain younger than her sister, etc. etc.

In brief, children at stage I have an egocentric and pre-operational conception of succession and duration, and therefore cannot base the former on the latter or *vice versa*. In other words, they are quite unable to say that A was born before B because A is older, or that A is older than B because he was born before him. This corresponds fully with what we have said about stage I in Chapters Three and Four.

§2. *The age of persons*

II. *The second and third stages*

The similarity between the development of the concept of age and that of physical time is even more striking at stage II. The reader will recall that this stage is characterized by the emergence of articulated intuitions, either of succession (the past in time becomes divorced from the past in space) or of duration (more quickly = less time), which, however, remain unco-ordinated. Now, in the case of age as well, the grasp of successions may precede that of durations (Type 1), or *vice versa* (Type 2). In the first case, the child is able to order the births but fails to deduce the permanence of age differences, in the second case, he discovers that age differences persist but fails to deduce the order of succession of the births.

Here are some examples of Type 1:

FILK (4; 11) (precocious) has an older sister: Are you the same age? *No, because we weren't born at the same time.* Who was born first? *She was.* Will you be the same age as her one day or will the two of you never be the same age? *Soon I shall be bigger than her, because men are bigger than women. Then I shall be older.*

ER (5; 8) thinks that his father is older than his mother *because he was born first and Mama last.* But neither his mother nor his grandmother are growing older. As for his father: *he grows older every year, but sometimes he stays the same.*

RAL (6; 9) has a brother who is 6 years younger than she is: Who is older? *I am.* Who was born first? *I was.* When you will be a lady, what age will your brother be? *The same as me.* The same age? *Yes.* Perhaps just a little older or younger? *A little older.* Is your mother older or younger than you? *Older.* Was she born before you? *Yes.* Or you before her? *No.* Is your father younger or older than your mother? *Older.* Have you been told that? *No, I've seen it.* Was he born before or after her? *Before.* Next year, will your father be older? *Yes.* And your mother? *Also.* And you? *Yes.* And your little brother? *Yes.* Who will be younger, you or he? *André.* Who will be older when you are both grown up? *André.* And today? *I am.* And when both of you are old? *We'll be the same age.* Are your grandmother and grandfather the same age or not? *Yes, more or less.* Who was born first? *My grandmother.*

MON (7; 10) has a friend, Eliane: How old is she? *9½.* And you? *7½.* Which one is older? *Eliane.* How much? *Two years.* Was she born before or after you? *Before.* How many years before? *. . .* How long before? *I don't know.* Is it possible to tell? *No.* Was it two years before? *No, not two years.* When you are a lady, will Eliane be older or younger than you? *Older.* By how much? *I don't know.* Two years like now? *No, more.*

VET (7; 10): *I have a little sister, Liliane, and a 9-month-old brother, Florian.* Are you the same age? *No. First of all there's my brother, then my sister, then me, then Mama and then Papa.* Who was born first? *Me, then my sister and then my brother.* When you are old, will Florian still be younger than you? *No, not always.* Does your father grow older every year? *No, he remains the same.* And you? *Me, I keep growing bigger.* When people are grown-up, do they get older? *People grow bigger and then for a long time they remain the same, and then quite suddenly they become old.*

We conclude with a subject who nearly succeeds in co-ordinating birth with age, but nevertheless keeps to the idea that age is defined by size:

CLAN (7; 10): How old are you? *7 years. I am big, people say I am 8 years old.* Have you a sister? *Yes, she's 6 years old.* Were you born before or after her? *Oh! Before!* When you will be a young man, will both of you be the same age? *No, when I'm 9 she'll be 8, when I'm 10, she'll be 9, when I'm 18 she'll be 17, there will always be a difference. My sister reaches up to here* (to his chin). *Me, I'm growing bigger all the time. When she reaches up to here* (to his forehead), *then I'll be there* (above his head), *and then afterwards we'll be here and there,* etc. Who is younger, your father or your mother? *My father.* (wrong) Was he born before or after your mother? *After* (wrong). So why is he the younger? *My mother is the tallest in our family.* Despite his brilliant beginning, Clan thus sticks to his confusion of age with size.

As we can see, all these children give the correct replies to questions involving the succession of births, equating 'older' with 'born earlier' and 'younger' with 'born later'. But, curiously enough, their grasp of this correspondence is restricted to the *actual* age of people, and does not imply a realization that age differences persist throughout life: it is therefore non-operational and simply represents an 'articulated intuition'.[1] A case in point is Ral's assertion that her younger brother will eventually outstrip her in age, or Vet's claim that his little brother (a 9-month-old baby) will not 'always' remain younger, etc. Now the reason for these strange opinions is very simple: though the subjects grasp the order of succession of births, they always think of duration in terms of spatial or physical developments and hence

[1] See the case of visual correspondences at stage II in the child's construction of number in *La Genèse du Nombre chez l'Enfant*, Chapters III and IV.

confuse age with size. It follows that their conception of lived duration or age is discontinuous: as Vet put it so suggestively 'people grow bigger and then for a long time they remain the same and then quite suddenly they become old'.

Unlike these subjects, those of Type 2 fully grasp the fact that age differences persist but fail to deduce the correct order of births (which is extraordinary from the operational point of view, but is easily explained when we remember that they still proceed by intuitive steps):

DOUR (7; 5): How old are you? *7½.* Have you any brothers or sisters? *No.* Any friends? *Yes, Gerald.* Is he older or younger than you? *A little older, he's 12 years old.* How much older is he than you? *Five years.* Was he born before or after you? *I don't know.* But think about it, haven't you just told me his age? Was he born before or after you? *He didn't tell me.* But is there no way of finding out whether he was born before or after you? *I could ask him.* But couldn't you tell without asking? *No.* When Gerald will be a father, will he be older or younger than you? *Older.* By how much? *By five years.* Are you getting old as quickly as each other? *Yes.* When you will be an old man what will he be? *A grandfather.* Will he be the same age as you? *No, I'll be five years less.* And when you will be very, very old, will there still be the same difference? *Yes, always.*

GIST (9 years) has a younger sister: *She'll be 7 years old on 8 January.* How many years younger than you? *Two years.* When you will be a big lady, will she be the same age as you? *No, she'll always be younger than me.* By how much? *Two years.* Are you absolutely certain? *By 21 months* (correct). Why? *Because it will be the same as today.* And when you are very old? *It will always be the same.* Well then, tell me, which of you two was born first? *I don't know.*

The reader will note the paradoxical character of these replies, which are not only much rarer than those of Type 1, but also far more instructive. We saw that Dour, who kept insisting that he would always be five years younger than his friend Gerald, was nevertheless unable to tell which of them was born first, and that Gist, who stated that her sister was 21 months younger, failed to realize that she herself must be the first-born. Their recognition of the conservation of age differences must therefore be based on articulated intuitions (dissociation of age differences

209

P

from physical growth, i.e. differences in height), while their grasp of the order of succession remains based on direct intuition.

Towards the end of stage II, we can, moreover, distinguish a sub-stage II B, representing a clear advance from stage II (Types 1 and 2) towards stage III. Children at this sub-stage set out with the same reactions as those at stage II, but then reach the correct answers by trial and error:

PHI (7; 8): Have you got a brother? *No, but I shall have one in February.* Which will be the older one? *I, because I was born first.* What will be the difference? *Seven years.* And when you become a father, what age difference will there be between him and you? *I don't know.* The same as now? *Oh yes.* Why? . . . And what about your mother, is she older than you? *Yes.* When you will be an old gentleman, will there be the same difference as now? *Yes . . . no, less . . . no, the same as now.* Is your father older than your mother? *Yes, one year older.* And when you were born, was there the same difference between them? *Mama was younger.* But the same difference? *No; yes; oh yes, the same.*

We see therefore that before it is fully taken for granted, the conservation of age differences can be adopted gradually, as an increasingly probable induction.

Here, finally, are some reactions at stage III, showing complete co-ordination between the order of succession of births and the colligation of ages:

GILB (7; 9) is an only child: Have you a friend? *Yes, he's seven years old.* Is he older or younger than you? *He's the same age as me, he was born in the same year, therefore he must be the same age.* Have you got another friend? *Remy. He's 15 years old.* Is he older than you? *Yes, much.* What's the difference? *Eight years.* Was he born before or after you? *Before.* How long before? (Brief hesitation). *Oh well, eight years.* When both of you will be men, will you be the same age? *He'll be older because he was born first.* And you and your mother? *She is older.* And when you grow up? *There will still be the same difference.* Why? *It never changes.* Don't all old men have the same age? *It all depends on when they were born, some are 50 others are 60. . . .*

POL (8; 3): *I have two small brothers, Charles and Jean.* Who was born first? *Me, then Charlie and finally Jean.* When you are grown up, how old will you all be? *I'll be the oldest, then Charlie and then Jean.* How much older will you be? *The same as now.* Why? *It's always the same. It all depends on when one was born.*

We see that, for these subjects, the order of succession (seriation of births) and durations (the ages themselves) are related by logical necessity, so much so that the conservation of age differences is no longer merely asserted but deduced from the very order of the births.

All in all, the facts described in §1 and §2 fully bear out the general progress with which we have become familiar in the course of this work. At stage I, the order of succession and duration remains completely unco-ordinated and gives rise to egocentric and distorting intuitions, determined both by the subjective viewpoint and by a spatial and physical phenomenalism from which time has not yet become differentiated. During stage II, progress in intuitive regulation leads to the grasp of either the order of births or else of the permanence of age differences. During stage III, finally, the simultaneous use of these two types of articulated intuition helps to transform the regulations on which they are based into operations proper, whose 'groupings' combine the succession and duration into a coherent, deductive system.

It is a striking fact that despite its verbal character, and though it is so strongly influenced by adult remarks, the child's conception of age should develop along paths precisely parallel to those described in Chapters Three and Four for the case of physical time. The problem is, moreover, the same in both cases: the construction of time calls for the co-ordination of motions and velocities: growth is, in effect, comparable to the spatial trajectories we met in our discussion of physical time, and the rate of growth (ageing) to differences in the velocity of two runners. Now, in both spheres, duration is at first confused with the path traversed—thus all children at stage I define age by size. In both cases, moreover, there is a complete failure to grasp the order of events, due to lack of differentiation between temporal and spatial succession: the spatial 'before' along the track (Chapters Three to Four), is, in effect, equivalent to an egocentric 'before' on the age scale. Then, at stage II, the emergence of articulated intuition results, in both cases, from the partial correction of the primitive intuitions, and hence from a regulation and not directly from reversible operations. Finally, stage III sees the appearance of operational co-ordination: thanks to the grouping of the relations involved, the subject succeeds in deducing ages from the order of birth and the order of succession of births from the colligation of ages.

Since the confusion of age with height underlies all the original difficulties children experience in formulating ideas about age, we must now look more closely at the way in which these two concepts become dissociated in due course.

§3. *The age of animals and plants and the dissociation of age from height*

A good way to check our conclusions is to ask our subjects to compare two trees belonging to different species and of different heights, and to deduce from their answers how precisely they discover that the age of these trees depends uniquely on the date on which they were planted and not on their present size.

But before we discuss this particular test, we must quickly show that children up to 7–8 years of age confuse the ages not only of plants, but also of animals and even of minerals, with their size, and that they believe that the process of ageing ceases with the attainment of maximum size:

PAU (4; 9): Do small dogs grow older? *I don't know. I don't have any. No, I think they always remain the same size.* And flowers? *They fade if they aren't given enough water.* And stones? *No, they remain the same. If you cut them in two with a saw, well then they change.* And you, do you yourself grow older? *When I grow bigger.*

KER (4; 6) thinks that birds grow older. And plants? *No, they always remain the same.* And stones? *Yes, because I saw one that grew bigger.*

ER (5; 8): Do plants grow older? *Yes, because they fade.* And horses? *Yes, they grow older because there are big ones and small ones.* And stones? *Some are older and others younger because there are big and small stones.*

DOR (6; 9) thinks that all the horses in the street are the same age because they are the same size.

GIS (6; 1) says that dogs grow older *because they grow bigger*, but that stones do not grow older *because they always remain as they are*.

FIN (7; 2) thinks that small dogs grow older. And do trees grow older every year? *Oh no, they don't have any age.* Why? *They don't grow bigger.*

On the other hand, from the age of 7–8 years, the idea of ageing begins to be dissociated from that of increase in size and height, and to be treated as a function of time:

DOUR (7; 5) thinks that plants, dogs, horses and he himself all age, and that from one spring to the next, they all grow 'one year older'.

DORB (7; 6) thinks that dogs and horses 'grow older all the time'. And trees? *Yes, because first of all there is winter and later all the leaves come back again.*

GIL (7; 9): *Everything grows older.* What about stones, don't they stay the same age? *No, they don't.*

It was in order to make these tests more precise that we first decided to ask our subjects about the age of two trees, represented by separate drawings. We produce two pieces of cardboard of the same size, one depicting a poplar (9 cm.) with a large and strong trunk, and the other depicting a different tree (6·5 cm.) with a thin and twisted stem and its leaves combined into a broad crown. Both trees have brown trunks and bright green leaves.

We tell the child the following story: 'One day, when I went out walking I saw these two trees, and drew them just as they were. Are they the same kind? (The child quite naturally says that they are not and is asked to specify the differences.) You are right, they are different species: one grows taller and the other grows thicker, one has a straight and thick trunk, the other has a thin and twisted trunk. They are like people, they don't resemble each other at all. And also like dogs: as you know, there are bulldogs, basset hounds, St. Bernards, etc. Trees, too, need not be of the same kind, they don't always grow in the same way.' After this preamble, we tell the child: 'Now I would like you to tell me, simply by looking at these drawings, which of these two trees is older and if you can be sure that you are right.' If the child bases his answer on the height of the tree, as many small children will do, we pursue the matter by raising as many objects as we can: 'But aren't there old and young people? Is a large man always older than a small one? etc.'

Now, of the forty or so 4–10-year-old subjects examined, all those over the age of 9 gave the correct answers, and all those from 4–6 years gave the wrong ones. At the age of 7, one in three was right, and at the age of 8 roughly two in three were right. The answers can be classified as follows: at stage I there is a complete lack of differentiation between age and size, and the subjects remain deaf to all arguments; at stage II, there is a gradual differentiation; and at stage III there is complete dissociation between age and size—presented with the two trees, the subject either refuses to guess their respective ages or else puts forward various hypotheses but, in any case, he is certain that only information about the date of planting can settle the question satisfactorily:

Here, to begin with, are a few examples from stage I:

ROH (4; 6): Is one of these two older than the other? *Oh yes, the tall one.* Why? *Because it is tall.* I think it may well be the other way round. *I don't know but I would say it's the taller one.* Can't a tiny tree ever be older than a big one? *Oh no, no, no!* (with an air of saying: you needn't mock me!).

ZUR (4; 5): *That one is 5½ and that one 4½.* Why? *Because it's bigger.* Can't one be older than someone and still be smaller? *Yes.* In that case, mightn't the big tree be younger than the other one? *No.*

LEA (4; 6). *The thick one is one year old and the tall one is two years old.* Are you quite certain? *Yes.* Can't one be bigger and yet be younger than someone else? *That never happens.*

CLAUD (5; 5): *It's the bigger one.* Can you be quite sure? *Absolutely.* Which one was born first? *The other.* Why? *Because it's smaller.* Does being born first mean older or younger? *Younger.*

ROB (5; 6): *This one is bigger.* Could the other one be older all the same? *No.* Are you sure? *Quite sure.* But Eric is bigger than you. Is he older than you or younger? *Younger.* But he is bigger than you? *Oh, only a little bit.* But you see that someone smaller can, in fact, be older, don't you? *Yes.* So can we tell which of these two trees is the older one? *Yes, the big one.*

ODE (6; 8): *The tall one is the older one.* Why? *Because it's bigger.* Are you sure? *Yes.* Couldn't the thick one be older? *Yes, the thick one could be older than the tall one.*

ARL (7; 10): *The tall one.* How do you know? *Because it's bigger.* But surely they're not of the same kind? *No.* So they don't grow at the same rate. So can we really be sure? *Oh yes, because it's bigger.*

DAR (7; 10): *The tall one is older.* Why? *Because it grows more quickly* (!) *than the other one.* So which one is older? *The tall one.* Were they born on the same day? *No, the big one was born first.* Was a dwarf at the circus born before or after you? *Before, but he didn't grow.* So is he younger or older than you? *Older.* So can't a tree be planted first and yet remain smaller? *It happens sometimes.* So could you swear that the bigger one is the older one? *Oh yes, it's the older one all right.*

Such then are the initial reactions: age is proportional to size. We have met this lack of differentiation in the case of the age of people, and these supplementary facts merely serve to emphasize how deep-rooted it really is. Now this type of reaction is fully comparable to the child's inability to distinguish weight from size;[1] in both cases he remains deaf to all arguments. Another striking point is the logical incoherence of these children: several of them agree that one can be both smaller and older, and yet fail to conclude that it is impossible to tell the age of different species of trees by their heights alone. For them the exception, therefore, does not disprove the rule. Their resistance is, so to speak, of a purely moral kind: they feel that a general law is at stake. More precisely, their arguments are transductive and ignore the logical 'whole' characteristic of operational generalizations. That is why Rob could say that though trees could be older and smaller, the big tree must be older all the same.[2]

Between these initial reactions and the correct ones, there exists an intermediate stage from which we shall quote a few examples. Here hesitant replies go hand in hand with a gradual differentiation of the two concepts:

GROS (5; 11): *The tall one is the older of the two.* How do you know? *Because it was planted first.* But how do you know it was planted first? *Because it's the bigger one.* But you must remember that they're not of the same kind. They don't grow at the same rate. So? *We should have to know their age. Still, it's the tall one which was planted first.* Are you sure? *No, because I didn't plant it myself.* Could the fat one be the older of the two? *Yes, because it didn't grow.*

[1] See Piaget and Inhelder, *Le Développement des Quantités chez l'Enfant*, Chapters VII and IX.
[2] Cf. the confusion, at the prelogical level of 'although' with 'because'; see *Le Jugement et le Raisonnement chez l'Enfant*, Chapter I.

VET (7; 10) is sure that the two trees are not of the same age *because they're not the same. The big one grows taller but the other one grows rounder.* Even so, he continues to judge by size. Could it be the other way round? *Yes, the tall one could become smaller and the round one bigger.*

MAR (5; 2: an advanced subject) thinks that the two trees *may perhaps be the same age because this one grows taller and the other one thicker.* So can you tell which one is older? *Yes, it may be the tall one because it grows upwards.* Can we be sure of that? *Only if the tall one grew thicker as well.* What do you think? *The tall one is older.* Are you sure? *Not altogether, because the other one could have been planted first.*

Let us briefly analyse these reactions. On the one hand, they bear witness to the emergence of a sense of relativity leading to the distinction between age and growth, and consequently between age and size: Gros argued that the small tree might have stopped growing, Vet that it might have grown 'rounder'. Mar concluded, and this is very remarkable for a child of his age, that before the age of two trees can be compared their growth must be reduced to a common form: 'only if the tall one grew thicker as well'. Nevertheless, each of these subjects stuck to the assumption that size varies with age, so that, all other things being equal, a big tree must necessarily be older than a small one. All in all, therefore, they had not yet fully succeeded in divorcing time from space and hence age from size, although the elements of this differentiation were already present.

Here, finally, are some examples from stage III, where the dissociation has become complete:

GIL (7; 5): *This one must be older, because it is bigger.* How do you know? *By the size, but I could be wrong, because some big trees are young, trees don't all grow in the same way.* Could they be the same age? *Yes, they could be, one might have grown taller while the other grew rounder, but one can't really tell because there are several things* (to be considered). *There are several kinds of trees. One can never tell.* Who can tell? *The man who planted them.*

DAR (7; 6): *They may be the same age, because one is thick and the other one is tall.* What do you think? *Perhaps the tall one is the older one, but that's just a guess: one would have to know when they were planted.*

BIR (8 years): *The big one may be older, but that's not certain because*

216

big trees can be old or young. So? *We have to know when they were planted.*

ED (9 years): *One can't tell, because yew trees grow very slowly and lime trees very quickly.*

We may therefore take it that it is thanks to the explicit (Gil and Ed) or implicit (Dar and Gir) introduction of the idea of different growth-rates that age finally becomes differentiated from size. This would be fully in accord with everything we have been saying about stage III reactions to physical time: the dissociation of duration from the space traversed based on the operational conception of differences in velocity. It is worth noting, moreover, that this dissociation is necessarily based on the order of succession (and *vice versa*): in the present case, each of our subjects, by his very rejection of the criterion of size, is, in effect, driven directly and spontaneously to the conclusion that the planting time of trees is the sole criterion for determining their age.

In view of this close similarity between the development of the concept of age and that of physical time, it seemed worth the trouble to look more closely at the operational mechanisms involved. The child's conception of people's age could, in effect, be based not simply on size but also on mental development: people's wisdom, knowledge, etc. Why then, although they appreciate that people can grow in stature as well as in grace, do children base their judgements on stature alone and this in face of perpetual contradictions? The reason, as we shall see during our discussion of psychological time, is undoubtedly that consciousness proceeds from the outside to the inside, that the construction of inner time presupposes a gradual process of 'subjectivation' and that it is not directly 'given'. But before looking further into this matter, we must first try to discover by what operations age becomes divorced from physical growth. We have just said that this is due to the intervention of the concept of 'growth-rate' (just as, with physical time, duration is divorced from space when differences in velocity are taken into consideration). But how, precisely, does this new concept arise and along what precise operational paths does it proceed? This is what we shall now examine more closely.

§4. *The correspondence of age to unequal rates of growth*

In the first two §§ of this chapter we saw that the child's conception of the age of people and of physical time develops along parallel paths: distorted intuitions of succession and duration are followed by articulated intuitions of one without direct effects on the other, and finally by operational co-ordination of the two concepts. Now, the reason for this complete similarity, as we suggested, was that in both cases time is a co-ordination of motions and velocities. Hence before this co-ordination has been effected, duration is necessarily confused with the path traversed or the work done, i.e. age is confused with size. On the other hand, the dissociation of age from size (like the dissociation of duration from the space traversed) must follow from this very co-ordination, i.e. from the introduction (see §3) of the concept of growth rate and above all from the appreciation of differences in this rate.

It is this hypothesis which we shall now verify and develop further. If the views we have presented are correct, the child begins by evaluating growth by its material results alone (height), and so comes to believe that greater stature necessarily corresponds to greater age, irrespective of the rate of growth. On the other hand, as soon as different growth-rates are introduced, age is no longer treated as being proportional to height alone, but to height relative to the rate of growth. In other words, just as physical time is equal to distance/velocity, so age is equal to height/growth rate.

We at first tried to check this hypothesis by presenting our subjects with drawings representing people at different times of life, whose ages could be computed by synchronization of their heights, but since the subjects produced too many automatic verbal responses, we decided to use the following method instead:

The child is presented with eleven drawings on cards measuring 10 × 15 cm., and depicting apple and pear trees. These trees are highly schematized (a high degree of schematization is essential if the child is not to become bogged down in unimportant details): they are drawn in the forms of circles of different sizes resting on a rigid trunk and bearing either small round and red apples, or small elongated yellow pears, both at equal intervals. The number of fruits is proportional to the size of the trees. There are six apple trees which we shall call A_1 (13 mm. diameter and 4 apples), A_2 (30 mm. diameter and 7 apples), A_3 (40 mm. and 13 apples), A_4 (60 mm. and 27 apples), A_5 (70 mm. and 36 apples) and A_6 (80 mm. and 44 apples). Their respective heights are 1·5; 4·5; 6; 9; 10·5 and 12 mm. from the base of the trunk.

There are five pear trees which we shall call P_1 (12 mm. diameter and 4 pears), P_2 (28 mm. and 7 pears), P_3 (60 mm. and 27 pears), P_4 (87 mm. and 46 pears) and P_5 (99 mm. and 74 pears); their heights are 1·5; 4; 9; 13 and 15 cm. respectively.

The children are told that the first set of drawings represents one and the same apple tree, 'photographed' each year on the same date: A_1 is the day on which the apple tree was planted (the children themselves use the term 'one year old' for that date and we have adopted the same convention); A_2 the year of its first anniversary (2 years); A_3 the year of its next anniversary (3 years); and so on. The children are than asked to arrange the 'photographs' by age and all of them (from 5; 0 onwards) manage to do so without difficulty, thus showing the purely intuitive nature of this problem.

Once the seriation of the apple trees has been completed, the children are told that, when the apple tree was 2 years old, a small pear tree was planted (P_1 is placed above A_2). Next all the remaining drawings of the pear (P_2–P_5) are placed on the table at random, and the children are told once again that this tree was photographed each year on the day of its anniversary. Next, we ask them to seriate the remaining four pear trees by first pointing out the 'photograph' that was taken the year after P_1, and then placing P_2 on top of A_3, P_3 on top of A_4, P_4 on top of A_5, and P_5 on top of A_6.

The correct spatial arrangement of the drawings therefore implies the simultaneity of P_1 and A_2, P_2 and A_3, etc., without our having to ask such questions as 'Which photograph was taken of the pear tree the day this one was taken of the apple tree?', and *vice versa*. The problem of correspondence will be examined in connection with a simpler test in the following §; here we simply concentrate on differences in the rate of growth, based on: $P_1 < A_2$; $P_2 < A_3$; $(P_3 = A_4)$; $P_4 > A_5$ and $P_5 > A_6$. The pear tree thus outgrows the apple tree from $P_3 = A_4$.

In other words, we simply try to find out when and how the child succeeds in dissociating age from height and thus comes to realize that duration (age) is uniquely determined by the date on which the tree was planted. But in this test, in contrast to the last, the child is forced, by the preliminary double seriation, to bear the growth-rates in mind, no matter whether he judges age by size alone or by the co-ordination of the starting and finishing points of the growing process (duration).

We accordingly ask our subjects (1) which tree is older during a particular year; and (2) by how many years. Up to $A_4 = P_3$, these questions present no difficulty, since the sizes are still proportional to the ages. But it is nevertheless important to start in this way, for it helps us to analyse the remaining reactions. It goes without saying, moreover, that in the course of our main questions, we also ask a number of peripheral questions on the subject of growth, etc.

Now, the reactions we have obtained are perfectly coherent and fully bear out our general theory. The correct answers, which call for the operational co-ordination of the growth-rates, are given by only some 50 per cent of subjects between the ages (6; 6) and (7; 6) and by more than 75 per cent of subjects between the ages of (7; 6) and (9; 0). Stage I is characterized by a total lack of differentiation between size and age, and stage II by an increasing differentiation due to articulated intuitions or intuitive regulations, but not to proper grouping.

Here are some examples from Stage I:

Joc (5; 6) succeeds in seriating the apple trees by saying *one year, two years, three years*, etc. Now look, when the apple tree was two years old, we planted this pear tree. Which of the two is older? *The apple tree.* And the next year? *Still the apple tree.* And the year afterwards? Look at these photographs which were taken on the same day ($A_4 = P_3$). *The pear tree.* Why? *Because it has more pears* (incorrect, both trees have 27 fruits). And what about here (A_5 and P_4)? *The pear tree.* How old is it? (Joc counts one at a time.) *4 years.* And the apple tree? (Counts while pointing with his finger.) *5 years.* Which is the older of the two? *The pear tree.* Why? *Because it is 4 years old.* Is four years older than five years?

Five years is older. So which one is older? *I don't know . . . the pear tree because it has more pears.*

Mic (5; 7) arranges the series by trial and error, and says that the apple tree is older until A_3. As for A_4 and P_3, he says: *Wait a minute* (he points to the two drawings). *They are the same age.* But do you remember when they were planted? *Yes* (he points to P_1 and A_2). So? *They are the same age.* And these (A_5 and P_4)? *The pear tree is older.* And in twenty years' time? *Both of them will be the same age.*

Gis (6; 1) arranges the two series correctly after an initial mistake which he corrects spontaneously. (A_3 and P_2)? *The apple tree.* And (A_5 and P_4)? *The pear tree.* Why? *Because it's grown more quickly.* But can a tree be older one year and younger the next? *Yes.* Could A_5 possibly be older than P_4? *No.* But which was born first? *The apple tree.* And does that make no difference to its age? *No.* How old is (P_5)? *5 years.* And (A_6)? *5 years, no, 6 years. The pear tree is older.* When is one older: at 5 years or at 6 years? *6 years.* Which is older (P_5 or A_6)? *The pear tree.*

Ode (6; 8) arranges the whole series correctly and declares that P_1 is one year younger than A_2, but that P_4 *is older than* (A_5). Are you sure? *Yes, because it's bigger.* But which is older (A_3 or P_2)? *The apple tree because it's bigger.* And when the two trees will be very old? *The pear tree will be older because it's already a little older here* (P_5) *and the apple tree is already a little younger* (A_6). Does it make no difference that the apple tree was born one year before the pear? *Yes. The apple tree was older at first.* And when they'll be very old? *The pear tree will be the older one.*

Phi (6; 8): *The pear tree grows more quickly: so here* (P_3) *it's become the same age.*

Jen (7; 2): *The apple tree is older first and the pear tree next.* How many years after the apple tree was the pear tree born? *One year.* And what happened during the years that I took the photographs? *The apple tree was younger because it is smaller.*

These replies show quite clearly that, these children who are quite capable of seriating the 'photographs' and though they understand perfectly well that there is a gap of one year between each set, nevertheless fail to dissociate the real (as opposed to the nominal) age of the trees from their size. On the one hand, they are not concerned with the order of births, as if it in no way influenced the age: (e.g. Mic, Gis and Jen). Ode and Jen even went so far as to say that the apple tree was older first and the pear tree next. Others again completely overlook the ages they themselves had mentioned (e.g. Joc). On the other hand, and this is the crucial point, the more rapid growth of the pear tree is interpreted as an inversion of the order of ages, and hence as being subject to a different time from that of the apple tree: 'It grew more quickly', Gis said explicitly of the pear tree and concluded that it must be older than the apple tree from the moment it starts outgrowing it. Similarly, Phi argued that 'the pear tree grows more quickly, so here (P_3) it's become the same age (as the apple tree)'. Whence the inversion of the actual ages: 'The pear tree will be older (at the end of its life) because it is already a little older here (P_5) and the apple tree is already a little younger (A_6)' (Ode).

In short, these replies represent the explicit assertion that time is heterogeneous, and that duration is independent of the order of succession. The same attitude was also expressed by children at stage I discussed in earlier chapters but only in an implicit way.

During stage II, the child becomes conscious of the real problem, and vacillates between undifferentiated, heterogeneous time, and homogeneous time divorced from the spatial order:

MIG (5; 11) after hesitating about the respective ages of P_5 and A_6, finally concludes that the apple tree is older *because it is 6 years and the other 5 years*, but adds by way of justification: *The apple tree grows more quickly because it was planted first.*

PIG (6; 8): (P_4) *is older than* (A_5). *Oh no, the apple tree is older, because it's 5 and the pear tree is only 4.* And what about these (P_5 and A_6)? *The pear tree is older because it has more fruits.* Is that right? *Oh no, it's the apple tree because it's 6 years old and the pear tree is 5 years old.*

SER (7; 5): (A_3 and P_2)? *The apple tree is older because it is 3 and the pear tree only 2.* And these (P_4 and A_5)? *The pear tree is older.* Why? *Because it's 4 years and the apple tree is 5 years. Oh no, it's the apple tree. No, the pear tree is older because it's bigger.* And which will be the older when both of them are full-grown? *The pear tree.* Look again. Tell me which of these two is older (A_2 and P_1)? (A_2). And of these (A_3 and P_2)? (A_3). And of these (A_4 and P_3)? (A_4) And of these (A_5 and P_4)? (A_5). Why were you wrong before? *Because I thought that the apple tree was* (must be) *older than the pear tree.* And can one tell which will be older in a few years' time? *No, because the pear tree is bigger in size but younger.* But which one do you yourself think will be older? *The apple tree all the same.*

ULR (7; 10): (A_4 and P_3)? *The apple tree is older.* And (A_5 and P_4)? *The apple tree, because it was born first. Oh no, that's not right, because the pear tree is bigger.* Think again. *The apple tree, because it came earlier.* And (A_6 and P_5)? *The pear tree, because it's bigger.* Mightn't the apple tree be older that year? *No.* Without looking at the pictures, can you tell me which one is older; you see, I forget. *The apple tree, because it came first.* And when both will be very old, will they be the same age or will one always be older than the other? *One will always be older: the pear tree. Oh no, the apple tree, it will always be one year older.*

These children therefore begin with a failure to dissociate age from size: 'The apple tree grows more quickly because it was planted first' (Mig) and 'I thought that the apple tree (must be) older than the pear tree' (Ser). Then, with Pig, Ser and Ulr, we see the emergence of dissociation, but by way of purely intuitive regulation: the pear tree is thought to be older or younger depending on whether attention is focused on the order of birth or on size. That is why Ser refused to predict the future age of the tree on the grounds that 'the pear tree is bigger in size but younger'.

At stage III, finally, all these contradictions are removed by the grouping of successions and durations, on the one hand, and of time, space and the rate of growth on the other hand (two syntheses which are in fact identical, since time is the co-ordination of motions:

PAU (7; 2): (A_5 and P_4)? *The apple tree is older because it was planted first.* And (A_6 and P_5)? *The same. It makes no difference that one of them is bigger. I have a friend who is bigger than me and who is only 6 years old.* And when they will be very old trees? *The apple tree will always be one year older.*

GIL (7; 9): *The apple tree is always older, because it was planted first. The pear tree grows more quickly, but the apple tree is older.*

GIST (9 years): *The pear tree grows more quickly, but one can be older and smaller or younger and bigger.*

More clearly than in any other sphere, the conception of time is here bound up with intuitive ideas of motion, first evaluated in terms of their end points (in this particular case the heights of the trees). Then, after a phase of differentiation, during which velocity is no longer simply linked to the intuitive idea of 'outstripping', time becomes divorced from space and acquires a special structure based on the systematic correlation of durations (ages) and the succession of events (births and anniversaries). That is why children at stage III apply growth-rates in quite a different way than do children at stage I. During the latter, age is equated to height because the rate of growth, like time itself, is assessed in terms of spatial end points alone—the starting points are completely ignored. At stage III, on the other hand, the growth-rate is treated as a ratio, and it is this ratio which permits the correlation of different growth-rates and hence the consideration of durations and ages independently of space and height.

§5. *The correspondence of ages with equal growth-rates*

At the risk of exhausting the reader's patience (who, moreover, is free to skip this final paragraph) we shall go on to describe a control experiment, in which the growth-rates of the two trees are kept constant.

To avoid complications resulting from the measurement of heights, we use drawings of two trees (a plum and an orange) that bear one extra fruit each year. In other words, the orange tree is represented by a branch bearing 1, then 2 ... 5 oranges (Or_1, Or_2, ... Or_5) corresponding to 1, 2, ... 5 years, and the plum tree by a branch bearing 1 ... 5 plums (Pl_1, ... Pl_5). We also tell the child that the plum tree (Pl_1) was planted when the orange tree was two years old (Or_2).

The problem is then simply to correlate the respective ages of the two trees. Now, the results we obtained were as follows: children from 4 to $5\frac{1}{2}$ years proved generally unable to solve the problem; 50 per cent of those from $5\frac{1}{2}$ to $6\frac{1}{2}$ years gave the correct replies; and so did more than 80 per cent of those from $6\frac{1}{2}$ to $7\frac{1}{2}$ years. This test thus provides us with excellent corroboration of what we have said about the differences between reactions at stages I and III: there is complete failure at stage I, during which temporal succession is still confused with spatial succession (in this particular case the order of births is confused with the number of fruits), but there is complete success with articulated intuition, simply because the order of birth in this test is no longer affected by differences in the growth-rate. The test therefore has no relevance for stage III where these complications do not matter in any case.

Let us note, moreover, that two distinct factors intervene in the double seriation of the drawings. There is first of all the seriation of the cardinal numbers 1, 2, . . . 5, for both oranges and plums. Now, this simple seriation can be performed by all normal children from the ages of five years onwards and often by younger children still. Thus only a few 4-year-olds had some difficulty, either because they could not count as far as five, or else because of fantastic personal ideas about age. But then there is also the problem of correlating Or_1 and O; Or_2 and Pl_1; Or_3 and Pl_2, . . . Or_5 and Pl_4 and finally O and Pl_5. It is evident that this kind of 'skew' correspondence causes all sorts of difficulties at stage I, which are highly interesting in themselves because they aid our understanding of the time relations involved (cf. the 'skew' correspondence discussed in Chapter One).

Here are some examples from stage I:

ED (4; 9) succeeds in arranging the orange trees in correct order. He is then told that the plum tree was born one year later. It was planted when the orange tree was already two years old, and we place Pl_1 on top of Or_2. Which of the two is older? *The plum tree.* Why? *Because it is darker.* But if it's born a year later? . . . Were you born before your little brother? *Yes.* So which of you is older? *Me.* And which of these two trees? *The orange tree.* Well now, each year, at the same time, we take a photograph of the orange tree and a photograph of the plum tree. Choose the photos which were taken at the same time as these (Or_3; Or_4 and Or_5). (He places Pl_1 —Pl_5 on top of Or_2—Or_5) Is this correct? . . . When was the plum tree born? *One year later.* (He now places Pl_3 on top of Or_3; Pl_4 on top of Or_4, and Pl_5 on top of Or_5. As for Pl_2, he puts it between Pl_1 [which is on top of Or_2] and Pl_3.) (His arrangement is corrected and the problem explained once again.) How old are (Pl_1 and Or_2)? *One year and two years.* And (Pl_4 and Or_5)? *The orange tree is older.* By how much? *I don't know.* And (Pl_3 and Or_4)? *The plum tree is older* Which one was born first? *The orange tree.* And when they will be very old, will one of them still be older than the other? *It'll be the same thing.*

Joc (5; 6). Same beginning. Pl_1 is older than Or_2 *because it is violet.*
Joc decides to match Or_3 with Pl_3, and after we have re-explained
the problem, he finally arrives at the following correspondences:
Pl_1 with Or_2; Pl_2 with Or_3; Pl_4 with Or_4; and Pl_5 with Or_5. He then
places the remaining plum tree, Pl_3 on top of Or_1. We correct his
mistake. Which of these (Pl_1 and Or_2) is the older? *The orange tree.*
Why? *It is two years old.* And will it always be a year older, even
when the two trees are big? *I don't know.* Is it possible to tell?
No.

We need not dwell on these initial failures, all of which are
much of a kind. Let us merely repeat that subjects at this stage
fail to equate 'first-born' with 'older', simply because they fail
to relate age with the order of births: Pl_1 is older than Or_2,
although planted after it, 'because it is darker', or 'violet', etc.
Let us also note the almost total failure to grasp the 'skew'
correspondence (shift of one year). No matter how often the
initial data are repeated, the subjects, even when they have
understood them, do not manage to keep them in mind. Finally,
let us mention the fact (which does not appear clearly from the
extracts we have quoted but which strikes one incessantly during
the test itself) that, as soon as the questions become at all complicated, subjects at this level have a marked tendency to erase,
so to speak, the identity of the tree as they pass from one
drawing to the next. True, they do not state explicitly that they
are looking at a different tree (for instance in passing from Pl_1
to Pl_2), but they reason as if they were. Now, when we followed
up a study by M. Luquet of the difficulties children under the
ages of 6–7 years have in grasping the method of telling a story
by successive drawings ('Epinal pictures'), we found that the
same difficulties beset their identification of people represented
by a succession of pictures,[1] and for the same reasons: the
problem of arranging past episodes in the correct time sequence.
The present observations confirm this view: because their ideas
of 'before' and 'after' are thrown out of gear by the shift of one
year, these children go on to distinguish as many trees and
individuals as there are drawings; in short, they find that the

[1] See Margairez and Piaget: 'La Structure des récits', *Arch. Psychol.* XIX,
pp. 232ff. and Krafft and Piaget: *L'Ordre des événements, ibid.,* XIX, p.
332. For the results classified by age, see Chapter Ten, §4, of the present
work.

events of the story are too complex to be fitted into a unique system. It goes without saying, moreover, that the age when this confusion appears and disappears varies with the nature of the story. In the case of our apple and pear trees, for example, it disappears earlier (at about 5 years) than in that of the orange and plum trees.

Between stages I and II proper, there is an intermediate stage characterized by correct replies as to the present ages of the two trees but not yet as to their future ages: the one-year difference in age is grasped in the present because there are no differences in the growth-rate, and because the number of fruits indicates the number of years. However, for lack of articulated intuition, these differences cannot yet be projected into the future:

GRI (6; 6) succeeds in co-seriating the two sets of drawings. Which tree is older (Or_3 or Pl_2)? *The orange tree because it has more fruits.* If here (underneath Pl_5) we had a photograph of the orange tree, how old would it be? *6 years and 6 fruits.* And what age will the two trees be when they are very old? The same age, or will one be older than the other? *The same age.*

CET (5; 11): Which is older (Or_3 or Pl_2)? *The orange tree because it is 3 and the plum tree is only 2.* (The drawings, which she had arranged correctly, are mixed up again.) Find me the picture of the plum tree which was made when the orange tree was 4 years old. (She chooses Pl_4 but immediately corrects it to Pl_3.) *But when they are old they'll be the same age.*

Here, finally, two successful tests at stage II:

ÉTE (6; 8) produces the correct series, observing the shift of one year straight away: Which tree is older this year (Or_4 or Pl_3)? *It's the orange tree because it came one year earlier.* They are going to grow into very big trees, soon. Will one of them be older than the other or will they both be the same age? *The orange tree will always be older because it was planted a year earlier than the plum tree.*

MARL (6; 11) also produces the correct series: (Pl_4 or Or_5)? *The orange tree is one year older, because it has an extra year.* Will the plum tree ever catch up with the orange tree? *No, they both grow the same way.* But what about when they are very old trees? *The orange tree will always be older.*

We see that these subjects have made progress in two related respects: they justify the greater age of the orange tree by the

227

fact that it was planted one year earlier and not only by the number of fruits, or by counting the years cardinally, and they think that the difference of one year will persist until the end of the trees' lives.

Now, while these two reactions occur together in the case of the last two subjects, we saw that they are not normally combined until stage III. How can we explain this exception to the general rule? It arises precisely because the rates of growth, in this particular case, are equal, so that the problem of the conservation of age differences does not involve the co-ordination of different velocities, but merely the conservation of a common velocity. As Marl put it so well, the orange tree will always be older than the plum tree because 'they both grow the same way'. The answers of these subjects, though quite correct, therefore do not involve anything more than an intuitive grasp of duration: they are based on the intuitive realization that the two growth-rates are equal. Our control experiment was therefore highly instructive: being much simpler than that described in §4, it provided us with an indirect proof of the rôle of the co-ordination of velocities.

§6. *Conclusion: The concept of age*

In our discussion of the child's conception of age, we arrived at two main conclusions, which, moreover, provide us with a useful bridge between our analysis of the development of physical time and that of psychological or inner time.

The first of these conclusions was that, far from setting out with a subjective conception of age, the child starts from the most external and most material criteria available to it: stature or height. One might argue that this is quite self-evident, and *a posteriori*, one is, in fact, justified in doing so. Nevertheless, when the age of persons is involved, and especially the age of the child itself and of members of his family, other criteria might have been used equally well. First of all, in comparing our own age to that of others, we often go by a kind of overall impression which, needless to say, is deceptive, but which the child might have applied far less critically than we do. Thus, as we saw, the child might easily have based his estimates on mental or moral development: older people know more than younger people do, they are less childish, play different games, seem wiser, etc. Finally, the child might have judged age in terms of memories: older people can recall many events that young people do not know about, etc. Now, far from proceeding from the inside to the outside, the child proceeds the other way round, and gradually corrects this false criterion (height) by the elaboration of true temporal concepts.

But what precisely is the nature of this elaboration? Here our second conclusion seems particularly illuminating: the construction of age follows a parallel path to the construction of physical time and, moreover, through fully comparable stages. The analysis of physical time has shown us that succession and duration are at first handled by means of incorrect and unrelated intuitions. Now, in the domain of age, one might have expected that the intuitive grasp of the order of births would lead directly to the grasp of corresponding ages, i.e. to the realization that a 7-year-old was not only born before a 6-year-old but that he was also one year older. However, our tests have shown that this is not the case, and that the two initial intuitions in this familiar field are as distorted and as incoherent as they are in that of physical time. Moreover, much as the gradual co-ordination of these two intuitions is based on the correlation of motions with different velocities and hence on the dissociation of temporal from spatial successions in the sphere of physical time, so it is the correlation of growth-rates which enables the child to dissociate age from height in the sphere of biological time. In the next chapter we shall see whether the same process also applies to the construction of psychological time.

CHAPTER TEN

Actions and Inner Duration[1]

The results described in the last chapter have shown us that children do not judge age by direct intuitions based on individual, inner time, but on height or size, i.e. by the most external of all possible criteria. This, as we suggested in the introduction to this section, is precisely what they do with the organization of psychological time, as well.

This view is borne out by everything we know about the memory of children, not least from the splendid work of Stern: the child retains a host of impressions and memories with a vivacity that is often disconcerting (because the impressions may be either correct or incorrect) but fails to fit them into a coherent system or to produce anything but the most confused estimates (or correlations) of durations. This is not at all surprising if we suppose that memory, far from being the pure object of Bergsonian philosophy and of early Freudianism, is, in fact, an 'elaboration', i.e. that it resurrects the past by a perpetual construction or reconstruction (Pierre Janet's *récit* or narrative). Now whether we accept this hypothesis fully or in part only, it goes without saying that inner time must call for the same organization as physical time, i.e. for the same seriations of successive states and for the same colligations of durations. Moreover, in classifying our memories, we must rely on the external results of our actions—i.e. on physical time itself—just as in classifying physical events we must necessarily rely on our memory.

As for the operational organization of psychological time, we could not possibly extend this already copious volume to include a systematic study of memory or of the structure of children's narratives, and must therefore refer the reader to two of our

[1] In collaboration with Mlle Esther Bussmann.

previous studies, namely *La Structure des récits et l'interpretation des images de Dawid chez l'Enfant* and our *La notion de l'ordre des événements et le test des images en désordre*.[1] Moreover, the experimental study of 'pure duration' by means of induced introspection comes up against the fundamental difficulty that this 'purity', far from constituting a 'direct datum of consciousness', is the product of a very subtle and highly intellectualized abstraction, and cannot therefore be examined directly as, for instance, a perception can. However, if we disregard intellectual reconstructions, psychological time becomes the time of current actions, rather than of dreams, reveries, or spontaneous memories, and is therefore open to experimental investigation.

In our tests, we ignore the problem of the order of succession, which is discussed in the two articles just mentioned, and simply concentrate on duration. To that purpose, we set our subjects a number of simple tasks and ask them to compare the durations (first method), or else we ask them to perform one and the same task more (or less) quickly but during the same time (second method). Now the results of these simple tests reveal one interesting fact at once: whenever the task is of a concrete rather than purely reflective kind, the youngest of our subjects do not assess its duration by direct introspection, but in objective, or rather in 'realist', terms: they rely on the results of the action or on its rapidity, i.e. on criteria that are fully comparable to those they use in estimating physical time. Older children, on the other hand, do use introspection, applying their internalizations of earlier concepts directly to the action under review, improving or correcting their estimates as they gain greater facility in performing operations with time.

§1. *The rapidity of actions*

To make certain that our subjects understand what we mean by duration, we begin by rapping out brief and long intervals on the table. Once the child has stated that the second interval is 'longer' or 'greater' than the first, or that there was a 'longer time' between the last two raps than between the first two, we can proceed with the test itself. We give the child a sheet of paper and ask him to draw a number of strokes, working as

[1] *Arch. Psychol.*, Vol. XIX (1925–1926).

neatly and carefully as possible. We stop the work after 15 seconds, and then ask the child to draw the strokes as quickly as possible. We stop him again after 15 seconds, and ask which, if any, of the two tasks took longer (first technique). Next we ask him to draw the strokes as quickly as possible and to stop as soon as he thinks he has drawn the same number of strokes as before (second technique).[1] The second technique has proved quite useless with most 4-year-olds, and often even with children of 5, because they are quite unable to judge time while they are busily working. However, though this is a statistical disadvantage, it proves highly instructive from the analytical point of view, a point to which we shall be returning.

The construction of psychological time does not proceed by way of the three distinct stages characteristic of the construction of physical time. There is, in fact, a much greater degree of continuity running through the entire process, and some of the original illusions persist, in the same qualitative forms, even into adulthood. Here we must distinguish three factors. First of all there is illusion as such, i.e. those systematic errors which cause our subjects to misjudge the duration of certain actions or experiences because of the inner tensions involved. Next, we have the reactions to the original illusion in the form either of precritical acceptance of the perceptive data or else of gradual corrections, first by the use of regulations and later by operational comparisons. Thirdly, and this is essential, we must distinguish between the child's impression of duration while the action is taking place, and subsequent assessments based on memory and hence on reasoning. Everyone knows that a given task may seem short while it is being done quickly, but very long and colourful in retrospect. Conversely, a period of idleness will seem long while it lasts, but short in memory, and this precisely because nothing at all was happening in it. It goes without saying that the subject's powers of introspection will, for that very reason, play a large part in the evaluation of 'lived' durations.

Now, while these three factors enable us to contrast the reactions of older with younger children, they do not, as we have said, help us to distinguish three clear stages of develop-

[1] In order to avoid systematic errors, we sometimes start with the first technique, and at other times with the second.

ment. Let us therefore examine the reactions age by age and simply note the gradual progress.

From 4 to 5; 0, all our subjects (with the exception of one exceptionally intelligent boy) were agreed that drawing the strokes quickly takes longer than drawing them slowly, thus judging duration purely by the results of the work and not by any kind of inner feeling.

ED (4; 6) represents the lowest level: Do you know what we mean by a very short time? *No.* And by a long time? *No.* When you come home from school, is that a long or a short time? *A long time.* (The table is rapped twice at different intervals.) Which took longer, the first two raps or these? . . . Now look, will you draw some lines as neatly as you can. (He works for 15″.) Were you working for a short time? *Yes.* And now will you draw the lines very, very quickly (he is stopped after 15″). Did you work for a short or for a long time? *For a short time.* Did you work longer this time or last time? . . .

ROS (4; 7) distinguishes between raps at intervals of 20″ and 25″. He is asked to draw the lines slowly and then quickly (for 25″ each time): Did you work for the same time? *No.* Which took longer? *These* (rapid strokes). Why? *I don't know.* Which took the shortest time? *These* (slow strokes).

MIT (4; 11): Did you work for the same time? *No.* When did you work longer? *When I was drawing more quickly.*

MIR (5; 0). The table is rapped at an interval of 20″: Was that a short time or a long one? *A short one.* (Interval of 25″.) Was that the same? *No, this one was longer.* (He draws the strokes.) Draw them neatly (20″). Did that take a long or a short time? *A short time.* And now draw them very quickly (also 20″). Was that a short or a long time? *A short time, but longer than before.* Why? *Because it was longer.* We repeat the experiment in the reverse order, to avoid the possible influence of the initial comparison: same results.

We see, therefore, that these children judge time simply by the results of their actions: because they produce more lines when they work quickly, they think that the quick work must have taken longer than the slow. One might object that they are simply missing the point of the questions, i.e. that they think we are asking them to assess the physical time needed for drawing 10 to 12 strokes instead of only 5 to 6, and not their inner sense of duration. However, this raises the question of whether these subjects are, in fact, capable of making this distinction, i.e. whether or not their awareness of time proceeds from the outside to the inside.

Before we try to decide this matter, let us first note that the best proof that some of our subjects at least, fully understand the verbal import of our questions is precisely that one of our 4-year-olds was not only perfectly capable of distinguishing between the sense of time during the action and time as evaluated after the action had been completed, but also based his evaluations on the latter. Let us now look at the reactions of the more advanced subject:

PAU (4; 9) can distinguish between raps at intervals of 20″ and 25″. He is asked to draw strokes slowly and then more rapidly: Did you work for the same time? *No, it took me longer here* (rapid strokes). Why? *It went faster when I worked more quickly.* Then which took longer? *These here* (rapid strokes). Why? *Because it took more time.*

Though Pau therefore had sufficient introspective powers to appreciate that 'it went faster when I worked more quickly', he nevertheless concluded that the rapid action took 'longer'. Pau thus clearly distinguished 'lived' time from retrospective time, applying the same systematic error to both (shorter duration during and longer duration after an action). Why then did he attach greater weight to the retrospective assessment, thus incidentally confirming that our questions are perfectly understood? The answer is that he may not yet have developed sufficient familiarity with introspection, and thus simply rely on the results of the action: more strokes were drawn, so more time was needed. Pau therefore remained a realist, and this reliance on realism rather than on introspection is in full accord with egocentric behaviour in general.

Let us also note, in parentheses, how largely this initial reaction explains why small children commonly equate 'more rapid' with 'more time'. Now, if this is true of psychological time, it goes without saying that it applies *a fortiori* to the case of physical time.

Their realistic and egocentric conception of time explains why our second method cannot be used with very young children. We

234

shall see that the same problem persists with slightly older subjects as well. Thus 90 per cent of those between the ages of 5; 1 and 6; 0 invariably believe that work done rapidly takes more time than work done slowly:

Pie (5; 6). We rap the table at intervals of 20″ and 25″ and then at 25″ and 20″: Which took longer? *The second lot.* (correct) And now? *The first lot* (correct). Now we are going to draw some lines. Draw the first ones as carefully as you can. Good. And now draw them as quickly as you can. Good. (20″ for both and 7 extra strokes the second time): Did one lot take longer than the other? *Yes. The second.* Did it seem longer to you while you were drawing? *Yes.* Why? . . .

Jap (5; 7): *A short moment* for the slow work, and *a big moment* for the rapid strokes. Was one moment greater than the other? *Yes, that one* (rapid strokes). Why? *Because it was longer.*

Fred (5; 11). Same beginning: *The second time I took longer.* Why? *Because there was more of it.*

Chel (5; 10) 15″ and 15″: *The second lot took more time.* Why? *Because there are more lines.* But did the first time seem longer or shorter? *Shorter.*

Gis (6; 0). We begin with the rapid strokes to make certain that it is not simply the second task as such that seems longer: Now draw some more strokes but do it very quickly (25″). Did it take you a long or a short time? *A long time.* And now draw them very carefully, without hurrying (also 25″). Did it take a long or a short time? *A short time.* Which took you longer to do? *These* (the rapid strokes). Why? *It took a long time because there were more lines.*

And now for some examples of the second method used in conjunction with the first:

Jan (5; 9). 20″ with slow strokes: *A short time.* (20″ rapid strokes): *This time I worked longer.* Why do you think so? *Because I can see that I've made more lines.*

Second method: We stop the slow strokes after 12″. Now you are going to work as quickly as possible and stop at the same time as before. (He fails to stop in time.) Let's start again, you didn't stop at the right moment. (Fails to stop again.) Let's do it once more (we stop him after 10″ instead of 12″). Was that longer or shorter than before? *It was longer.* . . .

Lil (6; 0). Working slowly (20″): *This one took a short time.* Now do the same work for the same time but working as quickly as possible. (Lil draws the same number of strokes and stops at 13″.) Was that the same time? *Yes.* (Naturally the first lot of strokes is hidden while the child produces the second, nevertheless Lil drew the same number of strokes on both occasions.)

Here, finally, a subject who vacillates between the typical belief that time varies as the speed of working and the opposite view:

CLAN (5; 8). Slow strokes (25″): Long or short time? *A long time.* And now draw your strokes very quickly (25″). Was it the same time? *No, longer than before.* So did one take longer? *Yes.* Which one? *The first.* Why? *Because I did more work.* When did you do more work? *Oh! It took longer the second time because I did more work then.*

The reactions of these 5–6-year-olds show that they have learned to reason more precisely than the younger subjects— with a few exceptions, all of them associate longer durations with more rapid working 'because it takes longer' (the younger ones among them) or 'because there are more strokes' (the older ones)—in either case because the results are greater. In that respect, Clan's hesitations assume a particular significance: he was certain of only one thing: that doing more work takes more time. But then he was not quite sure whether 'more work' meant higher quality (slow work) or greater quantity (quickness). It would seem that a glimpse of introspection caused him momentarily to come down in favour of the first alternative, but that the second won out in the end.

As for the second method, we saw that Jan's failure was due to his lack of introspection in assessing the duration while the work was actually in progress, while Lil's failure resulted from the fact that she judged the duration purely by the number of strokes, i.e. without bothering about speeds.

Between the ages of 6; 1 and 7; 0, 80 per cent of our subjects still contend that the quicker the work the longer it is:

ROT (6; 4). We start with the rapid strokes (20″): Was that a long time or a short time? *A short time.* Did the time pass quickly or not? *It went quickly.* And now (slow work: again 20″)? *It took longer before.* Why? *Because there are fewer strokes.*

JAC (6; 7): Try to draw them carefully (15″). *A short time.* Now, work very quickly (15″). Was that a short time as well? *Yes.* Did one take longer than the other? *The second one did.* Why did it seem longer to you? *Because it took me longer to draw* (the rapid strokes!).

SYL (6; 8). 5 slow strokes and 15 rapid ones, both in 20″: *These* (the rapid ones) *took much less time but I worked longer at them.* (Cf. the case of Pau at 4; 9.)

JOS (6; 9): *It took much longer when I was drawing the lines quickly.*

And here are some reactions obtained with the second method:

KAT (6; 10). Slow lines: 20″. Repeat in 15″: *It was the same thing.*

CHA (6; 11). Slow 20″. Rapid: stops at 20″ but thinks that he was wrong: *This one took longer because there are more strokes and also because I was much quicker.*

Now for an intermediate reaction followed by an advanced reaction:

AN (6; 3): *It took more time with these* (slow strokes). Did you work longer with one lot? *Yes.* With which one? *With these* (slow strokes). Up to what number could you have counted while you were drawing these (the slow strokes)? *Up to three.* And with these (the rapid strokes)? *Up to six.* (An, therefore, still thinks that the more quickly she draws the longer it takes.)

DOR (6; 9) with the second method, equated 20″ of rapid work with 15″ of slow work. He therefore considered that the first took less time.

We see that, with the exception of Dor, all these subjects produced much the same reactions. It should be noted that, though Rot and Syl, like Pau at 4; 9, thought the work 'short' while it was being done, they nevertheless judged it 'long' after the event. Another typical reaction was that of Jac, who asserted that it takes longer to draw more quickly.

Between the ages of 7–8, on the other hand, only 50 per cent of our subjects evaluate durations in this way, while 50 per cent have come to rely on introspective assessments. Here are some of the less advanced reactions in this group:

PHI (7; 2). Working slowly (20″). And now do it very quickly. *This one* (working slowly) *took a short time and that one* (working rapidly) *took longer.* Why? *Because there were more of them.*

FRA (7; 6) similarly: *A longer time because I drew more lines.*

Sel (7; 3). Working slowly: *A short time* (17″). Now draw as quickly as possible but for the same length of time. (14″). *That's the same time.*

Now for some of the more advanced reactions:

Aud (7; 4). 20″ working slowly and then rapidly (first method): *It took the same time.* Why do you think so? *Because there were more of these* (the rapid strokes) *and less of those* (the slow strokes) *but they took the same time to make.*

Til (7; 8). First method (20″): When did you work longer? *The first time.* Why? *Because I was working slowly.* Up to what number would you have counted? *One minute.* And the second time? *Also one minute.* So they're the same? *Yes.* When did the time pass more quickly? *The second time* (rapid strokes).

Ky (7; 3). Second method. Identifies 15″ with 15″: Is that the same? *Yes. I was working more quickly but it took the same time.*

These last three cases clearly represent an advance on the first three: all of them were able to identify equal intervals, and this despite the fact that they realized (and stressed) that working more slowly *seems* to take longer.

Finally, of all the 10–13-year-olds tested by way of control, only a third reacted like the younger children, while two thirds reacted like the last three subjects. Here are some inferior (backward) responses:

Mar (10; 11): *Less time here* (slow strokes) *because I was working more slowly.* And with the second method, he equated 11″ of quick working with 13″ of slow working.

Al (13; 1): *It took less time for these* (slow strokes) *because I was working more slowly.* With the second method: 10″ of rapid work seemed to take *almost the same time* as 20″ of slow work.

And here are some superior reactions:

Sim (10; 8). First method (20″ slow): *Fairly long.* And now (20″ working quickly)? *Was it almost the same?* Did one lot seem to take longer? *The first lot may have taken just a little longer.*

Od (12; 8). First method. 20″: *Not very long* (working slowly). And these (rapid strokes)? *Almost the same thing.* Did one lot seem to take longer? *No, almost the same.*

Second method. 20″ of rapid work = 21″ of slow work. Hence practically correct.

CEC (12; 2). First method: 20″ of rapid work: *That went very quickly.* And now (20″ of slow work)? *It's the same thing. I went more slowly but I rather think it took the same time.*

Three things strike one in these reactions (including those of advanced subjects between the ages of 7 and 8). The first is that older children evaluate the time of an action by relying almost exclusively on the impressions they obtain during the action itself, and no longer on its tangible results. This is also borne out by the fact that they use such expressions as 'almost', 'I rather think', etc.

In the second place, their estimates are very much more accurate than those of the younger subjects, and are no longer simply based on the reversal of the original systematic error, i.e. they do not simply argue that the *slower* work must take longer. Instead, most of these subjects hold that the two durations are more or less equal. No doubt, the original error is first compensated by a simple regulation, and since the accuracy of perceptive regulations in general increases with age[1] it is only to be expected that it should also increase in the case of inner time. However, that is not the whole story for, as we shall show in a moment, in this particular case, operations are involved as well.

This brings us to our third, general, point. If we compare the primitive grasp of psychological time with that of physical time or even with the qualitative and operational construction of physical time at stage III, we cannot but conclude that the former constitutes an internalized differentiation of the latter, and this in two ways: (1) the illusions accompanying the evaluation of 'lived' durations are nothing other than the extension of the systematic errors characterizing the early, intuitive and egocentric conception of physical time. Thus when the younger subjects say 'it took longer because I drew more lines', they merely repeat the error we encountered at stage I in the construction of physical time: 'quicker = more time = a greater distance covered or more work done'. Conversely, the mistaken belief that a slow motion takes more time, is simply the false generalization of the correct physical relation 'quicker = less time' (stage II). (2) Above all, if the systematic errors in the evaluation of psychological time are simply the internal expressions of the errors

---

[1] See *Arch. Psychol.*, Vol. XXIX, pp. 1–107 (1942).

besetting intuitive time in general, we are entitled to say that the correction of these errors, i.e. the construction of a more correct conception of internal duration, is the result of the same qualitative operations that lead to the construction of the objective and logical conception of physical time. In effect, when Aud (7; 4) said: 'There were more of these (rapid strokes) and less of those (slow strokes) but they took the same time to make'; when Ky (7; 3) said: 'I was working more quickly, but it took the same time'; and when Cec (12; 2) said: 'I went more slowly but I rather think it took the same time', etc., etc., they were, in fact, subjecting their own actions to an overall operational judgement, i.e. to a system of coherent logical relations similar to those by which, on the plane of physical time, velocity is related to the path traversed. To the extent, therefore, that action is made the subject of reflection and not merely of intuition, i.e. that reflective analysis replaces pure introspection, the results of the action, its rapidity, and the various events which constitute it, become fused into a coherent framework, in which the order of succession and the colligation of durations are interrelated in precisely the same way as they are in the case of physical time. More precisely, the child co-ordinates his own time by fitting his actions into physical time, just as he co-ordinates physical time by relying on his memory of, and active contribution to, changes in the environment of which he forms an organic part.

In brief, the development of psychological time is both the internalized response to, and the explanation of, intuitive physical time—the internalized response because it involves the same intuitions and later the same operations, and the explanation because it remains intuitive only as long as the subject remains incapable of dissociating his own actions from their external results.

§1a. *Appendix: Verification by metronome test*

In order to discover whether young children maintain that time is directly proportional, and older children that it is inversely proportional, to velocity, even when they themselves do no active work, but simply listen to sounds produced with different rhythms, we introduce a metronome, beating first slowly and then quickly for 15″, and question them by the same two methods we have described in §1.

Now, two-thirds of the thirty or so 4–8-year-olds examined, asserted that the metronome takes longer to beat more quickly:

PAU (4; 8): *It took longer the second time, because it went faster.*

MIL (5; 0): *It went on for longer because it went quicker.*

PRI (7; 0): *It took longer because it went more quickly.*

With the second method, Tan (5; 9) equated 10″ of the rapid beat with 20″ of the slow beat, and Rob (5; 9) 20″ of the first with 50″ of the second! Kat (6; 10) went so far as to equate 20″ of the rapid beat with 75″ of the slow one, and subsequently 10″ of the slow beat with 6″ of the rapid one. When presented with the slow beat for 15″ and asked to stop the quick beat after the same interval, he stopped it at 7″!

Of the remaining subjects, approximately two-thirds, or two-ninths of the total number, held that the slow beat took longer:

FRED (5; 11): *When it went quicker, it seemed to take less time.*

PAU (7; 8): *More time when it went slowly, because it took much longer.*

Second method: 15″ of quick beat = 10″ of slow beat.

And one-ninth of the total number decided in favour of equality:

GIS (6; 0): *Both took a short time.* Second method: 18″ of slow beat = 22″ of quick beat.

By contrast, half the 10–12-year-old subjects favoured equality:

ODA (12; 8): *Almost the same thing.* Second method: 20″ of slow beat = 19″ of the rapid beat.

The other half was divided into two-thirds who thought that the slow beat took longer (e.g. 20″ slow beat = 25″ rapid beat, or 20″ rapid beat = 13″ slow beat, etc.) and one-third (one-sixth of the total number) who reacted much like the younger children (though with the second method their errors were smaller).

In short, these reactions are fully comparable to those obtained with the earlier tests: gradual inversion of the time/velocity ratio, and gradual decrease in the degree of error.

§2. *Durations and tasks of varying difficulty*

The tests described in §1 and §1a were but two of a host of possible ones. But then it was not our intention to present an exhaustive analysis, but merely to show that there is a high degree of correspondence between the construction of physical and psychological time. To the same purpose, we devised two further tests, calling for the correlation of the speed of actions with their inherent difficulties.

We saw that when two actions are almost of the same simplicity (drawing strokes slowly or quickly), young children judge that time is directly and older children that it is inversely, proportional to velocity, an error they gradually correct. But what happens when they are asked to compare the duration of two tasks with unequal difficulties, for instance, when they are told to fit a number of rectangular lead discs or triangular wooden discs into a box, using small pincers? Since the transfer of the lead, which is both heavier and also more difficult to pick up on account of its shape, seemingly involves 'more work', will the children think that it takes longer, or will they rather argue that the transfer of the wood takes longer, seeing that more wooden pieces can be shifted in the same time?

Let us again examine their reactions by age groups (2 years at a time).

In the 4–6 age group, we found that children from 4; 0 to 4; 6 were completely stumped by the problem, and did not even understand our questions.

Ed (4; 6). Reacted as he did to the earlier test.

Ros (4; 7) who was able to compare durations in the stroke test, thought that the lead 'takes a long time' but could make no further comparisons: (After the experiment.) Did one take longer than the other? *Oh no.* Did one take less time? *Oh yes.* Did it take you longer to put the iron into the box than the wood? *Oh . . . oh . . . a short time.*

On the other hand, a small minority thought that it takes longer to transfer the pieces of wood.

Pau (4; 11) began with the lead and says: *That took a long time.* (Wood): Longer or shorter? *A little longer with the bits of wood because I put more of them in* (he was quite wrong on this point as well: he had transferred the same number of pieces in 20").

This is the same type of reaction we met in §1. On the other hand, the majority of these subjects (between two-thirds and three-quarters) thought that the lead took longer than the wood:

JEA (5; 6) worked assiduously with the lead: *A little longer for the lead.* Why? *Because it's bigger.* (20" and 20").

CLAU (5; 8). 45" for each transfer: *A little longer with the lead.* Why? *Because there was more of it* (wrong). Look for yourself. *Oh no.* Do you still think that one of them took longer than the other? *Yes, it took longer with the lead.*

ROB (5; 9) also thought that the lead takes longer. With the second method he first transferred the wood (37") and stopped the lead at 17". He even said: *It took a bit longer with the pieces of lead.* Why? *One of them got caught.* The experiment was repeated: same result.

FRED (5; 11): *The wood took less time.* Why? *It was less heavy.*

GIS (6: 0): *The lead took longer, there was more of it.* (wrong).

LIL (6; 0): *The lead took longer; it was heavy.* With the second method, he nevertheless succeeded in equating 33" (lead) with 34" (wood).

We see that despite the paucity of the introspective data, these subjects agree that the transfer of the lead takes longer because it is more laborious, i.e. because 'it's bigger', 'one of them got caught', 'it's heavier', etc. Moreover, several subjects thought they had transferred a larger number of wooden pieces. But this error (cf. Clau and Lil) is characteristic of the tendency of small children to think that the time it takes to accomplish a task is proportional to the speed and the work done. In this respect it is remarkable that the only subject who managed to equate the two durations based his judgement on the number of pieces and was moreover wrong in his count.

JEP (5; 6): *It's the same time.* Why? *Because I put the same number in.* Did you count them? *Yes. There were 15 of each* (in reality there were 15 pieces of lead and 17 pieces of wood).

All in all, we are therefore entitled to conclude that even in this test, children judge time by the work done which, in turn, is judged by its difficulty and the effort it demands rather than in quantitative terms (the number of pieces moved). But this last criterion is often used as well, and wrongly.

Between the ages of 6; 1 and 8 years, on the other hand, several subjects contend that the wood takes longer to shift, because a greater number of pieces can be transferred in the same time. A little more than a third of these subjects continue to think that the lead takes longer to shift, again simply because the lead plates are heavier:

Joj (6; 9): *It takes longer with the pieces of lead.* Why? *There were lots of them.*

UL (7; 8): *Longer when I put in the bits of lead, because they were heavier.* And with the second method: 13″ of transferring lead = 15″ of transferring wood.

Rather more than a third of these subjects, finally, came down in favour of equal duration, and interestingly enough, they were generally those who thought that the lead was slower to shift:

JAC (6; 7): *It ought to be the same time for both. It took rather longer with the lead, but the time was the same.* Second method: 15″ (wood) = 16″ (lead).

CHA (6; 11): *It took a long time with the lead because the pieces had to be fitted in one by one.* And less time with the wood? *No, because I fitted them in more quickly, but that made no difference to the time.*

If we compare the above reactions to those of a group of children between the ages of 9 and 12 years, we find that the latter (and adults as well) still tend to think that it takes longer to shift the lead, but that they generally correct their errors by reflection:

SIM (10; 8): *It must be the same time. I was going to say that the lead takes longer, but then I thought about it and found that it must be the same.* Why? *Because I put in more wood than lead.* (Cf. the opposite argument of younger children.) Second method: 25″ (wood) = 24″ (lead).

MAR (10; 11): the lead seems to take *fairly long. Time went more quickly with the wood than with the bits of lead, but I think that I worked for the same time all the same* (37″).

ALI (12 years): *A little longer for the lead because I put them in one by one.* And with the wood? *Almost the same time.*

In short, the results of this brief test concur with those described in §1. By introducing actions of various complexity, we implicitly lead our subjects to the correlation of time with the speed of their own movements (rate of activity) and thus free even the younger ones from their habitual belief that duration is proportional to velocity. Now, we saw that these younger subjects simply rely on the objective aspects of the work they have done (weight and size of the pieces of lead) much as in the case of velocities they rely on distance alone. Only the older subjects think of the shifting of the lead and wood in terms of the speed of their own movements, and generally correct their residual misconceptions by explicit arguments (Sim: the pieces of lead take longer to put in but are fewer in number) or by implicit ones (Mar). We thus arrive at the same conclusions as we did in §1.

§3. *Inactivity and interesting work*

The two preceding tests have shown that small children evaluate working time by the end result of their actions (e.g. the number of strokes they have drawn) or by the external difficulties (weight and size of the pieces of lead), i.e. by the work done, while older children rely more on their sense of inner duration. This brings us to the duration of tasks with no tangible results but involving periods of waiting or being absorbed.

We accordingly asked our subjects (a) to do nothing while sitting with crossed arms for 15″ and (b) to look at an amusing picture for the same time. (In some cases, we increased the waiting time to 30″ and the viewing time to 45″ simply to make sure that the differences were really as great as they appeared to be.)

Now, the results obtained are very simply classified: except for one or two subjects between 4; 0 and 4; 6 who proved quite incapable of comparing the two durations, most 4–12-year-olds thought the waiting time was much the longer of the two. There was one further exception, a boy of 7; 4 who, tired by the preceding interrogation, thought that it took less time to sit with crossed arms 'because I was left in peace'. All the others reacted much as follows:

CLAN (5; 8) thought it took *a long time* to do nothing and *a short time* to watch the picture. When he was told that the two were of equal duration, he refused to believe it: *No, the second was shorter.*

JAN (5; 9) crossed his arms for 30" and thought it took *a long time.* Then he looked at the picture for 45": *That took a short time.* But my watch tells me that it took longer. *Did it really?* Yes, so you must have been wrong. *No, it took much longer when I crossed my arms.*

NEL (6; 2): *It went much more quickly with the picture* (15").

PIE (6; 4): *I guess the one was short and the other one long.*

SIM (10; 8): *It was almost the same time* (30" and 45"!). *Waiting takes longer.*

MAR (10; 11): *The picture took a little less time* (45") *because it was such fun.*

CEC (12; 1): *The picture took much less time* (45"), etc., etc.

These answers speak for themselves, and there is no need for us to dwell upon them at length: older and younger subjects produce precisely the same evaluations. The only difference is that whereas, until about the age of 6, they base their opinions purely on external considerations, from 6–7 years onwards they use a degree of introspection: 'I guess', 'it was fun', etc.

But trivial though these observations are, they nevertheless call for two comments. The first is that, as we saw in Chapter Ten (Age), the child seems to think that time ceases to flow once a state has become permanent: why then does he attribute a greater duration to the immobile state of sitting around with crossed arms? The answer is simple. Seen from the outside, an immobile state represents the cessation of activity, and as long as time is conceived in terms of action, it is only natural that inactivity should be equated to null duration. However, for those who actually do it, waiting represents action and, indeed, a very 'costly' action, as P. Janet has put it: it means putting a brake on all motor activity, and holding one's energy in check. To sit with crossed arms is a kind of torture for the child, unless, of course, like our 7; 4-year-old, he has been plagued by questions and then finds that the time passes quickly 'because I was left in peace'. Waiting is therefore comparable to hard work.

As for the time spent on interesting tasks, it goes without saying that it will seem short if the stimulus, as Claparède has put it, acts as a 'dynamic generator' of reserve energy, and hence as a speed regulator in Janet's sense. The time spent on interesting tasks is thus comparable to the time of rapid or simple actions, even though it involves no more than perceptive attention.

It is therefore perfectly true to say that the sense of duration depends on the emotional regulators of the action—as P. Janet has shown so clearly[1]—and that the resulting illusions persist into adulthood, despite intellectual corrections. Thus we have found that people climbing mountains in thick snow think that they have spent twice as long as they do when their path is unimpeded and when, moreover, they can look round at the beautiful landscape. With children, such systematic errors are much more obvious still because children are far more susceptible to emotional stimuli than adults. However, as we saw in §1 and §2, in young subjects, these permanent factors in the evaluation of durations are opposed by the belief that the time of productive work varies as its results. Hence it is only in the case of two tasks producing the same results, or in the case of 'passive' actions, that the rapidity of the work seems to act as a brake on duration.

These factors alone should suffice to show that inner time is anything but 'primitive'. If, moreover, we remember that the elaboration of the practical time schema goes back to the level of sensory-motor intelligence,[2] it seems highly probable that the child's original conception of time depends both on his organization of the physical universe and also on his own activity, and hence on egocentric time which, as we shall show below, is anything but 'pure'.

§4. *Conclusion: Psychological time*

Let us now apply the above results to the problem we mentioned in the introduction to this chapter: are the illusions or systematic errors to which the intuitive conception of physical time is subject before the age of 7–8, due to the projection into the external world of a fully organized inner sense of duration, or is it rather true to say that inner time is constructed by the same operations that go into the organization of external time?

[1] P. Janet: *L'Evolution de la mémoire et de la notion du temps.* Paris, (Maloine), 1928.
[2] See *La Construction du Réel chez l'Enfant,* Chapter IV.

Like physical time, psychological time rests on two distinct and fundamental systems: the order of succession of events and the colligation of durations. The only difference is that, with psychological time, we are dealing with 'lived' events rather than with events divorced from personal action, but this is a difference of degree rather than of kind.

Now, the order of succession can be apprehended directly during the actual course of events, so that intuition will lead to correct evaluations except when very brief intervals are concerned (see Chapter Four, §4). However, as soon as the events are in the past, let us say after a lapse of ten minutes, a few hours, and *a fortiori* of several days, the order of succession has to be reconstructed. Can this be done simply by the act of remembering? Only if memory were indeed the total and passive recorder certain authors believe it to be, for in that case we should simply have to consult the 'record'. However, it is a well-known fact that young children cannot do so; though they may recall things better than adults can, they nevertheless stack up their memories in a confused jumble, and it is perhaps because we remember less and less as we grow older, that we are forced to supplement our intuitive memory with reflection.

This active part of memorizing, which certain authors at the other end of the spectrum mistake for the sole function of the memory, therefore involves the reconstruction not only of memories but also, and above all, of the order of succession: it is a 'narrative', i.e. the reconstruction of a series of events when the series can no longer be apprehended directly.

Now, the construction of this narrative, which we have discussed in several other contributions,[1] passes through the identical phases in the case of both psychological and also of physical time: it starts out by being intuitive or non-operational, simply substituting more or less correct or fabulated representations for perceptions, and ends up by being operational or logical in that it involves reasoned seriations.

Before the age of 7–8, children's narratives, including that internalized narrative, the active memory, remain purely egocentric, i.e. events are linked together on the basis of personal interest and not of the real order of time. If the child is asked

[1] See *La Langage et la Pensée chez l'Enfant*, Chapter II, and our two articles in the *Arch. de Psychol.*, Vol. XIX, 1925–6.

to retell a story, to construct one from two (Dawid's) pictures, or to re-arrange a series of shuffled drawings, he will simply jumble together a host of unrelated details, pairing two of them at a time. Is this due to lack of expository powers, or does it rather reflect a true state of mind? All we know about the relation between social and intellectual behaviour in children strongly suggests that these two types of failure are but a single one, and that it is by learning to tell stories to others that the child learns to tell stories to himself and thus to organize his active memory. To illustrate this point, let us compare the 'narratives' of children below the age of 7–8 with the way they tackle the problem of succession in physical time.

In Chapter Nine (§4) we saw that many of our subjects failed to identify a tree that was shown to them in successive drawings. Now, this failure was not due to lack of perceptive powers, but simply to the fact that children have less difficulty in arranging a series of little episodes than they have in constructing a single story in which the same individual re-appears in different situations. The lack of identification of objects or persons can therefore be considered as a sort of clinical index. It occurs at different ages with the following frequency (absolute numbers out of 120 narratives per age):

4 years	5 yrs	6 yrs	7 yrs	8 yrs	9 yrs	10 yrs	11 yrs
94	85	70	46	10	6	7	0

For the same reason, children below the age of 7–8 fail to seriate pictures, and children below the age of 8 fail to construct a story from pictures representing its beginning and end (Dawid's pictures).

It follows that the 'narratives' these children produce are neither chronological, causal nor deductive: their characteristic use of the conjunction 'and then' involves an 'and' that represents a half-way stage between the 'and' of serial addition (the non-communicative + operation) and the 'and' of simple association (the commutative +).

However, though the order adopted by these children strikes the adult as being so arbitrary, the children themselves come to consider it the only possible order. Here we have a process comparable to the 'rigid pairs' described earlier (Chapter One, §3 and §4). The reason is that the order which the child establishes reflects a syncretic schema that may sometimes give rise to nothing but incoherent enumerations, but nevertheless reflects an overall inner vision which becomes consolidated as soon as it is formed, in the way that perceptive structures are.

Finally—and this is undoubtedly the clearest lesson we can draw from these tests, once the child is shown and has admitted that he was wrong, he is nevertheless incapable of reconstructing his story by incorporating new data, but simply repeats it in part or *in toto*. Thus of a hundred reconstructions, the following percentages were mere recapitulations of the original story:

5 yrs	6 yrs	7 yrs	8 yrs	9 yrs	10 yrs
90%	84%	39%	15%	11%	9%

Now this difficulty in reconstructing a story, and hence in considering the old story as a mere hypothesis, is the direct result of irreversible thought and the clearest sign of its intuitive and pre-operational nature.

This brings us to the crux of our discussion: as we saw in Chapters One and Two, it is only the contents of time, i.e. the external or psychological events, that are irreversible—time itself is a system of reversible operations. In particular, the reconstruction of temporal successions necessarily involves the use of operations by which the events can be projected forward and backward in thought, since every series, however asymmetrical, must have two directions. In other words, seriating two events is tantamount to establishing not only that A precedes B; B precedes C; ..., etc., but also that C succeeds B, and B succeeds A. Now, to do that, we must go back from the effects to the causes or proceed from the causes to the effects, testing all possible combinations until we arrive at a solution that agrees with all the series we have previously constructed: it is in that sense that the order of succession presupposes reversibility of thought.

But why do we have to wait for the age of 7–8 before these facts can be appreciated? It is because the series of events involved in almost every story or memory, far from being simple and unique, is highly complex and entangled, and because the velocities, far from being common and uniform, generally vary from one series to the next and are, moreover, subject to positive or negative accelerations. A single series of events, such as progress in a particular school subject, can rapidly be reconstructed. However, since it interferes with other series such as work in different subjects, family events, social engagements, etc., etc., reconstructing the past calls for the co-ordination of a host of developments, each with a rhythm of its own. Now since small children show a lack of reversibility even in the case of a straight path covered at uniform velocity (cf. the seriation of levels described in Chapter One, §2), they cannot possibly be expected to succeed with the complex system of deductive operations involved in the reconstruction of events with complicated trajectories and variable velocities. The time of psychological actions, like physical time, is the co-ordination of motions and velocities and this is why children lacking operational reversibility have systematic difficulties in reconstructing either. With psychological as with physical time, intuition has a distorting effect: it tends to reduce everything to a simple process with a common and uniform velocity—hence the constant errors in establishing successions and durations.

From the age of 7–8 years onwards, however, there is a gradual change of mental attitude—subjects at this stage try to reconstruct their stories in the simplest possible way and by considering the most probable succession of events. Capable of reversibility, they will use all the data to make several constructions; in short, they will introduce into psychological time as into physical time, a rational succession based on operational methods and no longer purely on intuition.

It is this difference which explains the various reactions we have discussed in this chapter. 'Lived' durations are, in fact, nothing other than intervals between events. Their order of succession therefore corresponds to the operational colligation of durations in psychological or in physical time: both are based on the fact that if an event A precedes B, and if B precedes C, then the duration AB must necessarily be shorter than the duration AC. It is therefore only natural that the construction of successions should correspond to the construction of a coherent system of durations and *vice versa*.

But how precisely does the child develop its conception of inner duration? Let us imagine a creature who, from birth to death, does the same work, for instance building a long wall, at the same speed. His psychological time would coincide with his physical time: since the work proceeds at a constant rate, he could judge the durations simply by the size of the wall, and intervals simply by differences in that size. As soon as actions cease to be uniform, however, and different velocities are introduced, not only does psychological time become divorced from physical time, but different speeds or rhythms introduce new complications into the evaluation of durations and into the order of successions. We might even claim that differences in velocity dominate the problem of inner durations in exactly the same way as they dominate the problem of physical durations. If we think of several series of independent but overlapping events in our own past (for instance of important dates in our career, the dates of our publications, dates in private life and political events), we see that though all these series have remained very much alive in our memory, we must nevertheless use rational and hence operational reconstructions (1) to tell if a given event in one series came before an event in another series (even though the order of succession in each series is perfectly clear), and (2) to give an approximate evaluation (in terms of + or −) of the respective length of the intervals between two events in two distinct series. In brief, the overall system of past experience is comparable to the distances covered in a complex system of physical motions, the rhythm of a particular series of actions being comparable to a physical velocity. Hence the problem of psychological time, like that of physical time, reduces to the co-ordination of motions and velocities or, in our particular case, to the co-ordination of actions and the rate at which they are performed.

Things are even clearer with durations in the present, and the comparison of the latter with past durations supplies us with the key to our whole problem. In principle, when we perform a rapid or accelerated action, we experience a contraction of time, but when we remember the action we expand its duration (because we then judge it by the distance covered or the work done). Slow actions, and above all decelerated actions, give rise to the opposite estimates. As for the time associated with feelings of boredom, fatigue, emptiness on the one hand and with excitement, interest or of spontaneous effort on the other hand, it can, as P. Janet has shown so clearly, be reduced to changes in the speed of actions. All in all, the ego must therefore be considered a system of actions at different speeds or accelerations, whose durations are determined by comparisons among one another, velocity serving as the chief criterion in the case of simultaneous actions, and the distance covered (or the work done) becoming the more important the greater the interval between any two actions. These comparisons may remain unconscious, but they are nevertheless governed by perceptive and intuitive regulations, and later by intelligent and operational judgements.

It follows that children evaluate the duration of their own actions in the same way that they evaluate physical time. Here, as elsewhere, the child advances from intuitive and irreversible egocentrism to operational groupings or to the level of objective and reversible co-ordinations in which the ego is but one element among others. Now this explains why young children have introspective problems with the evaluation of time, and why older children are able to dissociate psychological time from physical time to discover the correct relation between time and velocity. In young children, the egocentric, i.e. the immediate and irreversible character, of thought, proves an impediment to introspection: the awareness of an action begins with the awareness of its results, and it is not until later that decentrations or comparisons lead the child back to the action itself. Hence small children begin by judging the duration of an action by its quantitative results (number of strokes drawn) or by the work done (the respective weight or size of the pieces of lead and wood) rather than by the speed. It is only when their actions produce no external results (e.g. waiting or looking at pictures) that they judge time like adults, i.e. in terms of boredom or interest, but without giving any reasons and in the firm conviction that they are producing objective judgements—once again for lack of introspective powers. Now, the same factors that impede introspection in small children and hence explain their 'realistic' evaluations of the time of actions, also prevent them from grasping the inverse relation between the rapidity of an action and its duration, and consequently from fitting velocities into a coherent time schema. In effect, thinking that 'quicker' signifies 'more time' as small children do, both on the physical and also on the psychological plane, is simply to liken the impression of the speed of an action (an impression which is naturally conscious because the speed is intentional) to its duration, judged, not during the action itself (we have seen why) but after the event and by its results: the greater the distance covered or the work done, the longer it must take. This confusion is quite natural for minds not given to introspection, and that is precisely why even adults, using retrospection instead of introspection, come to think that actions performed more rapidly and hence more packed with events, took longer than they actually did (at the time they were being performed these actions seemed shorter precisely because they were being performed quickly). With the appearance of articulated intuition at stage II, 'quicker' becomes equated with 'less time', because introspection now helps the child to distinguish between actual durations and the results of actions. This leads to the reversal of the previous error and to intuitive regulation. Finally, in the most advanced subjects, introspective regulation is joined to corrections based on operational reversibility, and so helps to turn psychological time into a particular case of that general co-ordination of motions and velocities which, as we saw, goes into the construction of time in all the spheres we have been examining.

Conclusions

From all the preceding discussions, we have learned that time is the co-ordination of motions at different velocities—motions of external objects in the case of physical time, and of the subject in the case of psychological time. When we say motions, we are thinking of real motions, and not of the displacements or ideal movements of geometry. The latter are simply changes of position or 'placements', in which the velocity can be neglected : that is why displacement is a spatial concept and why time only appears with real motions, i.e. with velocities. While the conception of time is not yet grasped operationally, i.e. as the ratio of the distance covered (or the work done, etc.) to the velocity, the temporal order is confused with the spatial order and duration with the path traversed. Conversely, before the temporal order has been constructed, the idea of velocity is often bound up with that of overtaking, i.e. with a purely spatial intuition involving a change in the respective positions of two moving bodies. The construction of time proper therefore begins with the correlation of velocities, be it in the case of human activity or of external motions.

I

The most elementary form of time is found at the sensory-motor level, and has been described elsewhere.[1] When it cries with hunger, the baby has its first experience of duration (waiting time) and when, trying to reach a distant object, it first gets hold of an appropriate tool (support or stick) it establishes a primitive order of succession between the means and the end. However, this does not mean that time, at the sensory-motor level, is constructed into a homogeneous scheme even on the

[1] *La Construction du Réel chez l'Enfant*, Chapter IV.

255

purely unconscious and practical plane: all the baby does is to correlate the succession or duration of particular actions with spatial displacements. At the primitive level, where objects are not yet endowed with permanence, the succession of events simply gives rise to motor responses, and later to those egocentric schemas that we have called 'subjective series': that is why, when it sees a person go out of the door, the baby will look for him by the side of its cot (where the person has just been). In spatial terms, therefore, displacements of objects are not yet 'grouped' into trajectories independent of the ego; and in temporal terms, there is a reversal of the order of succession, as if the 'watch' represented by the object suddenly ran backwards and its motion lacked all continuity. It is only once spatial groups of displacements have been constructed, that time itself can become objectivized or rather decentred on the practical plane and, it goes without saying, in one direction only. Thus, one-year-olds will look at the door or wave good-bye as soon as the name of a recent visitor is mentioned: the temporal construction of a course of events therefore goes hand in hand with its spatial construction. However, it cannot be stressed enough that, on the practical or sensory-motor plane, each action still has a time of its own, so that there are as many temporal series as there are schemes of action.

When, with the acquisition of language and verbo-motor concepts, the child's intelligence leaves the sensory-motor for the plane of thought, temporal concepts assume the form we have described as stage I. This includes a preliminary period (from $1\frac{1}{2}$ to 4 years) during which the child's reactions must be observed directly rather than elicited by questions, and it was in this way that Decroly and Mlle Degand were able to correlate progress in temporal conceptions with the child's use of language.[1] In particular, they observed a gradual extension of temporal notions to embrace both the future and the past, and also the gradual emergence (which C. and W. Stern had described previously) of relative conceptions by which the future becomes transformed into the present (tomorrow is changed into today) and the present into the past (today is changed into yesterday).

We see, therefore, that, in accordance with a general law

[1] O. Decroly, *Etudes de Psychogenèse*, 1932, Chapter IV.

governing the transition from the sensory-motor level to that of nascent thought (see *La Construction du Réel chez l'Enfant*, 'Conclusions'), the child begins to re-interpret what it had previously learned in action. Thus, having learned to anticipate successions on the practical plane (by localizing them in the immediate present) or to take certain durations into account, he must now reconstruct these concepts by substituting virtual for real actions, and appropriate signs and mental representations for their purely perceptive characteristics.

That is why, at the age of 4–5, children still have difficulty in arranging a series of symbols (and even drawings) into a simple time sequence, though they are perfectly capable of constructing such a sequence on the purely practical plane. Thus these children will be able to predict that, if water is run from one vessel into another, the level will drop in the first and rise in the second, but they remain incapable of seriating what drawings they themselves have made of this process (Chapter One, §2 and §3).

In short, at stage I, the child must reconstruct into concepts his elementary ideas of succession and duration. Now, at that stage his constructions remain exceedingly primitive: true, they are abstracted from their particular context and generalized by the very fact of their conceptualization, but they do not yet lead to the differentiation between temporal and spatial structures. In effect, time at stage I is simply the order of succession and the colligation of durations of a single series of linear events, irrespective of its own velocity or its intersections with other series with different velocities. In other words, the child watching a man walk along will say that the man reached B after A, and C after B; he might also say that the man took longer to go from A to C than from A to B. But in this particular case, it is clear that the temporal succession coincides with the spatial, and the durations with the displacements, so that the child can give the correct answer by relying on purely spatial considerations. Now, if we ask the same child to compare a motion from A to C with another motion, along the same path AC, but at a different velocity, he will be at a complete loss, i.e. he will be quite unable to tell us which of the two bodies will reach its destination first.

Time at stage I is therefore a localized time in the double

T

sense that it varies from one motion to the next, and that it is confused with the spatial order. It is, one might say, a time without velocities, or a time that is homogeneous only so long as all the velocities are uniform. As soon, however, as actions at different velocities are introduced, the terms 'before' and 'after' lose all meaning or else preserve their purely spatial sense (Chapter Three); simultaneity is denied (Chapter Four); the equality of two synchronous durations ceases to make sense (Chapter Five); the colligation of durations can no longer be performed (Chapters Six and Seven)—nor, *a fortiori*, can the measurement of time (Chapter Eight). Even the concept of age, which would seem to be based on what the child has heard from adults, is interpreted spatially, inasmuch as differences in growth-rate lead to failure in grasping the order of succession of births and the conservation of age differences (Chapter Nine). Finally, psychological time, too, may be assessed by such spatial criteria as the results of a particular action (Chapter Ten). All these findings lead us to the same conclusions, namely that the construction of homogeneous time involves the co-ordination of velocities, and that the temporal ideas prevailing before this co-ordination is achieved, must necessarily be bound up with spatial intuitions.

It is evident that while temporal concepts remain intuitive, the concept of velocity remains intuitive as well. This is a point to which we shall be returning elsewhere.[1] When one moving body overtakes another, or continues further along the same path, all small children are agreed that it goes 'faster': to elementary intuitive thought, velocity is therefore equivalent to the process of overtaking. As soon as this process becomes invisible (e.g. when the two bodies move in two tunnels of different length) or when there is no overtaking (i.e. when the two bodies move in opposite, or even in the same direction but on two concentric courses, the outer one of which is visibly greater) estimates of velocity become vague. It follows that velocity is not yet recognized as a relationship between time and the space traversed, and this cannot, in fact, happen before time as such has been constructed. Indeed, we are merely being tautological since, if time is, in fact, the co-ordination of velocities (or of real motions), velocity must remain a fragmentary

[1] See *Les Notions de mouvement et de vitesse chez l'Enfant.*

intuition before this co-ordination is achieved. In brief, it is the simultaneous construction of the operational conception of velocity (the ratio $v = s/t$) and of the operational conception of time ($t = s/v$) which alone enables the child to compare velocities when there is no visible overtaking, and also durations when the velocities differ.

But why precisely does the intuitive grasp of time remain spatialized for so long? To answer that question we need merely generalize our remarks about psychological time (Chapter Ten).

Grasping time is tantamount to freeing oneself from the present, to transcending space by a mobile effort, i.e. by reversible operations. To follow time along the simple and irreversible course of events is simply to live it without taking cognizance of it. To know it, on the other hand, is to retrace it in either direction. Rational time is therefore reversible, whereas empirical time is irreversible, and the former cannot embrace the latter unless this fundamental contrast is fully taken into account. Hence it is easy to understand why young children should have such difficulty in handling temporal concepts.

It is a characteristic of primitive thought that it treats as absolutes the particular perspectives it happens to be dwelling upon, and that it consequently fails to 'group'. This initial 'realism' is both a form of egocentrism, since it places current states of consciousness at the centre of everything, and also a form of irreversibility, because, in it, moment succeeds moment without leading to the construction of a general flux. More precisely, egocentrism and irreversibility are one and the same thing, and characterize the state of 'innocence' which precedes the phase of critical construction. In the field of psychological time, they mean living purely in the present and assessing the past exclusively by its results: whence the many problems of 'reflection' (in the literal sense of the term) we have been discussing, and also the inability to arrive at the correct order of succession and colligation of durations. In other words, the operational construction of inner time calls for the correlation of one's own time not only with that of others, but also with physical time, within a reversible system that has ceased to be egocentric and is no longer bound up with current events. In the field of physical time, too, reversibility takes the child beyond egocentric and local time, i.e. beyond the irreversible time characteristic of the motion of a single body, in which differences in velocity can be ignored. We repeat that egocentrism and irreversibility are but two complementary aspects of one and the same lack of co-ordination, and this fact alone explains the characteristic property of primitive time, i.e. the lack of differentiation between temporal and spatial successions.

This lack is gradually made good as the child passes from stage I to stage II, i.e. to the stage of 'articulated intuitions'. Here progress in intuitive regulation helps to reduce the excessive deformations that spring from the irreversible centrations we have just been describing. Articulated intuition thus marks the beginning of decentration and so prepares the way for operations. In the case of durations, it leads to the appreciation that time is inversely proportional to velocity and thus opens the way for the correct colligations. In the case of successions it leads to the anticipation and reconstruction of the motions themselves and deflects the attention from their end points. In short, intuitive decentrations introduce corrections and these, in turn, lead to certain correlations. However, as we saw, the correlation of velocity and duration does not automatically introduce the correct order of succession, or *vice versa*: these rudimentary correlations, far from being operations, are simply articulated intuitions, i.e. intuitions subject to relatively constant regulations.

II

Much as primitive intuitions of time are examples of irreversible thought, so operational time is the prototype of reversible thought, and perhaps the clearest example of the way in which rational operations tend, by their very construction, to take the form of 'groupings'. Thus while the operational fusion of the colligation of classes and the seriation of asymmetrical relations involved in the construction of number leads directly to a 'group' in the proper sense of the word, i.e. to a mathematical system, the colligation of durations and the seriation of the asymmetrical relations of succession do not become fused straightaway; they constitute two distinct logical 'groupings', in one-to-one correspondence on the qualitative plane, but capable of being combined on the quantitative plane.

From the psychological point of view, the construction of

temporal 'groupings' which marks the transition from stage II to stage III, is remarkable for two paradoxical facts on which we have dwelled at some length. The first is that the child succeeds in constructing one and the same system of temporal groupings in two distinct ways: sometimes he will discover successions before he is able to colligate durations, at other times he takes the opposite path; in both cases, however, he arrives at the same operational result, i.e. he learns to base successions on durations and *vice versa*. Now, here we have a most curious fact. In other spheres, too, we encounter distinct 'types', for example the abstract and visual types of mathematics, but they never express the same truths in distinct languages. The second fact worthy of notice is the relatively short period of transition between stages II and III, i.e. the relatively quick operational construction of itme. True, there is also a sub-stage II B, but we gain the impression that the moment when the child first succeeds in organizing a complete temporal system is so sudden that we can never actually put our finger on it: often he will correct an error, and in so doing trigger off a total process the speed of which is far greater than that of any conscious processes.

Now this total solution of the problem of time can be summed up in a single formula: operational time is constructed as soon as the order of successions is deduced from the colligation of durations and *vice versa*. How does this interpretation fit into our picture of the development of intelligence in general?

I. Let us start with the order of succession which, from the formal point of view constitutes an additive grouping of asymmetrical ('before' and 'after') relations (qualitative seriation). Now, a grouping of that type is by no means beyond the mental powers of children from $6\frac{1}{2}$–7 years, i.e. of children who still have great difficulty with temporal concepts as such. To fit sticks of increasing size into the series $A < B < C < \ldots$ is an example of this type of grouping. In the temporal field, on the other hand, children hesitate for a long time before choosing the correct order out of the possible orders ACB, BAC, etc. How do they eventually succeed in making the right choice? They can do so by the gradual dissociation of the temporal from the spatial order (stage II): if B went further than C, but C was still moving after B had stopped, the temporal 'before' and 'after' are no longer identical with the spatial, and the child must determine the correct sequence by trial and error. Thus while the data under consideration remain perceptible, seriation can be intuitive as well as operational. However, as soon as a temporal succession has to be constructed in retrospect, by means of drawings or other representations, operations intervene of necessity (see Chapters One and Nine) and observation shows that, as soon as that happens, the child also becomes capable of deducing the durations. (2) The child can equally well derive successions from durations, using the argument that, if A and B started simultaneously, and B went on longer than A, then A must necessarily have stopped before B. It goes without saying that, in this case, the successions have been established operationally.

But how precisely does the operational construction of temporal successions differ from the corresponding spatial operations? From our observations of young children, we know that they base their conception of time on spatial transformations (e.g. they judge age by height): to them the temporal order is simply the order of spatial transformations or rather the order of succession of the 'states' resulting from these transformations. A completely immobile universe would be completely lacking in time. To say that time is the order of spatial transformations is tantamount to describing it as a co-ordination (in the sense of simultaneous ordination) of motions—as we have shown at some length in this volume. In what follows, we shall therefore refer as 'state' to the absence of motion. We shall, moreover, use the term 'instantaneous' to describe a punctiform state (a point in time).

From the above remarks, it will be clear that the simplest grouping is the seriation of the instantaneous states either of a moving body passing successively through different spatial points, or of a spatial point through which different moving bodies pass successively:

(1)

$$a \quad a' \quad b' \quad c'$$
$$0 \to A \to B \to C \to \dots \text{ etc. where } a + a' = b; b + b' = c, \text{ etc.}$$

which may be read: A after 0; B after A; C after B, etc., hence B after 0; C after 0; etc.

Ia. From these relations it is quite simple to derive the particular case of simultaneity. The psychological factors we have been examining leave no doubt that simultaneity must, in effect, be considered a limiting case of succession, and this in the following senses:

(1) Whenever the states (or events) under consideration coincide completely or approximately, in the same point of space, simultaneity is simply a null succession, or a succession tending towards zero:

$$\overset{0}{} \qquad \overset{0}{} \qquad \overset{0}{}$$

(2) $\quad A_1 \to A_2$, whence if $A_2 \to A_3$, then $A_1 \to A_3$

(2) Whenever A_1 and A_2 do not coincide in space and whenever the comparison of these two events involves either an ocular movement or an exchange of physical signals, then A_1 and A_2 will be simultaneous if the shift from A_1 to A_2 causes A_1 to appear before A_2, if the shift from A_2 to A_1 causes A_2 to appear before A_1, and if the two reciprocal shifts cancel each other because they are of the same order (a, or b, etc.). We have:

$$\overset{a}{} \qquad \overset{0}{} \qquad \overset{b}{} \qquad \overset{0}{}$$

(2a) $\quad A_1 \to A_2 = A_1 \to A_2; \; A_1 \to A_2 = A_1 \to A_2$, etc.

$$\underset{a}{\underset{\leftarrow}{}} \qquad\qquad \underset{b}{\underset{\leftarrow}{}}$$

Let us note that this is precisely what happens with the simultaneous lighting of two lamps (Chapter Four, §4): when the subject centres his attention on one of the two lamps, he will gain the impression that it was lit first, but if his vision becomes 'decentred', really or virtually, i.e. if it oscillates between the two lamps, he will be able to correct this illusion.

(3) Now, since the succession of two events A_1 and A_2 always involves a fixed duration, we can equally well define simultaneity in terms of duration: either as the relation between two events separated by a null duration (cf. proposition 2), or else as the relations between two events such that the motion from A_1 to A_2 is of equal duration to the motion (with equal velocity) from A_2 to A_1 (cf. proposition 2a). Let us note here that this operation is in full accord with the corresponding psychological mechanism: when attention shifts from A_1 to A_2, and when the duration of that shift is cancelled out, we conclude that the two successive events are simultaneous.

Many authors distinguish between empirically discovered simultaneity and simultaneity that is deduced (or constructed) from succession or duration. M. Jean de La Harpe, in particular, has made much of this distinction, which nevertheless strikes us as resting on shaky psychological and axiomatic foundations:[1] simultaneity in both cases, is simply a limiting case of succession, in the sense of (2a) (proposition 2 only holds for one and the same point in space) and hence necessarily partakes of the nature of a construction, so that the difference is one of degree only.

Ib. Once the simultaneity of two events is given, the complete grouping of successions does not appear in the additive form (1), but in the following multiplicative form (co-seriation):

$$
\begin{array}{c}
\quad\; a \quad\;\; a' \quad\; b' \quad\; e' \\
O_1 \to A_1 \to B_1 \to C_1 \to \dots \\
\downarrow 0 \quad \downarrow 0 \quad \downarrow 0 \quad \downarrow 0 \\
\quad\; a \quad\;\; a' \quad\; b' \quad\; c' \\
O_2 \to A_2 \to B_2 \to C_2 \to \dots \\
\downarrow 0 \quad \downarrow 0 \quad \downarrow 0 \quad \downarrow 0 \\
\quad\; a \quad\;\; a' \quad\; b' \quad\; c' \\
O_3 \to A_3 \to B_3 \to C_3 \to \dots \\
\vdots \quad\;\; \vdots \quad\;\; \vdots \quad\;\; \vdots
\end{array}
$$

(3)

[1] J. de La Harpe, *Genèse et mesure du temps*, Neuchâtel, 1941, pp. 115 and 123. According to this author, 'quantitative' simultaneity is invariably constructed, whereas 'simple simultaneity is established by postulate': 'Two events are simultaneous if they are seized by a single act of awareness, though they remain completely distinct' (Postulate I), but 'two events are successive if they are seized by separate though closely linked acts of awareness' (Postulate II). Now, three objections can be raised against this formulation: (1) There is no way of distinguishing 'separate though closely linked acts of awareness' from 'a single act of awareness' bearing on 'distinct' events, and we might equally well argue that every assertion (unlike perception) that two events are successive constitutes a single 'state of awareness', and that, conversely, every assertion that two events are simultaneous involves two distinct acts of awareness. (2) What precisely are these 'acts of awareness'? If they are judgements, we are back with (1); if they are perceptions they have no general application to the problem of simultaneity (cf. Chapter IV §4). (3) In general, M. de La Harpe's axiomatic system treats as 'postulates', all the psychological constructions of time and thus introduces an irreducible dualism between postulates and theorems. From the purely psychological point of view, moreover, each of his postulates embraces a singularly complex process of constructions (as this whole book has tried to show). Now, it is the operations involved in these constructions which, we believe, are in need of axiomatization (cf.

i.e. in the form of several series of successions with simultaneous moments. The multiplicative form of this grouping does not moreover imply that time has two (or more) dimensions: since the vertical dimension (simultaneities) is zero, the non-dimensional nature of temporal successions is fully maintained (which, incidentally, is in full accord with the topological theory of dimensions).

II. Let us now look at the qualitative operations involved in the grouping of *durations*. As we saw, children succeed in this field even before they are capable of constructing quantitative time. Now, if two instantaneous moments A and B are successive, they must needs be separated by a duration and, unlike the order of succession which is asymmetrical (if B comes after A then A comes before B), duration appears logically as the interval between two successive terms and consequently as a symmetrical relation: the duration (interval) AB is identical with the duration (interval) BA, and any event occurring between A and B must necessarily occur between B and A as well.[1] In other words, the interval is independent of the order of events or of its mental reconstruction.

It is therefore quite simple to formulate the grouping of durations: to do so we must simply correlate the seriation of asymmetrical relations (successions) with the addition of symmetrical relations (intervals). The legitimacy of this procedure has been established elsewhere.[2] If $O \leftrightarrow | A$ is the interval between O and A (exclusively) we have

---

[1] When this interval tends towards zero, we have simultaneity, which is therefore still a limiting case.
[2] See our *Classes, relations et nombres, Essai sur les groupements de la logistique et la réversibilite de la pensée*. Paris (Vrin), 1942, Chapter VII, p. 120.

---

our *Axiomatique des opérations constitutives du temps*, C. R. des séances de la Soc. de physique de Genève, Vol. 58, 1941, p. 24). If we examine the logical structure of the operations themselves, instead of merely axiomatizing their results, we cannot agree with M. de La Harpe that, with the advent of relativity theory, 'simple and quantitative simultaneity have become completely divorced' (p. 149). In fact, Einstein's demonstration that simultaneity and velocity are indissolubly linked together, applies to perceptive motions no less than to the rest.

(4) $$ O \leftrightarrow \overset{a}{|} A \leftrightarrow \overset{a'}{|} B \leftrightarrow \overset{b'}{|} C \ldots \text{etc.} $$

where

$$ O \leftrightarrow \overset{a}{|} A + A \leftrightarrow \overset{a'}{|} B = O \leftrightarrow \overset{b}{|} B; \, O \leftrightarrow \overset{b}{|} B + B \leftrightarrow \overset{b'}{|} C = O \leftrightarrow \overset{c}{|} C; $$
etc.

Now there is a striking parallel between this logical formulation and the corresponding psychological construction, which, moreover, proves once again that the theory of operational groupings is simply the axiomatization of mental operations.

Let us recall that the great difficulty young children have in elaborating the concept of duration, is due precisely to its commutativity. Thus we saw (Chapter Two, §3, case of Mog) that some of our younger subjects refuse to compare successive durations on the grounds that, since the water has already disappeared, the time determined from the observable water levels cannot be applied to past durations. In this particular case, irreversibility of thought, therefore, goes hand in hand with a failure to grasp that the addition of durations is commutative, a fact that presents no difficulties at stage III.

The reader will recall how children tackle the problem of duration. At first, they assess durations by the path traversed, irrespective of the velocities: whence the negation of the equality of synchronous durations, the impossibility of colligating durations as such, and the absence of homogeneous time. Then, at stage II, they either discover the temporal (as distinct from the spatial) order of succession but fail to apply it directly to the durations, or else they discover that time is inversely proportional to velocity but fail to relate this relation to the order of succession. Stage III, and with it the grouping of durations, begins as soon as the child grasps that, of two bodies starting simultaneously, the one that moves for a longer time is also the one that stops last, or that age depends on the succession of births. Psychologically as well as logically, therefore, durations are partly treated as a system of intervals based on the grouping of successions. They nevertheless constitute an independent grouping from successions, in that their elementary relations are symmetrical and their formative operation is commutative.

In brief, the grouping of durations is engendered by the grouping of successions. However, successions can also be reconstructed from durations, and this fact fully accords with the psychological process. Now, as soon as the two systems can be correlated, both of them become operational at once, whence the impossibility of telling which determines the organization of the other at the beginning of stage III. The operational system involved in qualitative time thus constitutes an inseparable whole —psychologically as well as logically.

IIb. But duration is not simply an interval between two successive events—it can also be defined in terms of velocity, and this is a fact that quite a large number of our subjects take into account.

Now, it is true that the size of the intervals defined under II reduces to the set of instantaneous positions which a moving body occupies between the privileged states chosen to describe its motion. But these instantaneous positions are points in time without any duration, which comes back to defining intervals by distance alone, i.e. independently of the dynamic factors involved. In reality, the length of the interval between two successive points in time is nothing other than the motion itself related to its velocity.

This aspect of duration is, as we have just said, taken into consideration by quite a few of our subjects. To begin with, they treat duration as a simple function of the path traversed or of the work done, but as soon as articulated intuition enables them to dissociate actions and motions from the results, they treat duration as being inversely proportional to the velocity. In quantitative terms, this would mean that they put $t = s/v$, but since qualitative evaluations alone are involved, they simply make use of the logical expression $t = s \times (-v)$, meaning that (1) with equal distances any increase in time is equivalent to a decrease of velocity and *vice versa*; (2) with equal velocities, any increase in time is equivalent to an increase in distance, and (3) with equal times, any increase in distance is equivalent to an increase is time and *vice versa*.

From the quantitative point of view, all this is quite obvious, simply because time can only be expressed in terms of motions with a fixed velocity. However, it is important to stress that the same thing happens with qualitative time: we cannot see or perceive time as such since, unlike space or velocity, it does not impinge upon our senses. All we can perceive is events, i.e. motions, actions, speeds, and their results. Thus temporal successions are determined by the order of events, and durations either by the motions, i.e. by distances covered at given velocities, or else by actions, i.e. the work done at a given rate. Qualitative time, at the operational stage is based on velocity no less than quantitative time. It, too, is the relation between velocity and motion, or between activity and work, the only difference being that it is expressed by simple seriations and above all by simple colligations in the absence of a mobile unit by which alone the two can be combined. However, in both cases, time is essentially the co-ordination of velocities.

Now, since velocity is itself a relation between distance and time, how do we, in fact, help matters by asserting that duration is derived from it? Here we must bear in mind the distinction between the qualitative approach which reflects the actual construction of concepts, and the quantitative approach by which these concepts are given their simplest form. From the qualitative point of view, velocity, i.e. all judgements involving such terms as 'more rapidly', does not, in fact, involve the existence of durations but simply that of simultaneities: of two motions α and β which begin and end simultaneously, the more rapid is the one that covers the greater distance; and, if one of them should come to an end before the other, we need only determine the position of the other at that very moment, to obtain the velocity once again in terms of the path traversed. Needless to say, these remarks do not represent an exhaustive analysis of the qualitative conception of velocity; they simply show how the child manages to group velocities independently of durations. Now, this being so, let us suppose that the subject chooses as his standard of comparison the duration α in which one moving body covers the distance s_1 with velocity v_1, while a second moving body, starting and stopping simultaneously, covers the distance s_2 with velocity v_2. In that case, we can say that the child has an operational grasp of duration if it realizes that the duration $\alpha s_1 v_1$ is equal to the duration $\alpha s_2 v_2$, or, in qualitative terms, if it realizes that the difference in distance $s_2 - s_1 = s'_1$

is compensated by the difference in velocity $v_2 - v_1 = v'_1$, simply because the difference in velocity has been determined by the difference in distance (i.e. $v'_1 = s'_1$). Whence we have:

(5) $\alpha_{s_1 v_1} = \alpha_{s_2 v_2}$ because $s'_1 \times (-v'_1) = 0$.

The durations α, β, γ, etc., thus defined are then colligated by the method of addition of classes or parts, into hierarchical wholes:

(6) $\alpha + \alpha' = \beta$; $\beta + \beta' = \gamma$; $\gamma + \gamma' = \delta$; ... etc.

In brief, to define durations in terms of distances and velocities (or work and power) once again comes back to defining them as intervals between successive, instantaneous events, but with this difference, that the intervals are conceived as functions of their content, i.e. of the actions and motions whose co-ordination constitutes time.

III. We have so far ignored quantitative time as such. From the logical point of view, the construction of quantitative time is comparable to that of number: the iteration of the unit of duration results from the operational fusion of the colligation of durations (classes) with the seriation of successions (asymmetrical relations). However, in the case of qualitative time, these two operations are complementary, i.e. can be derived from each other, but do not become fused into a single grouping: if A, B and C are three successive events, and α is the duration AB and α' that of BC, we can seriate the successions and obtain the correct order ABC by comparison with BAC, etc. (non-commutative serial addition), or else we can add the durations to obtain $\alpha' + \alpha = \beta$ as well as $\alpha + \alpha' = \beta$ (non-serial commutative addition), but we can never combine the two additions without stepping outside the realm of qualitative time. It is, moreover, evident, that if the commutative addition of durations can lead to the reversal of their order, it can only do so because our mind has the power to jump from one duration to the next, as it combines them while maintaining the order of succession. But qualitative durations are so immobile that each of them can only be compared to the whole of which it forms a part and not to the following or preceding durations. In other words, qualitative operations can tell us that $\alpha < \beta$; $\beta < \gamma$; etc., because

$\alpha + \alpha' = \beta$; $\beta + \beta' = \gamma$, etc. but nothing about the relations between α and α', β', γ', etc.

Quantitative time, on the other hand, is characterized by the equalization of the successive durations $\alpha = \alpha' = \beta' = \gamma'$, etc. by repeated application of the initial duration α, chosen as the unit. In that case, the colligation (6) leads to the denumeration of units, because if $\alpha = \alpha'$ then $\beta = 2\alpha$ since $\beta = \alpha + \alpha'$. Colligation (6) is therefore transformed into:

(7)
$$\alpha + \alpha(= \alpha') = 2\alpha(= \beta);$$
$$2\alpha(= \beta) + \alpha(= \beta') = 3\alpha(= \gamma); \text{ etc.}$$

But how is the equalization of two successive durations effected? We saw that there is no such thing as temporal congruence, i.e. that durations, unlike distances, cannot be applied to one another (except in the equalization of two synchronous durations). Before we can therefore equalize a duration α and the subsequent duration α', we must define α, not only as the interval between two successive events, as in (4) but also in terms of its contents, i.e. in terms of a motion covering a given distance with a given velocity, e.g. as α_{sv} [(5) and (6)]. We must, moreover, be able to reproduce this motion by a new displacement s_1, such that $s' = s$ and its velocity $v' = v$. That is why, as we saw in Chapter Two, children cannot equalize two successive durations before they grasp the fact that water running at the same rate will produce identical differences in level. The situation is much the same with sand-glasses (Chapter Eight) and with the motion of the hand of a clock across the dial. In general, two durations

(8)
$$\alpha_{sv} = \alpha'_{s'v'} \text{ if } s' = s \text{ and } v' = v.$$

More generally still, we can equalize the durations of two successive 'tasks' r and r' if they are performed with the same 'power' p.

(8a)
$$\alpha_{rp} = \alpha'_{r'p'} \text{ if } r = r' \text{ and } p = p'.$$

(8a) is more general than (8) because it applies not only to the measurement of psychological time (II) but also to physical time, for if we simplify the ratio r/p by cancelling the forces in the numerator and denominator, we are back with the ratio s/v.

Now all these operations presuppose a new relationship between durations and the order of successions, i.e. they involve an operational synthesis of the two and thus go beyond simple complementarity. In effect, whereas in qualitative time, durations are colligated rigidly and the order of succession allows of no permutations, in the case of quantitative time the equalization of successive durations introduces a mobile standard of duration whose identity is unaffected by the order of the real successions. In that case, the only difference between the unit α and another unit α is that one precedes the other in the order of denumeration, which order is quite arbitrary inasmuch as, if the second unit were counted first, it would become the first unit. We can therefore say that the quantitative addition $\alpha + \alpha = 2\alpha$ is both serial and commutative, and that its serial character does not prevent it from being commutative.

In brief, in the sphere of time as in all other spatial and physical spheres, measurement appears as a synthesis of two fundamental systems of operation: displacement and partition. The reader may recall that number is the synthesis of the colligation of classes and the seriation of asymmetrical relations. Now similarly, when logico-arithmetical operations are replaced by spatio-temporal operations, and when the colligations of classes becomes the partition or colligation of parts into hierarchic wholes, and the seriation of relations becomes a spatio-temporal succession or placement (including changes in placement or displacement), measurement will result from the possible substitution of parts by their own displacement or by the displacement of a standard part chosen as a common unit. In the case of time, this unit is a motion at constant velocity that can be reproduced at will, i.e. that can be displaced in time and synchronized with the partial durations to be measured.

Now this is precisely how quantitative time is elaborated as the child develops its mental powers. To begin with, the child has great difficulties in admitting that a given partial duration, e.g. the time necessary for water to run between two levels (Chapters One and Two), can be equal to a prior or subsequent duration: before he can do so, he must be able to divorce the duration from its qualitative context and feel free to reproduce it in a context that did not exist during the first duration, and that subsequently abolishes the earlier context. When faced with

271

problems of this kind (Chapter Two, §3) children react as if they had been asked to equate an hour spent at enjoyable play with an hour spent on tedious calculations. And, indeed, the two are not comparable unless they have first been divorced from the actual events and related to, say, the motion of a clock.

This leaves us with the construction of the concept of motion at uniform velocity, which, as we saw, is an indispensable adjunct to the elaboration of quantitative time. Now, this construction seems to introduce a vicious circle: while the measurement of time rests on uniform velocity, the latter rests on the fact that two equal distances are covered in two equal durations. Hence how is it possible to establish that a given motion is uniform if we lack a unit of time? This particular psycho-genetic problem is the more interesting in that the same vicious circle appears in the scientific measurement of time: the adjustment of clocks rests on the regularity of natural motions, i.e. on the isochronism of small oscillations and the majestic periodicity of celestial orbits, but all we can say about this natural chronology is based on our own chronometry.[1] In point of fact, and this is characteristic of the operational organization of thought: the child discovers the conservation of uniform velocity simultaneously with the measurement of time, and by the identical operations (see our forthcoming *Les notions de mouvement et de vitesse chez l'enfant*).

IV. This new correlation between the construction of the concepts of velocity and of time, leads us to the psychological processes involved in the operational grouping of temporal relations and in the elaboration of the three fundamental attributes of rational time: homogeneity, continuity, and uniformity.

Now, just as the intuitive conception of time results from the egocentric and irreversible thought of young children, so the operational construction of time is the direct result of reversible correlations. The reversibility of thought is, in fact, marked by the correction of two tendencies, or, if you like, by the decentration of two types of centration. On the one hand, whereas the natural tendency of thought is to follow the course of the

[1] See J. G. Juvet, *La Structure de nouvelles théories physique*, Paris (Alcan), 1935.

action itself, reversibility involves the retracing of that course: whence the operational construction of the concept of succession or order. On the other hand, while the personal point of view constitutes a privileged centration, reversibility, in the field of symmetrical relationships, leads to the construction of reciprocal viewpoints: whence the emergence of the concept of synchronous durations. In brief, the two chief results of decentration and the resulting reversibility of temporal concepts are the unfolding of time in two directions, after the discovery that the present is but a single moment in a continuous process, and the co-ordination of all the intersecting trajectories that, at any given moment, form a common medium to a host of simultaneous events.

Even on the qualitative plane, therefore, temporal operations lead to two remarkable results: they render time homogeneous and they also make it continuous. Quantitative operations, for their part, help to render the flow of time uniform (at least in the case of the small velocities characteristic of our everyday world).

Since homogeneous time is common to all phenomena, it is no longer the local time of intuition. But homogeneity does not imply the uniformity of successive durations: time could be common to the entire universe, even if its flow were constantly accelerated or slowed down, and even if it varied from one epoch to the next. The homogeneity of time results from synchronizations and other qualitative operations, and since such operations are limited to the colligation of the partial duration α or α' into a total duration in the form $\alpha + \alpha' = \beta; \beta + \beta' = \gamma$; etc., they cannot ensure the uniformity of successive durations—quantitative operations alone can tell us anything at all about the relation between α and α', β', etc.

As for the continuity of time, it is a remarkable fact that it, like homogeneity, should not be taken for granted at all levels of mental development: for young children, in effect, time is discontinuous as well as local, since it stops with any partial motion. That is why adults are thought to have stopped ageing, why a tree is thought to age if it still grows but not otherwise, etc. It is only with the introduction of operational time that duration is treated as a continuous flux, which shows that, far from being an intuitive concept, the continuity of time calls for

273

U

a special construction. Now this construction is simply the system of qualitative colligations, which leads to the partition of durations and ensures that it can be continued indefinitely and at all times. True, the various topological interpretations of the continuum introduce extensive quantity (e.g. Dedekind's or Cantor's axiom) or even metric quantity (Archimedes' axiom). But since the idea of continuous time is not grasped at the earlier stages of mental development, it follows that the mind must construct a qualitative continuum (intensive quantity) based on colligations (proposition 6) before the latter can give rise to mathematical quantification.

As for the uniform flow of time, it is based on uniform velocity, and its construction therefore calls for quantative rather than qualitative operations. However since, in the temporal as in all other spheres we have been investigating (number, mass, weight and volume), quantitative and extensive operations emerge the moment the grouping of qualitative or intensive operations has been achieved, the uniformity of time is recognized just as soon as its homogeneity and continuity have been constructed.

Reversibility of thought thus helps the child to unfold successions or asymmetries in two directions and, by gradual progress in decentration, to construct a general grouping, both qualitative and quantitative, of temporal relations that ensure the homogeneity, continuity and uniformity of time (on our scale). As Kant put it so profoundly, time is not a concept, i.e. a class of objects, but a unique schema, common to all objects, or, if you like, a formal object or structure. However, on the grounds that time is not a logical class, Kant argued that it is an 'intuition' (see Chapter Two, §2), i.e. an '*a priori* form of sensibility' like space, and hence unlike the categories of the understanding, e.g. unlike quantity. Now, genetic analysis has led us to a quite different conclusion, namely that time must be *constructed* into a unique scheme by operations and, moreover, by the same groupings and groups as go into the construction of logical and arithmetical forms. The only difference is that, with time, the operations are not wholly logical (colligation of classes or seriation of relations) or arithmetical (correlation of invariant objects) but infra-logical (partitions and displacements), i.e. identical with the operations used in the very construction of objects, or rather in their colligation into that total object which

the universe of space-time.[1] This is why time, though forming
unique object, or one of its structures, is operational neverthe-
ess. This is equally true of space, with which, however, we are
ot concerned in this volume.

III

Vhen it comes to psychological time, finally, we saw that it is
iot simply intuitive, as so many authorities claim, but that it
nvolves the same operations as physical time: the evaluation of
lived' duration calls for a host of conscious or unconscious
omparisons that lead to continuous progress from the level of
erceptive or intuitive regulations to that of operational group-
ng.

The seriation of instants, first of all, is as essential in psycho-
ogical as it is in physical time. The well-known idea of the 'flow
if consciousness' should not be allowed to disguise the fact that
very particular moment in this inner flux does not represent a
oint on a line, but a multiple and complex state resulting from
he intermingling of a great many diverse currents. At any
articular moment, we can be happy about our work, unhappy
bout the political situation, confident about the welfare of a
iear relative, etc., all at once, so that each slice of our inner time
ontinuum appears as a tissue of simultaneous events, or as a
napshot. The reconstruction of a series of inner events thus
nvariably involves the process of co-seriation.

But it is in respect of durations that the operational character
if psychological time is most often overlooked. This is due to
he common error of confusing the implicit qualitative opera-
ions with intuitions, and of the explicit qualitative operations
vith measurements: since inner durations generally lack a com-
non measure, we imagine that they do not involve operational
olligations. However, it must be clear that, whenever we are
ible to arrange internal events in their order O, A, B, C, etc.,
ve are introducing the duration α (between O and A), α' (be-
ween A and B), β' (between B and C), etc. Now while we may
iot be able to evaluate these durations in numerical terms, or
:ven tell if they are uniform, or what precisely is the relation

For a further discussion of infra-logical or spatio-temporal operations
ee *Le Développement des Quantités chez l'Enfant*, 'Conclusions'.

between α, α' and β, we do know that $\alpha + \alpha' = \beta$ (β being the duration between O and B); $\beta + \beta' = \gamma$ (the duration between O and C), etc., and hence that $\alpha < \beta < \gamma \ldots$ etc., i.e. that these durations can be colligated. One might say that this is very little knowledge, indeed, but it is, in fact, all that is needed for the logic of classes in general. And above all, it is this knowledge which, joined to the seriation of successive moments, enables the child to construct physical time before it can tell hours and minutes.

Nor is that all. Lived durations are not simply intervals but, as Bergson so rightly put it, the 'very stuff of reality'. However, this in no way differentiates them from physical durations, since the real content of both is identical, i.e. the work done at a given rate (cf. proposition 5). True, in the case of psychological time, the work does not take the form of a distance traversed, because inner time is not spatialized, nor is it usually measurable since we never count our ideas or perceptions, but it can nevertheless be assessed in terms of plus or minus. 'Time is creation, or it is nothing at all', Bergson said, and this is perfectly true, provided only we remember that mental, unlike physical, creation can only be translated into duration in terms of power (and hence of rapidity). That this translation is subject to systematic errors, as a result of which intense work seems short while it is being done and long in retrospect, no one will deny, but these illusions are partly corrected—thanks precisely to those operational comparisons which the mind performs incessantly and almost automatically.

Operations in psychological time would therefore seem to be mainly of a qualitative kind. Does that mean that there is no such thing as quantitative inner time? Bergson borrowed most of his imagery from music and, whenever this master of introspection wished to show that creative duration involved irreducibly intuitive and anti-rational factors, he did so in terms of melody, rhythm and symphony. But what else is music than an inner type of mathematics? Long before Pythagoras discovered the numerical ratios which determine the principal musical intervals, ancient shepherds, singing their songs or playing an air on their pipes, busily constructed musical scales and realized, without being able to put it into so many words, that a minim equals two crotchets and a crotchet equals two quavers. Musical rhythm is, in fact, the most intuitive of all time measurements and is most certainly not imposed on us from outside.[1] The same is true of stress in common speech and quite particularly of metre in poetry. Here, too, it was not the theorists who invented the metre but the bards, thus showing that there is no contradiction between elementary arithmetic and the expression of rhythms in inner life. The case of metre even provides us with a good example of the continuous links between perceptive rhythms and spontaneous temporal operations.

All this points to the common nature of temporal operations in all spheres, and to the close relationship between psychological and physical time: both are co-ordinations of motions with different velocities, and both involve the same 'groupings'. This is only to be expected since both are derived from practical or sensory-motor time which, in its turn, is based on objective relations and on personal actions. As the external universe is gradually differentiated from the inner universe, so objects and actions become differentiated as well, but remain closely inter-related.

It goes without saying that the development of psychological time involves physical time, since the co-ordination of actions performed at different rates presupposes that some work has been done in the first place, and since all work is sooner or later incorporated into the external world. Hence personal memory is the memory of things and actions in the external world as much, if not more so than, the memory of things and actions in the inner world. What is far less clear is that physical time implies psychological time: the succession of psychological phenomena can only be grasped by an observer who goes beyond them and so resurrects a physical time that is no longer. Stueckelberg, in a recent study, has even tried to show that since mechanical time is reversible, and the time of thermodynamics and of micro-physics is subject to fluctuations, the direction of physical time can only be determined by the correlation of external trajectories with a series of psychological or biological memories, which latter alone have an unequivocal direction in time. It is significant that a physicist should have felt the need to base physical

[1] In his suggestive 'Sur les operations de la composition musicale' (*Archives de Psychologie*, Vol. XXVII, p. 186), A. Mercier has tried to show that tone and rhythm represent two fundamental musical 'groups'.

on psychological time,[1] whereas psychologists, who know about the active reconstructions of external events that go into every act of memory, tend to look upon physical time as the basis of inner time. In fact, the two are closely interrelated and both alike involve reconstructions of the causal order of events. Time, in both cases, is therefore the co-ordination of motions, and the direction of its flow can only be deduced from the causal chain because causes necessarily precede their effects. Now, if causality is the general system of operations enabling us to correlate physical events, it is clear that before we can establish the existence of a causal relationship by experiment, we must first be able to correlate our measurements and this involves appealing to our memory or to reconstructions characteristic of psychological time. This is precisely what we mean when we say that physical time implies psychological time, and *vice versa*.

As for the time of relativity theory, far from being an exception to this general rule,[2] it involves the co-ordination of motions

[1] See E. Stueckelberg, *La Notion de temps*, in Disquisitiones Mathematicae et Physicae (Bucharest) 1942, pp. 301–17, and especially pp. 302–3. In much the same way as we have defined the colligation of durations as a qualitative grouping (see Proceedings of the Société de Physique, Geneva, Vol. 58, 1941, pp. 21 and 24), Stueckelberg treats psychological time as a colligation of sets of memories in the manner of transformations in affine geometry. Every sub-set of $A < B < C \ldots$ would then be defined not only by the present memories of a given period, for example by the memories of C, but also by memories, in C, of B and of A. The class A would therefore include only the oldest memories (because it does not yet contain memories of memories) while the increasingly general classes B, C, etc., would include, apart from direct memories, memories of memories of different degree. Of two intervals, that with the greatest past is therefore also the most recent, whence the unequivocal character of this 'psychological clock'. However, we see no need for introducing affine geometry, whose fundamental group involves the conservation of parallels, of anharmonic ratios, etc., none of which have any psychological connotations, when the 'grouping' of the logical addition of classes or of infra-logical partition fully accounts for the colligation of durations. Moreover, we are entitled to ask what else these 'memories of memories' are except operational reconstructions of past actions, partly by their results, i.e. whether psychological time is indeed wholly independent of physical time, as M. Stueckelberg seems to think.

[2] It is significant that Bergson, far from applauding the fact that Einsteinian time presents physics with a much closer model of psychological time (we might say of Bergsonian time) than Newtonian time did, challenged relativity theory with the claim that relative time was a characteristic of life alone.

and their velocities even more clearly than the rest. Let us recall first of all that relativity theory never reverses the order of events in terms of the observer's viewpoint: if A precedes B when considered from a certain point of view, it can never follow B when considered from a different standpoint, but will at most be simultaneous with it. Einstein's refinements of the concept of time bear solely on non-simultaneity at a distance, and consequently on the dilation of durations at very great velocities. Now both these consequences follow directly from our definition of simultaneity as a limiting case of succession, i.e. as the result of two signalling motions in opposite directions, whose relative successions cancel out (proposition 2a). Simultaneity must therefore be relative to an organic or physical instrument (moving eye or optical signals, etc.). Now, since the relative velocity of light is constant and so constitutes a kind of absolute standard, simultaneity, in the case of great velocities, depends purely on the relative motions of the observer and the phenomenon he observes, as well as on their distance apart. And if simultaneities are indeed relative to velocities, it follows that the measurement of durations will itself depend on the co-ordination of these velocities. Relativistic time is therefore simply an extension, to the case of very great velocities and quite particularly to the velocity of light, of a principle that applies at the humblest level in the construction of physical and psychological time, a principle that, as we saw, lies at the very root of the time conceptions of very young children.[1]

---

[1] The reader will forgive us if, in a book devoted to the development of time concepts in children, we ignore the subject of microphysical time, with which we shall be dealing in a separate work.

Index

Actions and inner duration, 230–54; children's evaluation of duration of their own actions, 253; durations and tasks of varying difficulty, 242–5; emotional regulations, 247; inactivity and interesting work, 245–7; psychological time, 234, 240, 247–54; rapidity of actions, 231–41

Additive and associative composition of durations, 160–72; and synchronization of elementary durations, 169–70; experimental methods and general results, 161–3; failure to effect compositions, 164–70; first and second stages, 164-70; immediate grasp, 170–2; third stage, 170–2

Age: age and height, 212–17, 228; analysis of children's ideas, 201; concept of age, 201–29; correspondence with equal growth rates, 224–8; correspondence with unequal growth rates, 218–24; of animals and plants, 212–17; of persons, 202–12; parallel path to construction of physical time, 229

Age and inner time, 197–254; actions and inner duration, 230–54; concept of age, 201–29

Archimedes' axiom, 274

Aristotle, 119; and subjective time, 49

Articulated intuition, 40, 43–52,

92–3, 208, 260; beginning of operational co-ordination, 94–6

Attention, synthetic and monoideic, 158

Auersperg, A., 97, 117

Bergson, Henri, ix, x, 197, 230, 276; on lived durations, 276; on pure memory and intuitive ideas of duration, 5

Cantor's axiom, 274

Causal processes and time, 5–6

Centration and decentration, 107, 110–11, 117–18, 120, 158, 159, 171, 181, 272; operational decentration, 48

Chance, definition of, 5

Claparède, 246

Colligation of durations, 55–63, 66, 77–9, 122, 141–51, 160, 173–5, 195, 268; and psychological time, 248, 251; first stage, 142–5; operational seriation, 150–1; second stage, 145–9

Continuity of time, 273–4

Co-placements and co-displacements, 26–7, 29, 32–4, 39–40, 59–60, 66, 70, 74, 175; grouping of co-displacements, 75. *See also* Displacements

Co-seriation (serial correspondence), 27–34, 63; operational, 28, 30–4

Cournot, 5